MANAGERS AND THEIR WIVES

A STUDY OF CAREER
AND FAMILY RELATIONSHIPS IN THE
MIDDLE CLASS

J. M. and R. E. Pahl

ALLEN LANE THE PENGUIN PRESS

First published in 1971 by
Allen Lane The Penguin Press
Vigo Street, London W1

ISBN 0 7139 0183 7

Printed in Great Britain by
Fletcher & Son Ltd, Norwich
Set in Monotype Garamond

Contents

Contents

Preface

THIS book arises out of my work and the ideas I began exploring in 1964 and 1965 when I was still with the University of Cambridge Board of Extra-Mural Studies. I acknowledge with gratitude and affection all the kindness and help my colleagues gave me, particularly, of course, in enabling me to be associated with the Madingley course for managers. Some of the pilot work on the relationship between family and work was done with the help of students in some of my Hertfordshire university extra-mural classes. Partly, perhaps, because this book arose out of the interests of the people about whom we are writing we have tried to write it so that those with no previous knowledge of sociology will not be deterred from reading it: I hope that my professional colleagues will understand and perhaps sympathize.

It is difficult to express adequately our appreciation of the help and cooperation we received from the managers and their wives about whom this book is written: we dedicate it to them. To Mrs Marie Corbin, who interviewed the sixteen couples in their homes, we owe a great deal: quite literally the book could not have been written without her. She has read the book in draft and has contributed a note on the method which appears as Appendix 3. Of course she is in no way responsible for the interpretation of the material we have made. Similar absolution of responsibility applies to Robert and Rhona Rapoport, Colin Bell, Peter Willmott and Michael Young, who also read all or part of the book in draft. Jill Norman of Penguin Books has been constructively helpful throughout and has given us encouragement at black moments.

The expenses of Mrs Corbin were met by a small grant from Political and Economic Planning and we would like to thank Professor Michael Fogarty and John Pinder for coming to our assistance when all else had failed.

Preface

I have received many ideas from my colleagues at the University of Kent at Canterbury: the influence of some of them has been much stronger than perhaps they suspect. They have been indulgent as sounding boards for half-formed ideas, as indeed have the students. We probably get more than we realize by trying to make our ideas explicit to students. The University has also helped by providing generous secretarial assistance: the administration of the postal questionnaire as well as the typing of Mrs Corbin's interview material imposed a more than usually heavy burden. Mrs M. Waring and her staff have been cheerfully efficient in coping with all this, often when heavily pressed.

Finally I would like to stress that this is the only part of the book for which one of us takes individual responsibility. It has been written equally between us: each author contributed different qualities but there is no part of the book which is more the responsibility of one than of the other, even if there was a necessary, and probably obvious, division of labour in the actual writing. It might be helpful for some readers to know that our main themes are developed in chapters 4, 8 and 9. Certainly the last two chapters were the hardest for us to write.

Patrixbourne   R. E. Pahl
Nr Canterbury   August 1970

CHAPTER I

Background to the Study

THIS is a book about a part of the middle class: it is about the men and women who typically live in privately built houses on suburban estates round the major industrial cities of Britain. We view the man in his 'career' as a manager and at home as husband and father. We view the woman as 'a manager's wife' as well as a mother or employee in her own right. We try to present some of the dilemmas, which such people face in relating their work life to their family life, and what they consider to be rewarding and valuable. Inevitably, chapters have to follow each other, but we would prefer them to be considered in parallel. The chapters about the husband's 'career' – Chapters 2 and 4 in particular – come before the chapters on the wife's social and domestic world more by accident than by logic. Chapters 3 and 7 link the two themes together but are only extended discussions of examples – the family facing mobility and the company's conscious attempts to bring benefits to the family and to relate the manager's wife to her husband's activities. The two concluding chapters draw the whole book together: in the first we focus on the manager and his wife as a married couple and consider types of marriage in relation to the men's work or 'career'. Finally we consider the elusive concept of ambition and the attitudes of the managers' wives to 'success'. We try to answer why, for example, some men seem married to their work and spend long hours at the office or work at home, saying that they do all this for their wives. Is more money gained at the expense of less home and family life?

Is the middle class as competitive and materialistic as those devising incentives for managers in industry assume? We could not finally resolve this issue, but we have certainly detected a degree of ambivalence and uncertainty towards the basic materialistic values which are often assumed to be dominant by certain politicians and spokesmen for British industry. That so many of the middle-class couples we studied showed such ambiguity towards the basic values of a competitive society has far-reaching implications. It could affect the whole role and purpose of Britain in the world economic and political environment. However, before throwing all academic caution to the winds, we must elaborate in some detail how we came to write this book, how we set about it, and the limitations and advantages of our method.

We realize that for some people this book may be painful to read; it may be a comfort for such readers to know that it was painful to write. However hard we each tried to escape from our own culture to consider our evidence objectively, we had constantly to struggle with our own values and attitudes. To some extent we are making conscious the processes of which we ourselves form a part, and some of the tensions which the men and women in our study experience are common to us too. Since we are writing for the people we are writing about, we expect and hope that readers will be critical and compare what we say with their own experience. Indeed, the development of such a critical awareness would be some justification for writing this book.

Given that we expect our readers to be more critical than they would be if reading about some 'colourful' peasant society, we think that it is important to be as explicit as we can about our assumptions and preconceptions. This is particularly necessary since we are not setting out to prove specific hypotheses. We have tried to record the questions and problems which interested us in the early stages of the study in order to show how the material that we gathered dissolved some questions but raised others. We make no apology for our study being shaped by our material; we admit being uncertain ourselves, particularly at the start of the study, as to how to define and determine our area of interest. We simply want to write a book which is sociologically informed and which will help those who read it, whether or not they have studied social science, to understand the middle class better. We have been particularly conscious when writing this book that the people we are writing about, and many others like them, will read and react to what we have written. This has forced us to consider the impact of what we write on people's feelings, so that we have perhaps erred on the side of caution: less ready to generalize about and more ready to sympathize with the men and women we describe, we may have lost a degree of objectivity. Yet by being forced to see their lives in the way they themselves see them we may have gained an unscientific but perhaps valuable empathy. We suspect that sociology is sometimes disliked, or perhaps feared, because it appears to be so insulting to people: it implies that one or two variables such as 'years of education received' or 'father's occupation' determine a large proportion of people's lives. Such a sociology makes people appear two-dimensional and flat and it is perhaps this that is most resented.

We wanted to go beyond this two-dimensional approach, but we were not inclined simply to extend the list of 'factors' and quantitatively to assess the relative importance of each. In striving for a multi-dimensional sociology we believe that correlations do not constitute explanations; that what people say they do is not necessarily what they are doing; that attitudes and behaviour change over time as situations change; and that what may appear to be true at one level of abstraction becomes less so as the level of analysis changes.

Sociology then may be an uncomfortable subject both for those who read it and for those who write it. For us there has been combined the pain of producing a novel with the discipline of a scientific method. In this chapter we outline some of the discipline that guided our work.

Generally the middle class live some distance from their place of work and this is one of the ways in which they differ from the working class; as a result there have been few studies that attempt to relate together their various spheres of activity, which are physically if not socially discrete. Those concerned with the work life of managers do their studies in the industrial or commercial context; those concerned with family life work in the residential areas.* Separate sociologies deal with separate spheres – the sociology of work and organization, the sociology of the family, the sociology of religion, and so on. The interconnections between these spheres are not very clearly articulated. Indeed there is some danger that inexplicable variations in attitudes to work are ascribed to unexplored variables related to the non-work situation; similarly variations in family and community behaviour which are not understood are assumed to have their roots in the world of work. Thus the very fact of being in an academic discipline appears to create blinkers, which direct the gaze to specific problems in specific institutional spheres, and literature grows up on specific topics with very little cross linking or reference to other spheres. For example, Glaser's book on *Organizational Careers* (1968) includes no paper among the sixty-three selections which discusses the significance of a man's wife and family in relation to his career. It is as if sociologists have assumed that men are cut off in the world of work from the rest of society and their personal ties. One sometimes gets the impression from some textbooks in sociology that men and women have lives which are as separate as the divisions between the chapters. Thus 'family life' imposes its own pattern of rules, obligations and sanctions and there are certain times in the day or week when these constraints operate. At other times men and women are able to escape from these constraints and enter other equally well-defined spheres, such as 'the economy'. Indeed there is a current argument, which gives added force to this point, which maintains that true individual autonomy is only possible in the interstices between these institutional spheres (Luckmann, 1967). According to this view there is a pervasive social control provided by the objective autonomy of social institutions: individuals may be obliged to withdraw into the private sphere to gain a sense of personal autonomy. These private meanings, fantasies, explanations and justifications may be in conflict with, or

* Notable exceptions are the article by Robert and Rhona Rapoport, 'Work and Family in Contemporary Society' (June 1965) and also their book with Michael Fogarty, *Sex, Career and Family* (1971).

separate from, the main social institutions of society which are 'out there' dominating the individual. True autonomy is found, as it were, between the chapters of the textbook.

EARLY LINES OF THOUGHT

We must acknowledge that our approach to the study of the middle class was coloured by earlier studies of managerial and professional people in Hertfordshire commuterland (R. E. Pahl, 1965, 1970). We were impressed by the enthusiasm and satisfaction such people expressed for a particular environmental situation and pattern of social life. A certain style of life could seemingly develop only in certain contexts: the quality and style of shopping which is available in places such as Saffron Walden, St Albans or Windsor, the high density of Good Food Guide restaurants and the ease of access to London from a large part of South East England are all factors which seem to be increasingly important to the senior salariat. A certain style of house in a certain sort of district, with the likelihood of finding other people of a similar sort, seemed to be essential ingredients in this valued style of life. The study of 'Dormersdell' in central Hertfordshire suggested to us that the men and women who lived there might be reluctant to move away to other parts of the country; we felt that there might be a potential source of conflict here between the demands of the company for whom a man worked and his own and his wife's demands for a particular pattern of family and community life. This point was put by the Social Sciences Adviser to Unilever as follows:

Ideally managers and specialists should be as widely deployable as capital within the total organization. In practice, differences in the situation of different affiliates, differences in the experiences they demand, together with the personal and family situations of many managers, offer severe constraints to the wide deployment of a considerable proportion of managers. (Wilson, 1966, p. 9)

This theme dominated our early approach to the subject: we wondered whether the most able men in a company were penalized by being obliged to be 'spiralists' (Watson, 1960), that is to move house to another part of the country as they moved up the hierarchy of large-scale organizations. Since R. E. Pahl was working as a tutor on A.E.I. staff courses in the early 1960s it was not surprising that informal discussion should centre on the usefulness of community studies. Practical-minded managers were quick to see the connection between career mobility and family or community ties and a great wealth of anecdotal material or saloon-bar sociology was accumulated. Undoubtedly some of the ideas on which this study is based arose out of these informal conversations with managers at Oxford and, later, Cambridge. Unfortunately it is the bizarre or striking detail that sticks in the mind and we may have suffered by the unsystematic way in which our ideas towards the subject developed.

A more structured approach to the problem began in 1966 when we asked the managers who attended courses in Cambridge in 1965 and 1966 to complete a form which simply asked for documentation of their social background and previous career. We hoped that the men would continue to keep us informed as their career developed and we promised to write regularly twice a year in order to keep track of developments in career and family. We needed funds to enable us to interview men and women in their homes before and after they moved and the initial approach to the managers was simply to ensure that we kept in contact as a more elaborate research project was established. The central focus was originally on 'spiralling' and its effect on the manager's domestic life, and a detailed research strategy was prepared. R. E. Pahl was a director of studies on the courses of 1965 and 1966 and had lectured to the course in 1967, so there were few difficulties in gaining the men's cooperation. There were 113 married British managers on the three courses and very few refused to cooperate. There were, however, about twenty who promised to send the form back but nevertheless failed to do so. Very often this was simply due to pressure of work at a particular time or the result of a recent promotion or move. Despite this general goodwill it became evident in the summer of 1967 that unless the research developed more rapidly and more systematically the sample was likely to be whittled away by the success of men who were moving on in their careers. It was likely that the men in whom we were most interested would be the men we were most likely to lose. Alternative strategies to enlarge the scope of the study by getting support from research sponsors in or outside industry all failed. Plenty of lip service was given to the importance of the topic and so forth, but financial backing was not forthcoming. Thus we were in the galling position of having the support of some ninety to a hundred managers, while being unable to proceed through lack of funds. Under these circumstances we felt it preferable to do as best we could without research funds by sending a postal questionnaire to the wives of our managers, which we did in the autumn of 1967. We had an astonishingly high response rate and eighty-six wives returned completed questionnaires which could be matched with the other information already gathered from their husbands. A copy of this questionnaire is reproduced in Appendix 1. In the end we had only two or three men's forms without the matching form for their wives.

As we analysed the questionnaires completed by the wives we realized first, that there were discrepancies between what the husband claimed his wife felt about, for example, mobility and what she herself actually felt about it. Secondly, some wives were clearly highly articulate, enjoyed thinking about their situation and had much more to say than could be elicited by a postal questionnaire. Finally, there were some internal discrepancies within the questionnaires which only a face-to-face interview could unravel. Since our couples were scattered all over the country interviewing would inevitably be a very costly business. Happily in the spring of 1968 a small grant from P.E.P. enabled us to get lengthy interviews in the homes of sixteen of our couples later in the summer of 1968. We were particularly fortunate in finding a trained social anthropologist, Mrs Marie Corbin, who was free to undertake this arduous but essential part of our work. Frequently Mrs Corbin arrived at the homes of her interviewees soon after lunch and did not leave until midnight, and during this time the wives and their husbands were interviewed both separately and together. An outline of the main themes developed in the relatively unstructured interviews is reproduced as Appendix 2 and a more detailed account of this phase of the research by Mrs Corbin is presented in Appendix 3. We have given our respondents the names of Kentish towns and villages and made certain other minor changes to preserve their anonymity. We have also emphasized certain phrases in the verbatim comments to illustrate our themes and hope that this does not distort what our respondents said.

THE SAMPLE

This book is based on material gathered from only 172 men and women and undoubtedly this raises questions about the general validity of the material. Before giving an account of the Cambridge course and the kind of men it is likely to attract, it is perhaps worth considering some alternative strategies of gathering a sample. Most studies gather their respondents from specific companies or specific localities. There are, however, many reasons for not taking one or two companies. First, different companies have different policies and different 'cultures' and it would be difficult to know how typical the companies selected were of a larger universe. Secondly, the cooperation of the companies concerned would probably be necessary and this in itself might create problems as the men might be less prepared to talk to researchers about their true relationships to colleagues and superiors if they knew that these same colleagues were also likely to be interviewed or that a final report would be presented to the company. Alternatively, of course, the more 'successful' the research, the less enthusiastic the sponsors might be about seeing it published. There are, of course, compensating advantages: the man who claims he is a dynamic leader of men may appear less so when he is actually observed in action or when his views of himself are compared with what his colleagues say. Working with a small number of companies would have produced a different kind of study. There are different drawbacks about a study with respondents selected from a middle-class area such as a suburban housing estate. This was the approach adopted by Colin Bell in his *Middle Class Families* (1969) when he reported on two estates in Swansea. Bell has recently been criticized for limiting himself in this way; certain categories of the middle class are unlikely to live on new housing estates. Bell is concerned to create a typology of patterns of social mobility based on a specific residential milieu and it is reasonable to expect that old established middle-class areas of towns would have distinctive social elements not found in the newer areas.*

Arguments can run either way: should as full a knowledge as possible of the *context* of social behaviour be a fundamental requirement if one is trying to understand such behaviour, or should one try to get a sample reflecting as many different contexts as possible so as to neutralize the compositional effect in particular localities or work milieux? Certainly among the middle class the local context is perhaps less important for certain categories, who may be less concerned with what they do at a particular time than with what they are in terms of their biography and future potential. This longitudinal conception of social reality extends such middle-class people out of immediate contexts so that, although they may be constrained by a local configuration of social relationships, a broader perspective must be taken into consideration.

The method of selecting respondents which was used here has certain advantages, which are worth mentioning, although to do so may appear to be wringing too much virtue out of necessity. First, we have the advantage that our managers are more or less of similar age and stage in the family cycle: eighty-five per cent of the men are between thirty and forty years old. Secondly, we have men from a wide variety of backgrounds, scattered throughout the country and working in organizations of varying sizes and functions. Our respondents lived in northern industrial towns and southern commuter villages, in new estates and old-established suburbs. They worked in large, nationalized industries and in smaller,

* F. Bechhofer, *Sociological Review*, November 1969, p. 451.

rapidly expanding companies; in banking, insurance and the Civil Service as well as in large manufacturing enterprises. Some were well-established members of local communities and others were the ideal-typical spiralists, moving on from job and community. It is clear from our analysis of a whole range of characteristics that our managers do not fall into an obvious mould. Indeed the very diversity of our sample has created one of the most difficult problems in the analysis: invariably the cells of complex tabulations were too small to be significant. However, we feel it is better to try to capture this diversity than to give a falsely homogenous picture of a typical manager and his wife.

THE MADINGLEY MANAGERS' COURSE

We were concerned lest the Cambridge course attracted only a certain sort of manager – for example those who had been fairly rapidly socially mobile and had been sent to Cambridge for 'tone'. The prospectus for the University of Cambridge Board of Extra-Mural Studies Managers' Course lists three categories for whom the course is intended.

1. Managers whose full-time education ended fairly early, and who have moved to positions of responsibility but have had little opportunity of examining problems outside their own areas of immediate practical concern.

2. Managers (including graduates) who have concentrated on developing their skills in specialized fields but who are now likely to take on different kinds of responsibility (e.g. research workers entering general management).

3. Managers who are rising to positions of higher responsibility and are therefore facing the task of making decisions in unfamiliar fields.

The course is held in Madingley Hall and lasts for a month. Since 1953 the Board of Extra Mural Studies has administered the course and has provided the basic academic framework. Basically the course is designed

to help members to think systematically about those aspects of the national economy which primarily concern managers. It is expected that over the next five or ten years those attending the course will become increasingly concerned with the more general problems of management, and with the external relations of their companies in the national and international economy. The course therefore aims at throwing light on the economic, political, social and human background against which these problems should be seen.*

Certainly, if most members of the course came into category 1, we would be less confident that our results reflected the more typical pattern revealed in previous studies of the social origins and backgrounds of British managers (Clements, 1958; Clark, 1966). Happily there are no signs that either the companies or the organizers viewed it as a finishing school. We document the detailed situation in Chapter 3 and it is clear that, if anything, categories 2 and 3 have been dominant, although over a number of years the pattern is well balanced.

In content the course is clearly academic rather than practical in its basic assumptions: the concern is to educate managers rather than to train men for management. The course seeks to provide a general broadening of intellectual horizons and this mind-stretching may be as painful for the graduate technologist as for the sales manager with few formal qualifications. Most men undoubtedly found the course tough going but rewarding and some had come on the course on the recommendation of senior colleagues who had participated in previous years. However, problems of communication and continuity in the training field being what they are, it is unlikely that any two companies viewed the course in the same way. From our point of view this is an advantage, since it ensures a more diverse and perhaps more representative group of managers. Most see the course as a preparation for more responsibility in the company and certainly not as a reward for meritorious service. The well-known joke about only those whose presence would not be missed being able to get away for a course does not apply to this one. On the other hand, Cambridge is a good brand image which sells the course somewhat indiscriminately.

* From the letter sent to successful applicants who are selected to join the course.

However, since all nominated applicants are interviewed, it is unlikely that serious misunderstandings of the nature of the course can arise. It is mainly the larger firms who provide the applicants and so our material is not representative of the small-scale, entrepreneurial element in British industry.

Thus we would argue that since the universe of 'British Managers' is unknown, and since there are serious difficulties in taking a sample from a particular firm or a particular area, our method is probably as good as any. It would be difficult to get such a broad spread in any other way and since our managers, as we shall see, are particularly heterogeneous, any generalizations which can safely apply to them would seem to have a much wider validity. The peculiar advantage that one of us had in spending a month's residential course with two out of three groups meant that a degree of sympathy and a willingness to cooperate could be assumed from the start. If we had had research funds to help with full-time secretarial assistance it would have been possible to follow up those who promised their forms but for one reason or another did not send them; we would certainly have achieved a response rate of well over ninety per cent. However, we are well satisfied with what we have got. The rates of response were similar for each year. Of course we do not know the degree to which the course is self-selected in the sense that some wives would strongly oppose their husbands being away from home for a month during the summer.

A NOTE ON METHODOLOGY

One problem is that there is no clear way of precisely relating our managers to a broader universe. We make no attempt to use systematically census and other data as a means of enlarging our scope. Similarly, and perhaps more seriously, we do not spell out precise hypotheses or relate our material to a precise scholarly universe. There are few elegant propositions and we do not set out our findings in such a way that they can be easily verified by replication. Those of our managers trained in one of the more quantitatively exact sciences are likely to be scathing of our intuitive and, to them, sloppy methods and procedures.

Our view is that advances in the understanding of middle-class life are not held up through lack of mathematical sophistication and methodological rigour, however valuable these may be in their place. We are depressed by some of the methodologically sophisticated but intellectually arid sociological literature, which to our minds dehumanizes the 'respondents'. Too often studies present the author's interpretations of respondents' interpretations of questions which the author thinks are significant and which he thinks tap 'real' problems and issues in the minds of the respondents. There has been a reaction within sociology both against the methodology of the survey (Cicourel, 1964) and against prejudging results by the over rigid formulation of initial hypotheses (Glaser and Strauss, 1967).

Our problem, in common with all research workers, is to make the best sense of what we have got. We believe that at this stage in our understanding of a complex field, imagination is as useful a tool in aiding understanding as mathematics. We are less interested in showing precise correlations than in suggesting patterns of relationships which have not been considered in that way before. We believe in the importance of social variables in determining social patterns and social behaviour, but we do not want to become so obsessed by the search for the exact amount of variance which may be attributable to any given factor that we forget to describe the whole. Much of what we have written we recognize to be tentative and exploratory. We were dissatisfied with much of what we read on the subject and we expect those who come after us to be similarly dissatisfied with what we do. That is as it should be. We expect sociology to advance in its ability to provide a satisfactory understanding of complex issues. At the moment we are not sure what is 'satisfactory'. Hence we are unable to measure our own success.

There is one final point to be made on our method. We are trying to bring together the findings of the literature on managerial careers with the literature on middle-class family

life and to develop the important work of Bell and the Rapoports. Career and family are generally kept apart – the former
is studied by tough-minded industrial sociologists and the
latter by tender-minded students of the family. This tension
between the two approaches perhaps provided the dialectic
out of which our particular approach developed. Frequently
R. E. Pahl argued for the man, his career and the needs of the
company against the more expressive and affective approach
of J. M. Pahl who argued for particularistic, familial values.
Both of us felt our individual identities and values were bound
up in the stances we adopted, and the differences which
emerged between us made us more alert to attitudes towards
the study in general and the interpretation of the specific case
material in particular. We are not sure whether we would have
been equally alert and sensitive to these in-built biases if we
had each been working alone; thus we feel that whatever
merit this book might have owes a great deal to our joint
efforts to persuade the other. All our own personal crises
during the time of writing the book became case studies to be
analysed: it was small comfort for one of us to be told by
the other, 'Write it all down and don't complain.' Being participant observers in our own career–conjugal role conflicts
had its strains, but fits in very well with current sociological
thinking in ethnomethodology!

ATTITUDES TO THE MIDDLE CLASS

This rather intense personal involvement in our work and the
lack of any satisfactory literature on which we could build
made us wonder why there had been so little research on the
themes that interested us. Perhaps it is the case that *too many*
people have written about the middle class in a popular or
intuitive way, so that the field has become devalued. Clearly,
if every feature writer on the *Sunday Times* or the *Observer* has
offered views on some aspect or other of middle-class life,
this may be a deterrent to more serious study. Many sociologists seem to prefer to study social situations or occupational groups with which they are not familiar. The lives of
deep-sea fishermen or lorry drivers are more romantic to

academics than those of regional sales managers or accountants. Furthermore sociologists who find themselves more
sympathetic to left-wing political ideologies may prefer to
study the 'true' workers, perhaps in the hope of discovering a
clue to their 'false consciousness' or some such politically
useful theme. And even sociologists of mildly reformist bent
are more likely to find 'problems' connected with the working
class, and that the more applied the research project the easier
it may be to get research funds. (We may be a little sour on this
point owing to our lack of success in persuading industry or a
foundation to support us.) Even the very rich may be more
interesting to left-wing sociologists than the middle class, for
though they have little sympathy with the rich, they still feel
that knowing more about them may ultimately help to change
things. But the bourgeoisie:

> How beastly the bourgeois is
> especially the male of the species –
> presentable, eminently presentable –
> shall I make you a present of him?

Many sociologists seem to join with D. H. Lawrence in des-
pising the middle class. A colleague at another university
admitted that he would need courage to write a book about the
middle class: 'How could I justify it to the students?' Simply
to have an academic interest in a cultural style is not, it seems,
enough.

However, polemics aside, perhaps the main reason for the
neglect of the middle class is that it is an extremely complex
collection of different status groups, each of which is sure of
its distinctiveness in relation to others. Lower-white-collar
workers in a South London suburb, the affluent industrialists
of the West Riding and the upper-middle-class 'county' of
Northamptonshire are uneasily brought together under the
label 'middle class'. In this book we are simply exploring some
of the themes for part of the middle class. Hopefully it might
serve as a building block for some larger construction.

However, though the middle class may have been relatively
neglected by professional sociologists, we have found that

there is a wide general interest in our subject. Thus two preliminary short pieces which we published in relatively unob-
trusive places were reported and commented on by most
national newspapers and were the subjects of television and
radio features: for example, *The Times* headed its six-inch
double-column report 'Manager and his Wife Worlds Apart'
(27 November 1968), while the *Morning Star* headed its report
'It's Not All Joy for the Wives of Big Earners' (24 November
1968). It is likely that this response is itself of considerable
sociological significance. Part of the reason for the interest
may simply be that journalists themselves find it interesting
and many of those with whom we spoke confessed that our
descriptive analysis fitted their own personal situation. To
some extent the publicity we received was simply a self-
indulgence on their part and we should be a little sceptical
before we assume that we have really touched on problems
of wide and deep significance. Nevertheless it is still possible
that the issues we are probing are becoming more and more
central to people's experience. As men and women increasingly find their sense of identity through personal relationships it may be that we are writing about what is most
meaningful in people's lives. Berger and Kellner have explored
this theme in their perceptive article 'Marriage and the construction of reality' (1964). As Luckmann (1967) puts it:

In the 'private sphere' the partial sharing, and even joint construction, of systems of 'ultimate significance' is possible without
conflict with the functionally rational norms of the primary institutions. The so-called nuclear family prevalent in industrial societies
performs an important role in providing a structural basis for the
'private' production of (rather fleeting) systems of 'ultimate'
significance. This holds especially for the middle-class family ideal
of 'partnership marriage' of which it is typically expected that it
provides 'fulfilment' for the marriage partners.

This then provides something of the context in which this
book developed. The following chapter is basically an account
of the sociological literature on the career, and readers who
are more interested in our empirical material may like to move
straight to Chapter 3, perhaps returning to Chapter 2 later.

The Sociology of the Career

FOR the middle class the career is 'the supreme social reality', in the words of one of the most distinguished contemporary sociologists, Dahrendorf (1959). Later in this chapter we have some cause to question this assertion, but for the moment it is worth considering in some detail the sociological importance of the career, as it has been developed and used as a concept by other scholars. One of the most stimulating contributors to this field is Wilensky, who has reported empirical findings of the greatest interest over the past decade. He offers the following definition (1960, p. 554): 'A career, viewed structurally, is a succession of related jobs, arranged in a hierarchy of prestige, through which persons move in an ordered, predictable sequence.' Wilensky thinks there may be a quarter or a third of the population of the United States in such careers. The prospect of continuous, predictable and increasing rewards provides an incentive to undergo prolonged training, to defer immediate gratifications and to struggle to achieve 'good' careers. Since the most able and skilled in the workforce are slotted into some developing life plan they are less likely to jeopardize their future by objecting to the system: thus careers provide a major source of stability for modern society and may be said to be helping to prevent rebellion, revolution – or even social change.

The organizational career provides for people a stability in life plan, style, and cycle, engendering their motivation to work. This stability is one of the sources of a stable organization and thus leads to stability in the organizational sectors of society. This stability is clearly seen in the continuity of employment, style and plan of life in the governmental sectors of civil service and the military.*

* Glaser, 1968, p. 15.

Thus the career, viewed objectively, will have 'typical sequences of position, achievement, responsibility, and even of adventure'.* It is important to remember this emphasis on *typicality*: simply moving between a number of unrelated jobs does not necessarily constitute a career. Similarly there are problems of accommodating horizontal movements to positions at the same level in different firms or organizations. Are these to be seen as advances in a career? Potentially such lateral moves open up opportunities for advancement in larger or more rapidly expanding organizations. However, until the man has actually got his promotion it may be difficult, according to the criteria we are adopting, to decide whether he is enjoying a 'career' or simply a succession of jobs.

Careers may also be considered from the point of view of the social actor concerned. This subjective approach will see the career 'as the moving perspective in which the person sees his life as a whole and interprets the meaning of his various attributes, actions and the things which happen to him'.* This personal interpretation or re-interpretation of biography produces a *longitudinal perspective on life*. The individual's private plan or project may not necessarily coincide with the objective career or typical sequence of positions which the organization has labelled a 'good' career. Thus a man may plan over a number of years to get a job in Scotland to enable him to be closer to relatives or to pursue some private interest. Others may define this as an unsuccessful career since it may be that opportunities for further advancement to 'better' positions have been or will be forgone. But to the man himself he has been a success, since he has achieved the personal aim he set himself. This constant dialogue between private plans and public expectations will be a continuing theme in our discussion.

Whether the career is viewed objectively or subjectively, some degree of commitment is involved. It is this *long-term commitment* which could be seen to be typical of the middle-class style. Thus it is not what the middle class do which is of greatest significance but what they *are* or what they are in

* Hughes, 1937.

process of becoming. The past, the present and the future are linked together by personal projects or organizational careers. Perhaps such a longitudinal perspective is becoming a necessary part of biological maturity. After all, modern man cannot prove his manhood by killing a wild boar or felling a huge tree. His wife may be able to achieve adult womanhood in terms of her sex role through pregnancy, childbirth and the early years of motherhood. But manifestation of womanliness through the obvious physical cycle of conception, expansion and production is hardly matched for the man, whose abdominal expansion may seem to match his wife's but for reasons little connected with vigorous maturity but rather with corpulent decline. The developmental sequence of the career may serve as a compensation, particularly if its most rapid development is coincident with his wife's child rearing and producing so that he gets promotion to, say, regional sales manager as she gets their second child. The phasing of family life-cycle stage with career development is another important theme.

We now try to create an over-simplified model of the stages in a typical career path, making some attempt to link the objective with the subjective situation and drawing on research material where this is available. We view the career as the strand which links personal history or biography to the major institutions, such as school, family and employing organization with which the individual comes into contact.

THE EDUCATIONAL CAREER

The educational system inculcates a view of life as a series of stages; each form or examination is partly concerned with preparing each age cohort for the next stage – pre-eleven plus exams, eleven plus, mock 'O' levels, 'O' levels, mock 'A' levels, 'A' levels, university entrance, a preliminary examination, Part I, Part II, M.A., M.Phil., Ph.D., diplomas and qualifying examinations to get membership of the appropriate professional organization whether of accountants, engineers or market researchers. 'Work' is experienced as the effort required to get over intellectual hurdles of increasing size, difficulty and complexity. Those who become good academic hurdlers are not only learning that deferred gratification is the price of success, although this may certainly be true, but also the acceptance and expectation that life is made up of stages. A rhythm develops of preparation, trial and objective self-rating; each success serves as the passport to permit entry to the next stage.

Of course this does not necessarily imply that those who succeed are the ambitious strivers, living in a state of lonely and intensive struggle to master physics or economics, while their peers go necking at parties. Many are simply carried through on the conveyor belt of a bright form, all the members of which fill in their university entrance forms at the same time. Turner in his exploration of *The Social Context of Ambition* (1964) distinguishes between differing elements in both social mobility and ambition and argues that involvement in so-called youth cultures may be ritualistic and segmental for ambitious young people who are acquiring at the same time the values of self-reliance and deferred gratification. Thus such young people are not totally committed to the roles and styles they adopt but simply 'fit in' as it suits them.

ANTICIPATORY SOCIALIZATION

Embryonic careerists will be concerned to acquire the attitudes and values of the groups to which they hope to belong in the next stage before they are actually members of such groups. By learning in advance about these *reference groups* such people are said to undergo anticipatory socialization. Indeed behaviour appropriate to the next stage may be acted out in advance: this may be described as precocity, presumption or maturity, according to choice. By the time those who are committed to a successful career reach university they have become skilful in managing a variety of situations to their long-term advantage. This is how Dalton (1959, p. 164–5) describes the development of managerial skills at an early stage.

Anticipatory socialization

Long before he completes high school, the student has learned that in our society he must participate or be a 'grind' in danger of becoming 'introverted' or 'maladjusted' or even 'antisocial'. Social activities take time but may pay unexpected returns.... Taking part in campus politics gives the student an experience he may not get outside of college, at his age, short of entering professional politics. He tries his hand at helping select and elect officers, and may himself serve. His part in the intra- and extra-organizational struggles is educational. He learns to move in and out of cliques and organizations with minimum friction. . . . If with all these activities he is still able to make good marks, he has learned how to function inside limitations. Probably he has become adept at analysing his professors and utilizing his social contacts whether he is consciously calculating or not. If his limited time demands more shortcuts to maintain his grade-points, he studies his professors to (a) isolate their pet theories; (b) outguess them in preparing for examinations; and (c) please them. Although apple-polishing may not always pay off as expected, the exercise in grappling with the unknown still enlarges his executive potential. He compares notes and impressions with other students. . . . He becomes sensitive to intangibles, and learns to live with the elusive and ambiguous. This unofficial training teaches him to get in his own claims and grace-fully escape those of others that he must. He learns to appear sophisticated and to adjust quickly to endless new situations and personalities.

There is a difference between anticipatory socialization and simply using one's free time in one stage to acquire the skills appropriate to the next. Thus the man who intends to go into television and who works with his university dramatic society, or the man who works on a student newspaper before going into journalism is simply acquiring skills and experience. Where, however, the educational process is taking a man away from the norms and values of his family or stratum of origin to a new and higher level he may, but not necessarily, move towards the acceptance of the new values and the disavowal of the old before he actually achieves membership of the group with the new values. Turner (1964, Ch. 7) makes the distinction between the acquisition of the material benefits of social mobility and participation in a culturally 'superior' way of life. Only ambition for the latter is likely to lead to, for example, an intrinsic interest in education, a conscious attempt to listen to 'good' music or a concern for elitist culture in any other form.

THE EARLY PERIOD

A man in his twenties is less likely to be 'settled' in his career. This is the period of testing, switching, experimenting and gaining experience. This period may be used to gain experience, gain accurate knowledge of the job situation in an appropriate limited area, make contacts, get further formal qualifications; thus career considerations may be allowed to override all others. For those from lower social origins, who are reluctant to change their norms and values, commitment to a specific identity such as research scientist – in academic or industrial life – or a profession requiring high expertise – such as certain types of technologists or accountants – will help to stabilize their central identity in terms of the one occupational role. Hence the obsessive, almost compulsive, young research worker, creating his own self by the research publications he achieves: being a scientist may be the chief and only sign of his social mobility. In other aspects of his style of life he may have more in common with the style of his social origins.

The image of the scientist tends to be a classless one, and hence it can be embraced by a working-class student without involving a denial of his biographical self . . . as the student-scientist learns to play the role of scientist he acquires the motivations of a scientist – motivation directed towards recognition – and ultimately may embrace the scientist's identity. Finally the dominant norms and values of science are, like those of religion, sufficiently ecumenical to act as anchorage points for other life areas.*

This is the period of so-called 'spiralling'.† Different types of experience in different types of organization typically take

* Box and Ford, 1967.
† It is symptomatic of the scant material on the middle class that this notion should have retained currency. See Watson (1960) and the discussion in Bell (1968).

a man for short periods to various plants and establishments throughout the country. This is the spiralist in the strictly geometrical sense of the word since these geographical moves are not necessarily associated with a movement up the occupational hierarchy. Rapoport (1964) reports from a study of a sample of engineers that several moves in the early years following graduation are important for giving them a well-rounded competence. This high frequency of moving with, in the case of the civil engineer, possibilities of work in isolated areas, together with relatively low pay makes early marriage less likely. While not all engineers and technologists would echo Brunel, 'My profession is, after all, my only fit wife',* it is nevertheless true that professional engineers have a higher marriage rate than the population as a whole when they are over thirty, but a lower rate before. Rapoport showed that engineers trained at technical college married earlier than those trained at university but that the former were more likely to come from working-class backgrounds. When asked if they thought that getting married would affect their career, two thirds of all Rapoport's sub-groups felt it would, especially if they had children. They might be less prepared to travel and more likely to play safe in the work situation and not jeopardize their position by challenging those in authority. The majority felt that marriage would make them less ambitious.

This early period of uncertainty and change may be very unsettling and stressful. Links with home and college or university friends may be broken or stretched. As friends who have gone into safer or less demanding occupations get married the dedicated careerist's loneliness may be emphasized, as all the friendly faces in his biography marry one another. He returns to his landlady's daughter in desperation if not deliberation. To some extent we caricature to make our point, but the break from the free and easy sociability and sexual freedom of student days, to the situation where most work colleagues are both older and married is not unlikely to turn the young careerist into the arms of his typist or of the

* Quoted by Rapoport (1964).

loyal girl from back home. Our data do suggest that this is not just a women's magazine myth.

The very early period of a young manager's career with a company has been demonstrated to be crucial. A recent article in the *Harvard Business Review* was entitled 'How to break in the college graduate'.* A more recent study was concerned with the relationships between early job challenge and early performance and later success; it was demonstrated that the amount of challenge in the first-year job correlates strongly with success.† The authors of this study argue that new managers are socialized by the companies they join and that the company's initial expectations of young managers has a direct and lasting effect on their future careers. As they put it (p. 223): 'Never again will he be so "unfrozen" and ready to learn as he is in his first year. For the benefit of the individual and of the investment in him, no organization can afford to treat this critical period lightly.' According to this initial-socialization argument, any company which neglects or under-stretches its trainee managers in their first year may produce lasting effects on a man's career, wherever he works. However, men are not puppy dogs which have to be house trained and the personal plans of the typical careerist must also be considered.

THE EARLY PRODUCTIVE PERIOD

Unless a man has been exceptionally able during his early period of experimentation and switching, he will be obliged to establish his career by some 'solid' work or complete a major job as proof of his total potential. What he does in this period may be a result of his past experience and future expectations, but the sense of continuity will now be stronger. One of the most distinctive aspects of this phase may be the need to co-operate with colleagues with whom he is also, in a sense, in competition. In previous jobs the degree of commitment to the job and work situation may have been less, since both the man and his colleagues would know and accept that his stay

* Schein, 1964.   † Berlew and Hall, 1966.

24

was temporary and that his identity or created self-image in this situation was not of central importance.

Now, however, the typical career man is forced into a love–hate relationship with colleagues: too much of his sense of personal identity is involved in this particular work situation for him to be able to ignore his colleagues. They, in their turn, need his energies and efforts; but to some degree the greater his success, the greater will be their implied failure. The more the man is committed to his career the more he will be committed to alliances with his colleagues as an extension of this commitment. As Burns (1966, p. 14), who has written so perceptively on this issue, puts it 'It reflects, by way of being an alternative way of pushing self-interest, his need to groom himself for organization acceptability.' This is a time when he must work out some boundary between 'licit ambition and illicit careerism'.

Men are objectively open to three main sources of strain or tension at this period. Assuming that they are married, which most of them will be, it is likely that this will be the peak of the baby-producing period. A man's wife may have trouble with her pregnancy and become tired, irritable and less 'wifely' in various ways. All the clichés may apply with greater or lesser force: the weepy, post-parturiant wife, the sleepless nights, the mess of baby stuff everywhere. It is easy to exaggerate the amount of havoc two or three tinies in a small, neat, suburban house can create, but certainly it is the exceptional wife who is ready to serve nightly as a tame geisha girl for her work-wracked spouse.

Secondly, as we have suggested, the work situation may be stretching the man more perhaps than at any other time. Unable to hide behind lack of experience, but equally without actually having the experience, the job of pushing up sales in a new area or getting a new plant operating efficiently falls heavily on his shoulders. Not only must he be effective, but he must be seen to be effective. Work probably has to come home in the evenings and the physical strain may be heavy. We enlarge on this in relation to our managers in Chapters 8 and 9 below.

Finally there is the new situation of operating in the cliques and cabals arising from conflict and cooperation with colleagues.* What sort of man is he? What personality traits do both he and they define as desirable to enable him to become the kind of man he should be? This may be the most intense period of adult socialization our typical man passes through. Later on men must take him more as they find him: at this stage they are moulding him as they, his colleagues, are also being moulded themselves.

THE MIDDLE AND LATE PRODUCTIVE PERIODS

In the early period the man is under stress, as we have seen: by his middle or late productive periods he will have come to terms with himself, and his sense of career and personal identity will be fixed. He will probably have re-written his biography or mental picture of himself to suggest that all previous stages in his career have logically led to his present position or the next one to which he aspires. He will have rehearsed this new identity with his wife or other confidant to make sure the career story remains consistent. It may be possible for him to present this new identity to a new company and new colleagues formally through his *curriculum vitae*, and informally by all the clues and signs to his most favourable identity which he is now practised at controlling.

We are not suggesting that all men with careers are successful; indeed the pyramids of most organizational structures ensure that if success is defined as 'getting to the top', then most men will not be 'successful'. A difficult question to decide is what we mean by 'successful', since it is one of the main themes of this book that company success and personal success need not coincide.

Given that men are under the three sources of stress in their early productive period, some men may at this time feel obliged to withdraw from one or more stressful situation. Retreating from the world of work may lead to experiment in

* Burns, 1956, pp. 467–86. Sofer, 1966.

the private field, and this may be a time for sexual adventures. Alternatively the man may become more deeply involved in the sphere in which he feels most secure, perhaps over-compensating by driving himself in a narrow work role. Finally he may cling to his work colleagues for security, spending time on the golf-course or drinking when he might otherwise be at home facing up to difficult work problems. With the fear of being bypassed for promotion, or even of demotion, becoming a real possibility we leave the productive period for the final period of contrasts. Before coming to this we digress briefly to discuss organization career lines.

CAREER LINES

Individuals pursuing a career combine vertical and horizontal movements: the latter widen experience; the former add responsibility. Some positions, whether achieved by vertical or horizontal movement, are more critical than others, since performance at these points will determine the type of career line to be followed later. Different types of organizations have different structures, with different career lines and opportunities for mobility: the size of the company, the nature and pattern of its relationships with its subsidiaries, if it has them, the geographical distribution of its plants, all make for variety. Furthermore, companies with fairly similar structures may operate with different policies: some may have a policy of recruiting from outside the company at certain levels to inject 'new blood', whereas others may believe that recruitment from within provides more incentive. Even for those men whom the company wants to keep, one organization may argue that it is in the men's interests to move frequently to gain a wide experience; another organization may feel that the best men should not be moved too much, first, since they are unlikely to get better men to replace them and secondly since they see little point in unsettling a man and risking his leaving the company. Vertical mobility in an organization is not always achieved by physical mobility. However, this varies again according to function: it may make better sense when promoting a man to regional sales manager to move him to a new region so that he will not be the immediate superior of his erstwhile colleagues and drinking partners. Alternatively in other branches – on the technical and production side – a man's experience of the research work of his colleagues or detailed knowledge of the operation of a plant may make it appear more sensible, or indeed necessary, to promote him without lateral, physical movement. Martin and Strauss (1956) have provided a good discussion of this issue and they conclude 'a relationship holds between mobility structure, technology, organization philosophy and type of training. It becomes a major problem in management to achieve the right blending of these components.'

In growth industries it is very difficult for career lines to develop into typical patterns and all managers may simply move up the escalator together. In other, more stable and structured organizations individuals may be expected to follow fairly predictable patterns or career timetables and there are strong pressures not to promote people if they are 'too young' (or, for that matter, 'too old'). Youth may be a positive barrier to promotion in some organizations, where it is argued that the promotion of one young man leads to dissatisfaction and relative deprivation among his contemporaries, some of whom may decide to leave if they too do not get advancement. It also puts pressure on the older men, who fear that 'experience' is being devalued. Some firms combine both methods so that, for example, young men are promoted very rapidly in the commercial side as a result of their energy and effectiveness. As they get up to higher levels of management they are likely to come into conflict with other 'line' managers who have come up from other functional branches of the organization where age is an essential prerequisite to promotion. Age differentials may then underline other sources of potential conflict within the organization and there may be pressure to bring the part of the organization which promotes 'too rapidly' back into line. This in turn leads to demands for more functional autonomy as the price for more efficient selling and rapid expansion.

The more clearly that career timetables become institutionalized in a company, the more easily men can assess their own success and advancement within the organization. This again can work in two ways: on the one hand it can provide stability and continuity within an organization, so that rather than operating the system and engaging in personal battles and stratagems to outwit colleagues in the struggle for promotion, men can simply get on with the job, building up experience and effectiveness which will eventually be rewarded. On the other hand the necessity to wait, as it were, for dead men's shoes may cause the young manager to lose patience. The ability to judge the rate of advancement which is likely, early in his career, may encourage a man to leave an organization, not because he does not enjoy his job or because he is not doing well, but simply because prospects seem less encouraging than they would be if he were doing a similar job elsewhere. This may cause a man to suffer a short-term drop in salary in order to change onto a better career ladder.

It is for such reasons that organizations prefer to have considerable ambiguity surrounding the whole question of salaries, appropriate career lines and so on. The greater the ambiguity or secrecy the less likely it is that men will know who their chief rivals in the organization are, how their salaries compare with those of colleagues and contemporaries and whether they would do better elsewhere. This confusion and ambiguity in the characterization of the market may, paradoxically, create more stability than, say, a nationally negotiated wage rate for managers. The more salaries are known and the criteria for advancement made explicit the more dissatisfaction and relative deprivation there is likely to be. The more salary comes to be the sole determinant of a man's worth and the more the knowledge of a man's salary is shared the greater the concern with it. In some senses apparent justice is harder to bear than unexplained injustice: when a man can argue that he was unlucky, or not in the right place at the right time, he may find it easier to put up with lack of promotion. However, when it is made explicit to his colleagues that his salary has been pegged simply because he is less effective as a manager, no matter how objectively true this may be, it is harder to bear.

Of course, most men want the best of both worlds: a stable and secure career and a high salary. These two goals may be incompatible. It is interesting in this context to consider the role of the management selection organizations. Such organizations work partly through an incredibly effective and diffuse grape vine which taps sources of knowledge about successful and aspiring managers through a broad cross-section of British industry. They also advertise extensively in the daily and Sunday papers. It is partly their function to make the young manager uneasy and to feel that the grass may be greener elsewhere. Particularly for those who are in, and move between, smaller companies the management selection organizations provide all the career planning they are likely to get. A chance meeting may be followed a year later with a phone call about a possible job which may be interesting. This, of course, makes these organizations very powerful in deciding whom to phone or whom to shortlist. The nervous laugh with which men tell the story about the man who applied for his own job gives some indication of the situation. There is need for serious sociological investigation of this particular aspect of managers' careers.

THE PERIOD OF CONTRASTS

Since, by and large, most organizations taper fairly sharply at the peaks of their hierarchies there are likely to be sharp contrasts between those men in their late forties and fifties who go on to positions of the greatest power and responsibility and those who level off at some lower peak or operate some strategy of withdrawal, so that their work is no longer their central life interest in the way it may have been during their thirties. The less successful may settle for being big fish in a small pool, as chairmen or directors of small subsidiaries, or they may make a late career switch to something related but different. Others may get involved in family and community activities, retreat into private fantasies, or regress to have an affair with someone the same age as their daughter.

Few men are able to judge the future development of their careers very accurately and a high proportion are likely to 'over-aspire' even if they will not openly acknowledge it. Hence some kind of 'cooling out', as it has been called,* is needed to square expectations with reality. This is seen in its most acute form with the problem of demotion. It is in this context that we can see the sharpest contrasts between the pressures for competition and efficiency and the pressures for stability and security. A recent study by Goldner (1965) of the Graduate School of Business at Columbia University sheds some light on this problem. As senior managers develop an ideology of 'adequacy' – that is, the idea that now they are on the 'plateau' of their career they can take it easier for a time – those rising in the hierarchy become dissatisfied with low rates of demotion. Those accepting adequate performance rather than excellence are likely to take fewer risks, aiming always at the safe decision. The company's reaction to this situation is to pursue a policy of demotion but not to discharge any manager. Goldner quotes one of his respondents as follows:

No one is getting fired if his intent is right. This is damn important. We are all stockholders and all of us have chosen this company as a career company and some of us have passed a point of no return. If we get fired where do we go?

Goldner suggests (p. 717) that

comments like these suggest that extreme anxiety is alleviated by combining employment security with uncertainty of position, while at the same time personnel are motivated to produce, to remain flexible and to innovate. If employment security were at stake the pressure would be to work hard but also to 'play it safe', and security, of both employment and position, would weaken incentives to produce and innovate.

Most of the men interviewed in Goldner's study were prepared to accept that demotion would be likely for them, with

* Goffman, 1962.

sixty-three per cent of the headquarters executives believing they had a good chance of demotion. The interesting theme raised by this particular research report is the way both the organization and the individual accommodated the uncertainty about demotion with the need to be efficient. The organization did much to disguise the demotion by making the career situation more ambiguous, thus making effective demotion less visible. Lateral movements are as frequent as promotion and the men are simply not sure whether a given move was promotion, demotion or a lateral move. Hence men sometimes genuinely do not know when they have been demoted, and with a great deal of overlapping of responsibility in the company, it might be difficult to give an objective answer. The status of particular positions may be in a state of flux. The positive functions of ambiguity were illustrated by a situation where one part of the company's organization became known as a 'dumping ground' for men who were becoming less effective. This stigmatizing of one division was lost when the company started sending evidently upwardly mobile men there to mix with those who were in fact demoted. This mixing of the upward and downwardly mobile creates ambiguity when new or ambiguously rated positions are not available. Ambiguity is also created by 'rewarding' men, by sending them away from the company for a period of 'training'. Not all men on managers' courses are potential high-flyers: some are simply those who will not be missed from their desks or who are being compensated for demotion.

Where it is quite possible to be promoted after demotion the individual may be able to withstand a particular demotion, even if it is perceived as such, without too much loss of self-esteem. As Goldner puts it 'this "zig-zag" mobility is a natural phenomenon in a widely dispersed diversified organization that contains many lines of "skill" and authority as well as a social acceptance of demotion'. The vaguer the criteria for advancement, as we suggested above, the less the strain on the individual. The more explicit the criteria the less easy it may be both to justify what is done and to rectify mistakes. The managers themselves are likely to develop an ideology of 'moderate success' by commenting on the 'price' which must be paid for moving up the career ladder. Defensive reactions discussed above and the rewriting of biographies to emphasize another identity in his personal hierarchy are likely to emerge at this period. It is almost impossible for the researcher to discover whether a man 'really' planned to withdraw from total involvement in his work life during his forties or whether this alternative was in effect forced upon him by the organization. When does necessity become a virtue? It can be argued that only when a man has achieved a fair measure of success can he allow himself to shift attention to family, community and leisure interests. This development of a man's 'real' self in his forties is a somewhat doubtful proposition and one to which we shall return when considering the 'careers' of some of our sample of managers.

This study by Goldner has been referred to in some detail, since it is central to the theme of this book. Clearly his work is limited in relating simply to one organization, which is perhaps unusual in having less clear lines of authority than would be the case in many other organizations. He does not probe the tensions the men themselves may suffer throughout their careers between two equally strongly culturally endorsed values – success in career and involvement with the family. He simply urges (p. 724) that investigation should be directed to the development of alternative and perhaps conflicting goal systems, 'If all societies – and organizations – require some system of stratification, to place and motivate individuals, then consideration of the dysfunctions produced by stratification may suggest that alternative *unstratified* systems are also necessary.' This is a valuable insight and underlines the necessity for an understanding of what is subjectively important – the private plans, projects and fluctuating hierarchies of identities – to the men concerned.

It is evident that at this period in a man's career there can be a wide diversity of situations and responses. There has been some interesting work on this stage during the last decade. One of the nicest accounts is that by W. E. Moore in *The Conduct of the Corporation* (1962). This book has been somewhat neglected in Britain, perhaps because of its detached and gently mocking tune. In his chapter on 'Climbers, Riders and Treaders' Moore points out (p. 168) that 'there is no reason to suppose that the coincidence of capacities and opportunities is always neat and orderly, that chance plays no part in the outcome, or that mismatches do not occur. Between the extremes of outstanding success and miserable failure lie many middle courses.'

Moore goes on to describe some of the characteristic types and compares the 'strainers' with the 'secure mobiles' – the latter 'provide assurance of modest progress not by doing nothing but also not by doing anything exceptional'. Those who opt out at this stage to do a less demanding job are 'treated with patronizing sympathy or open contempt'. It is always assumed that those who are not 'successful' are 'frustrated'. Moore comments (p. 175):

> In the American ideological baggage the man who professes to be satisfied has 'given up'. He has left the rat race and entered the treadmill, where progress is foredoomed. Contentment is not a permissible goal; in fact it is downright immoral.

The acceptance that there may be different orientations to success and career is an interesting theme and there have been other typologies related to the American situation.*

Other studies have documented the mobility orientations of managers and have shown that only a minority are strivers: a high proportion are prepared to look back on their careers and congratulate themselves on how far they have gone. There is also a higher degree of ambivalence towards the idea of career success than some research workers have expected.†

SOME OTHER VIEWS OF MANAGERS IN MID-CAREER

This diversity of orientation and situation of men in mid-career provides certain problems for those who see managers primarily as 'a resource' which needs to be exploited to the full in order to meet 'the demands' of industry, the system,

---

* For example in Presthus (1962) and Downs (1967).
† See, for example, Tausky and Dubin (1965).

the country and so on. Perhaps the best example of this approach is provided by the British Institute of Management report by Alistair Mant on *The Experienced Manager* (1969). The report is primarily concerned with the most appropriate training and education for the

man who has probably had at least five years in management and has reached his position largely through success in jobs below his current one. He is probably no longer in a company promotion fast stream. His success has arisen from a mixture of experience, intuition and knowledge built up by dealing with situations. His management techniques and skills have been developed by necessity rather than any planned process. He is most commonly, but not necessarily, in middle age and middle management. (p. 7)

The report then goes on to develop a typology of these men which is worth considering in greater detail than those in the American sources mentioned above. We reserve our comments until we have reproduced the typology in full.

(a) Mobile Manager I (Internal)

This type is still on a reasonably 'fast track', probably in a growth industry. Aided by rapid expansion and shortage of managers in his company he is able to see himself as 'a man on the move'. He is likely to be 'deeply committed, politically sensitive and trusted in high places . . . largely thanks to his mobility, he has developed the knack of quickly picking up the small quantity of factors in successive jobs which account for most of the results'. He is probably between thirty-five and forty-five. Such a man 'will need (and seek) increasing access to the top'. He is thought to represent only a small section of the experienced manager population.

(b) Mobile Manager II (External)

Apparently also known as 'the hopper' or 'the wheeler-dealer' this man has loyalty primarily to himself. Most forms of company indoctrination will be wasted on him.

(c) The Thwarted Manager

In a stable, conservative and bureaucratic organization, or perhaps in a declining industry, such a man 'has or had drive and ambition but is now getting to be too good at his job'. Since he has good standing in the company and is 'basically loyal' he needs to become a mobile manager of some sort before it is 'too late'. Companies should consider rotating him from job to job.

(d) The Specialist/Technocrat Manager

The specialist's main problem is to resolve the choice of career paths between a future based on technical or managerial expertise.

(e) Recessional Manager (The Hidden Redundant)

This manager does just enough to get by: he 'is politically sensitive and quite cynical about promotion and "getting on". He may in fact be less talented than his colleagues or a combination of early bad luck and career path blockage may have transformed him from any of the previous types.' If he goes on a mid-management course this 'far from being a benefit or an act of philanthropy belongs in the medical department as a kind of elixir for the sick manager'.

(f) The Old-Boy Manager

He tends to come from 'rather slow, friendly companies of a fair size, operating in the gentler markets. The firm is characterized by woolly objectives and a "system" of informal criteria for promotion – the road to the top is paved with mimicry.' Such men are said to need a 'jolt'.

(g) The Backbone Manager

'He tends to be in his forties – past the first flush of ambition but not yet on the "run home". . . . He is responsible and willing and has probably made a rational accommodation to limited prospects in the company.' Firms with a training department who send him on a company course for 'conditioning' or 'reindoctrination' are wasting his time, 'when his real need is to think about, and improve, his own performance of his own job, using yardsticks that make sense to him'.

Of course certain types – such as the 'high-flyer' or 'brilliant technocrat' are not included in the typology by definition. However, it is clear that the author does consider that it is a representative and exhaustive list and from discussion he found that even the smallest companies could have examples from each type.

We must now examine certain assumptions that are made in the report. First, it is assumed that most men ought to be 'committed', 'loyal', 'ambitious' and so forth. Indeed the author states '*In a perfect world, all managers would be Mobiles and Backbones*' (p. 16, our italics).

It is unquestioned that work must be a central life interest, and indeed it is one of the purposes of the report 'to ensure that all managers reach their own personal summit, however mediocre that might be'. Thus the report has a particular value position or ideology and the typology reflects that ideology. As a resource to be exploited some managers need 'indoctrination' or a change of attitude, some need 'a jolt', others need to be made artificially mobile by rotation, and so forth. These things are needed for men to get on and get up. The type who is described as 'politically sensitive and quite cynical about promotion and "getting on"' is said to be 'sick'. The second assumption is that where men are less committed and so forth this is generally due to the nature of the company. Thus the thwarted manager is in a 'declining industry', the old-boy manager is in 'gentler markets' and so forth. There is no indication that men might be affected by their own private plans based on family or community roles and identities. The assumption is that the firm moulds the man. References to indoctrination are frequent, perhaps implying that the moulding influences have to be aided now and again.

Of course this is not a sociologist's typology but is devised by someone preparing a report for the British Institute of Management to provide a guide to the training requirement of perhaps the majority of British managers. It is clear, however, that both within the company and outside there is a conception of an ideal-typical career orientation and attitude to the firm which is 'normal'. This is clearly a move towards the American pattern which the report itself recognizes – 'the aim of "professionalism" in American management education implies a widespread professional *commitment* to the business world which has not shown itself in Britain on any scale'. While accepting that 'any manpower system generates relative "failures"', the report does not face up to the problem of what would happen if all managers really did share the same striving attitudes. If they were all active movers, measuring their success by the speed of promotion, totally committed to their work and constantly striving to innovate, surely there would be widespread discontent and unrest. A diversity of ideologies is essential: if all the ambiguity is destroyed the British Institute of Management might find, no doubt to its great surprise, that it had turned into a trade union. It is perhaps just as well that the assumption that all managers have 'been conditioned to expect more or less continuous advancement' is not true.

We have been sceptical of Mant's report but see it as inevitable in its context. Clearly it is related to quite different purposes from that which we have in this book. We take a man's orientation to 'success' and 'career' as problematic: those who view managers as a resource have an understandable bias to managerial ambition and commitment. However, even if we accept their goals, we are not convinced that the most ambitious or committed men are necessarily the most efficient. The assumption that the man who takes work home and cultivates business connections at all times is necessarily better or more efficient than the man, say, who prefers to go home at five-thirty to his family and garden should perhaps be questioned. The cool, detached approach to work, based on a more instrumental attitude, need not necessarily be less effective. A senior 'backbone manager', quoted in the report, claimed that he was stretched to his limits by working on a second job. This is supposed to illustrate the point that new challenges should be presented in order to get this desirable stretching. This taut view of efficiency is questionable.

It is useful to have this statement of assumptions for British managers as so much of the literature in this field is related to the American experience and is of only limited usefulness. We are aware of the dangers of using previous research done in a different context with different norms and values as an introduction to our material. A recent work by Cyril Sofer (1970) illustrates the dangers and inadequacies of this approach very well. This is a study of eighty-one men in two large British companies. The actual reporting on these men's views is preceded by a very thorough review of the literature.* He moves between British studies and American studies, between studies in large, complex organizations and small organizations, between studies based on samples of different sizes and so on. So much material is presented that the limitations of the study in terms of its general applicability to British middle managers, which Sofer acknowledges, are easily overlooked. As it happened we had men in our sample who worked for the two companies Sofer was concerned with, but of course we had a much wider spread of British industry. Sofer's study suffers from the fact that all the interviews were held at the workplace and there was no contact with the men's wives and their home environment. In terms of our present argument we do find it of great interest that thirty-eight out of the eighty-one men have significant reservations about the work they are doing and mention some form of retreat or private plan.† Total company commitment, even in the large companies which stress and value it, seems less widespread than is perhaps assumed. This applies particularly to the scientists in Sofer's sample, who are not so readily prepared to have their whole lives dominated by their work. Some of Sofer's respondents make this point quite clearly:

I dislike situations where there is a high spillover of work into life

I don't believe in belonging to the firm heart and soul. It's not good for the firm. . . . I don't live to work. I work to live

I want to go up a bit, not too far. I want to live a bit. A more extended life, spare time to enjoy family life and weekends

* This present chapter had been drafted before Sofer's book was published and we do not take account of his work in our approach to the career in the foregoing pages.

† ibid., pp. 193–7.

39

I'm pretty satisfied with the whole balance of my life. I have a job that is interesting and can carry on all my outside interests. This would affect my reactions to a geographical move. I would consider resigning because of my church commitments . . .

There must be a point where the next step is not worth the worry. . . . One thing I don't want to do is to climb on the bandwagon of ambition to the extent of destroying happiness at home. It happens at about my level.

However, Sofer does little more than note such reservations. This may be because in his pilot study he had discovered that men in another company wanted to be used more unambiguously as organizational resources; thus, not expecting such responses, he did not build into his study ways of probing the tension between family and work. This is particularly unfortunate since a substantial proportion of his sample live to a significant extent in occupational communities* but the implications of this were not explored. Therefore, since his pilot study was in one company with a distinctive culture, and his full study was in two other companies with distinctive characteristics of their own, Sofer's study has limitations. His review of the literature is uncritical and much is quoted with the implication that it has relevance for the interpretation of his findings. It is, perhaps, worth quoting Riesman (1964, pp. 187–8), if only to balance the conception of American management described in the Mant report:

. . . One sees developing in certain occupations a more complex concept of what one might do with one's life, a concept that requires that individuals achieve self-realization as well as a certain position in the community. Attention to the family and the community tend to become elements of this new aim, though perhaps insufficient in themselves. What is clear is that the individual who has only his work is thought to be one-sided, possibly sick, and certainly unfortunate. Similar attitudes may be spreading in the ranks of middle management, where junior executives may realize that they are not indispensable and that, in an increasingly complex and bureaucratic society, they may be fools to drive themselves only in order to achieve a moderately greater income and vastly greater responsibilities.

* ibid., p. 312.

If we can understand the reciprocal relationships between career and work experience and family and community patterns of behaviour we may be getting closer to an understanding of the principal determinants of styles of life. It is to this issue that Wilensky (1960, p. 550) addresses himself: 'I believe that . . . in the study of the links between economic order and life style, with attention to change within the biography of persons and the history of structures, lie some of the most fascinating clues to the shape of modern society.' Wilensky goes on to argue (p. 555),

It is likely that with continuing industrialization careers are becoming on average more discrete and are characterized by more numerous stages, longer training periods, less fluctuation in the curve of rewards (amount, timing, duration), a more bureaucratic setting and more institutionalization but are less widely visible (fewer, smaller publics recognize them). Each of these dimensions of career is related to life style and thus to the types and levels of integration of persons and groups into community and society.

Wilensky analyses the work of Riesman (1961 edition) and Whyte (1956) in this context, arguing that the organization-man syndrome can be explained by certain structural attributes of organizations. The sort of factors which seem to be important are tall hierarchies, giving many positions and opportunities for mobility, a high ratio of managers to managed, a diversified or indispensable industry with a high growth potential, and so on. The characteristics of expedient conformity and a pseudo-community style of life with shallow roots are said to follow from such structural features, particularly for middle managers. Wilensky gives some interesting clues to this overconformity among the men in the middle. Such men are not only less involved in the day-to-day tasks of the men at the bottom, they also lack the overview of the whole enterprise which is available to the top executives who are responsible for the major goals of the organization, such as profit and long-term growth. It is difficult to assign such responsibilities to men in the middle and those beneath them are more clearly accountable in terms of prescribed processes and by regular checks on output and quality. Nevertheless competition amongst middle managers is keen and, as Wilensky (1960, pp. 556–7n.) significantly remarks, 'Strong competition for vaguely defined jobs breeds insecurity. Insecurity breeds both overconformity and underconformity and encourages "politicking". The insecure fear change and seek safety in fixed rules (whether they fit organizational needs or not), or if sticking to useful rules makes the boss unhappy, they underconform.'

More specifically Wilensky elaborates the conditions which are likely to lead to strong community ties, participation in voluntary associations and the like. If the technical and social organization of work provides a degree of freedom and variety, giving wide-ranging contacts with customers or clients, thus making the work role visible to significant others, and, finally, if also the career is *orderly*, with each job leading to another related in function and higher in status, then such community ties are more likely. The analysis and classification of complete work histories by the degree of orderliness enables Wilensky to create a typology of careers, which cuts across all types and sizes of organizations as well as across diverse age grades and economic strata. He found that the categories he devised fitted the data better than distinctions between 'bureaucratic' and 'entrepreneur', 'old' or 'new' middle class and the like. Wilensky demonstrates convincingly that those with orderly careers join more activities, spend more time being engaged in them and are more likely to be involved with local school or church activities than those with disorderly careers. Furthermore, those with orderly careers will have a wider range of social contacts both within and outside the family; they are more likely to be in circles of friends where each knows the others and their friendships are likely to be more long-lasting. These patterns could not be explained by education, age or income differentials. Such factors as the present income or occupational status of a man or his father appear to be less good predictors of patterns of social relations and styles of leisure-time activity 'than career pat-

tern, mobility orientation, and work milieu – and the associated educational experiences'.*

Without doubt an understanding of the relationships
between the structure and style of work and the pattern and
style of extra-work activities and relationships is still confused.
So much depends on the personal plans and self-images which
a man brings to the work situation that it is difficult to see
how a particular set of structural conditions can in themselves
have the strong determinative effects which Wilensky's data
demonstrate. However, we must remember that he is simply
showing that the associations found in his typology of a particular cluster of variables is better than that found in other
typologies. Sociologists are fond of typologies and dichotomies, each with subtle differences in meaning, some of which
may be listed as follows:

Traditionalists	Non-traditionalists
Orderly careers	Disorderly careers
Burgesses	Spiralists
Locals	Cosmopolitans
Entrepreneur	Bureaucrat

There has been much debate on the finer distinctions of
these 'catchy neologisms which often get confused with
knowledge' to borrow a phrase† and the degree to which they
may be uni- or multi-dimensional‡ or the way in which they
may be subdivided. For example, one particularly fine study of
the 'latent' social roles of 'locals' and 'cosmopolitans' among
faculty members in a small liberal arts college in America was
able to sub-divide the former into 'the dedicated', 'the elders',
the 'true bureaucrats', and 'the homeguard', whereas the
latter were sub-divided into two: 'the outsiders' and 'the
empire builders'.§ This is an extremely valuable and perceptive study but there appears to be no end to the different
forms and patterns of these latent roles and identities. In their
context they are useful to clarify the different-patterned

* Wilensky, 1961, p. 539.   † Hauser, 1965.
‡ Goldberg, L. C. *et. al.*, 1965.   § Gouldner, 1957 and 1958.

responses to similar structural situations. Clearly there is an important difference between say, an industrial scientist, who has as his reference group his colleagues and peers within the academic discipline within which he works, and the scientist whose reference group is company-oriented and not necessarily tied to his specific field of competence. Of course any group of industrial scientists is unlikely to be divided between the two types, but it is nevertheless an important distinction to make.* Certainly we are not against the use of typologies or even neologisms: they can often be aids to understanding within a given context. However, we must be careful lest a knowledge of a certain pattern is mistaken for an understanding of the processes which caused that pattern. We have made an analytical distinction between the objective characteristics and structures of organizations, which give rise to typical careers, and the subjective meaning-complexes which typical actors bring to these situations. The individual is shifting and changing his definition of himself and his private life as he experiences changes in his family and work situation. Similarly, the organization, or the 'structure' of the world into which the actor moves, is changing. A continuous pattern of interaction and bargaining, between actors with different biographies, expectations and definitions of the situation, serves to modify and change the structures within which the actors operate. Social life is less fixed and static than many sociologists would have us believe, but any descriptive study is bound to categorize and simplify – not to put a non-existent order on complex reality but rather to highlight the pattern which is there *at the appropriate level of analysis*. Much confusion has arisen in contemporary sociology because scholars working at different levels of abstraction have talked past each other. This is not the place to enlarge on this theme but it is certainly important to be aware of the difficulties.†

Our aim throughout this book is to make the sort of men

* See the admirable study of Glaser (1964).

† The following provide a good introduction to the problems we have in mind, Berger and Luckmann (1967); Blau (1964); McCall and Simmons (1966).

and women about whom we write more conscious of the processes of which they form a part. Description is necessary as a context within which we can analyse the processes operating. This may help towards a general understanding of how society works, which we take to be one of the chief purposes of sociology. In this chapter we have sought to raise a number of issues about the career, more to give readers a feeling for the subject and some of the central concerns of those working on it, rather than to provide a definitive contribution to a text-book. We turn in the next chapter to our own material on the 'careers' of eighty-six managers in British industry.

CHAPTER 3

Managers and Their Mobility

In this chapter we explore in some detail the issue that first aroused our interest in the interrelationships between career and family life: mobility. However, before discussing the effects of physical mobility on the wives and families of our managers, we must supply some essential background information. We must attempt to provide the reader with some salient points on the general characteristics of the managers, which should be borne in mind in relation to our discussions in the chapters which follow.

WHO ARE THE MANAGERS?

We do not want to weary the reader with a detailed statistical exposition, particularly since the totals in sub-groups of our sample are small and without much statistical significance. The most accurate way to present the characteristics of our men is probably in the form of a series of tables, simply showing the actual numbers in each category. This we do in an appendix to this chapter. We now draw out some of the most relevant points, hoping that those who want to read the tables in detail will forgive us if we have painted with rather too broad strokes on occasion. (Page 108 gives comparable information about the social backgrounds, and educational and work experience of the wives.)

Most of our managers are in their thirties: only two men were under 31 and two were over 50 (Table 3.1). They were fairly evenly spread between the commercial, administrative and technical branches of their respective companies (Table 3.2). We were particularly interested in the social origins of our sample, since it is frequently asserted that managers are more likely to come from the middle class.* We gathered

* e.g. Miliband, 1969, pp. 44–5.

Who are the managers?

TABLE 3.1. The Ages of the Managers

The Manager in 1967 was	No.	Per cent
Under 35	28	32
Between 36 and 40	30	35
Between 41 and 45	17	20
46 and over	11	13
	86	100

information on the chief occupations of the fathers of our managers and this showed that 36 out of the 86 were themselves sons of managers or professional workers. A further 27 had fathers who were in junior non-manual occupations, personal-service workers, foremen and so on. We have classified these as 'intermediate'. Finally, 22 were sons of manual workers, but only 6 of these had fathers who were semi- or unskilled workers (Table A).* Generally our managers were now well qualified, even if they did not have a degree (Table 3.3). Only 13 men had simply 'O' or 'A' level, or an equivalent, as their highest qualification.

However, even if they are reasonably well qualified now,

TABLE 3.2. Type of Manager's Present Job

Manager's present job is	No.	per cent
1 Commercial, sales, publicity	26	30
2 Production	6	7
3 Administration and financial	19	22
4 Technical	18	21
5 Combination of 1 and 3	2	2
6 Personnel, welfare, education	6	7
7 Banking and insurance	7	8
8 Civil Service	2	2
	86	100

* Tables designated by a letter appear as an appendix at the end of this chapter.

47

many men had to work their way up and acquire these qualifications while in employment. The two most likely starting
jobs were either junior clerk (30 out of 86) or graduate
entrant (32 out of 86). This latter starting point was virtually
inevitable for the specialist scientist. A very small minority
had worked their way up right from the bottom: 5 men

TABLE 3.3. The Managers' Qualifications

	No.	Per cent
None	1	1
'O' or 'A' Level or Matriculation	12	14
Professional qualifications – diplomas, etc.	28	32
Technical qualifications at less than degree level	10	12
Degree but no further qualifications	16	19
Degree and further qualifications or Ph.D	18	21
Other	1	1
	86	100

started as manual workers on the shop floor and 6 as craft
apprentices. Table B shows that those from the solid middle
class were more likely to enter industry as graduates, and those
from 'intermediate' backgrounds to enter as junior non-
manual workers. It is worthy of note that 8 out of the 22 men
of working-class background started their careers as graduate
entrants. These statements are not by themselves very illu-
minating: in our next chapter we describe some typical career
patterns, one of which is a graduate from a working-class
background.

We now turn to mobility, the theme of this chapter. Table C
shows that 19 of the managers have moved their workplace
once every 2 or 3 years and a further 28 have moved, on
average, every 4 or 5 years. Thus just over half our sample
have been faced with a change of workplace at least every 4 or
5 years. Table D shows that for 27 men moves have also

involved frequent changes of company, since they have already worked in three or more firms. On the other hand, 31 men have remained with the same firm throughout their careers. If we now relate this mobility to the men's qualifications we see (Table E) that graduates were likely to be the least mobile – 15 out of 34 had either not moved at all or had moved less than once every 6 years. Thus our data show that it is the *least qualified* who are more likely to move. Of our 13 least-qualified men 6 had moved their workplace at least every 4 years. Clearly one must be careful not to assume that 'spiralists'* are necessarily the most successful or best-qualified men. However, if it is the case that the most qualified men can afford not to move frequently, there is an indication that men from middle-class backgrounds with few qualifications are under most pressure to move. Such men, as we show below, are most likely to be on the commercial side of their companies. As might be expected, the *rates* of mobility are higher for those aged 35 and under. Presumably this is related to the need to get wider experience in the early stages of their careers (Table F). We compared the social characteristics of those aged 35 and under with those aged 36 and over and found to our surprise that there was no tendency for a higher proportion of graduates to appear in the younger group: 10 out of the 28 younger managers are graduates, as against 24 of the 58 older men. We discovered from our analysis that there is a distinctive category of men from solid-middle-class backgrounds who are 35 or under but who do not have degrees. Ten out of our total sample fall into this category. Perhaps, for the middle class, a degree was still not so very important ten or fifteen years ago, when most of this category came into industry. Alternatively, it is possible that young, confident and articulate non-graduates make good candidates to send on managers' courses. We return to this category, exemplified by Mr Ickham, in the next chapter. It is

* The full definition derives from Watson (1964): 'the progressive ascent of . . . specialists of different skills through a series of higher positions in one or more hierarchical structures, and the concomitant residential mobility through a number of communities'.

perhaps significant that 6 out of the 10 middle-class non-graduates are working on the commercial side of their companies in sales or publicity.

Although the proportion of graduates is much the same between the younger and older categories of managers, there is a striking difference in social background between the two groups. Table F shows that, of the 28 managers aged 35 and under, 17 (61 per cent) come from the solid middle class, whereas of the 58 managers aged 36 and over only 19 (33 per cent) came from such a background. This suggests that, on the basis of our sample, it is becoming proportionately *more* difficult for men from working-class backgrounds to get into managerial positions. This finding is not likely to be due to an eccentric sample since, first, one might expect a higher proportion of men from working-class backgrounds to be sent to the Madingley course to acquire 'polish'. Secondly, this general trend has been confirmed by other studies.*

As might be expected, those with middle-class social origins were more likely to be on the commercial side, whether graduates or not. Presumably the verbal skills and self-confidence acquired during the early years of socialization have an effect throughout the career. By contrast, of the 22 men from solid-working-class origins, 9 were on the production or technical sides of their companies and 6 were on the financial and administrative sides, all jobs requiring formal, advanced training (Table G). Ten out of the 22 men with working-class backgrounds are graduates (all non-Oxbridge) and, of these, seven have doctorates or the equivalent. We enlarge on this category, again in the next chapter, through the case study of Mr Frith, a highly mobile scientist from a working-class background.

Men will be more or less mobile depending on the nature of their jobs: certain companies, or branches within companies, are more mobility-prone. We found that those in the commercial or administrative sides of their organizations are more likely to move their workplace than those in the technical or production side of the enterprise. Thus 12 out of 23 (52 per

* e.g. Clements, 1958.

cent) of the latter type had moved less than once every six years or had not moved at all since marriage, whereas 10 out of 44 (23 per cent) in the former category were similarly immobile (Table H).

We have seen that scientists are less likely to move than salesmen and also that those from working-class backgrounds are more likely to be scientists and those from middle-class backgrounds salesmen. This therefore suggests that middle-class parents are likely to be somewhat more separated from their sons than those in the working class. However, there was very little indication that those who had made frequent changes of workplace were any further from their parents than those who had made few moves. The situation for the sample as a whole is shown in Table 3.1. From this it can be seen that about the same proportion of parents live within 20 miles as live over 200 miles away; half of all parents of the managers in the sample live within 100 miles of their sons. Even in the case of the 32 men who had moved at least once every four years and whose parents were still alive, 14 of their parents live less than 100 miles away. The largest proportion of those parents who live near their sons live in the South East: of the 21 parents who live within 20 miles of their sons 12 (57 per cent) are in the South East and Eastern regions compared with the 21 out of 73 (28 per cent) for the sample as a whole living at this degree of proximity. We wondered whether the salesmen are more likely to move to the South East or whether those in technical and production jobs drift to the Midlands or North West. Our data did not confirm this hypothesis, since the numbers in the cells at this level of analysis were very few.

We now turn to consider the physical mobility of our managers in geographical terms: the men came from all over the British Isles (except from Northern Ireland), but the fact that 25 of them at present live in South East England reflects the concentration in that area of head office and management jobs. A further 25 at present live either in the Midlands, Yorkshire or the North West, and the rest are distributed as Table 3.4 shows:

TABLE 3.4. Origins of the Madingley Managers by Present Address and Distribution of S.E.G.s 1, 2 and 13 for England and Wales in 1966

Standard region	Madingley managers No.	Per cent	Proportion of the population in S.E.G.s 1, 2 and 13 for England and Wales 1966 living in each region
Scotland	3	3	0
North	6	7	5
East and West Riding North West	14	16	21
Midlands	11	13	16
Eastern	11	13	3
London and South East	25	29 ⎫ 38	⎫ 42
Southern	8	9 ⎭	⎭
South West	4	5	8
Wales	3	3	5
Other	1	1	
	86	100	100

Note: The proportions for England and Wales are taken from the table in M. Waugh (1969). This in turn is based on the 1966 Sample Census.

It is reassuring that the national distribution of professional and managerial workers is not markedly different from that of our own sample, and the slightly higher proportion in our sample from Eastern standard region is perhaps a reflection of the fact that the courses were held within the region at Cambridge.

Very few of either the men or the women in our sample live now in the place in which they were brought up: for them adulthood meant physical mobility as they left home, either to obtain training, or to go where their own or, in the case of the wives, their husband's career took them. Table J shows how few of the men are now living even in the region in which they were brought up, and, though it is, of course, based on very small numbers, this table does also permit an interesting comparison between the regions. Only the South East region has been able to keep more than half of those born there; at the other extreme none of those men born in the Northern region is still living there. This perhaps illustrates the lack of opportunity for managerial advance in the less prosperous, or more agricultural, regions of Britain, and the capacity of London and the South East in particular to provide a wide range of opportunities.* This may mean that close relationships between parents and their grown-up children, or between other extra-familial kin, may be maintained more often in the South East, as we suggested above, than in those regions which have a narrower range of opportunities for the middle class and therefore fewer opportunities to reach middle-class status.

This pattern of mobility contrasts with that documented, for the population as a whole, by the Harris and Clausen (1966) government social survey of *Labour Mobility in Great Britain, 1953–63.* Using a stratified random sample, this showed that the percentage of people born in the region and still living there varied from over 80 per cent in the North and North West, Wales and Scotland, to less than 54 per cent in London and the South East, and the Southern and the Eastern regions. This contrast must reflect chiefly the different proportions of each social class in the different regions and the fact that our sample is taken from the middle class while the *Labour Mobility* survey dealt with the population as a whole.

MANAGERS AND THEIR FAMILIES MOVING HOUSE

The majority of our managers, then, have experienced relatively long-distance mobility during adult life; for some moving house is almost a part of everyday life: 'when the curtains begin to get dirty, I begin to think of moving', one wife said. Table K shows the frequency with which the managers have moved since marriage and the distance which they have moved. There is a great variation, from the 28 who have on average

* The growing dominance of the South East is well shown by Waugh (1969).

moved less than once every 6 years, to the restless 26 who have, on average, never stayed more than 3 years in each place, and from the 31 who have spent all their married lives in the same region, to the 22 who have already lived in 3 or more regions (Table L).

What does mobility involve for the manager at home and his family? What are the patterns of interaction between husband and wife when a move is contemplated? To begin with, the characteristics of a move depend very much on the stage in their life cycle which the couple have reached. There is a characteristic sequence in which the couple move from living as newly marrieds in rented accommodation, to their first semi-detached and their first baby: then, as the children grow both in years and in numbers, better housing is sought: at the time of the survey about a third of our managers were living in detached houses with four or more bedrooms.

Because moving house for the manager is often associated with moving his job, it tends to be a point of crisis for the family, a time when conflicts become more open and when cooperation and understanding between husband and wife are more necessary than usual. Only 6 of our managers have not experienced any move since marriage. The attitudes of the wives to moving varies from the deeply antagonistic: 'I would hate to leave this area where I am so happy; I really feel it would be the end of a good life' through the acquiescent, 'I do not mind particularly where I live so long as I have my family and a good home' to the enthusiastic, 'I have learnt to make friends more easily and I look forward to seeing and living in different countries. There is also the point that in moving about the children are less likely to develop a strong dialect.' Husbands more often look at a move in terms of their career, seeing it as a necessary preliminary to a better job; for them the domestic side of a move tends to take second place in their comments. Their wives, on the other hand, will be thinking of a move primarily in terms of friendship and kinship links, their own shopping patterns, their children's education, and whether the old carpets and curtains will fit the new house. Some wives, identifying themselves closely with their husband's career, may make such comments as 'the advantages of moving are the reflected enthusiasm of my husband for his new job', or 'I rate my husband's career and happiness at work much more important than my own feelings. I accept a move as essential to his career.' A move, then, may emphasize the differences between the worlds of husband and wife, and may heighten any conflicts; where consensus between the couple exists it tends to focus on the prime importance of the husband's career, the career which has been the cause of the move.

A problem to be faced at an early stage in many moves is simply that of visiting the place where the new job is to be to look at houses, when both husband and wife have commitments which make such visiting difficult, that is a job and children, respectively. Often the husband, less often the wife, will make two or three visits to the new area and will provisionally decide on a house, the final decision about its purchase being taken after both have seen it. Many couples mention the difficulties involved in choosing a house when time is short, and give this as one reason for choosing a house on a modern estate. Time becomes an even more serious factor when a man is expected to start work on a new job soon after being given it – so soon that it would have been quite impossible for the family to have moved house in time. In these cases the wife must remain behind, perhaps for many weeks, to sell the old house, see the children through till the end of term and pack up the family's belongings. Mr and Mrs Ash, for example, moved from Southern England to the North in 1963, Mr Ash staying in a hotel in the North for three months before his wife could join him; then in 1965 he moved back to the South, and again they were separated for about two months. Such a time of separation may be one of great strain for the family, a strain which can be greatly lightened by a thoughtful employer.

Many firms do indeed make provision for easing the moves of their managers. They may pay all or part of the removal expenses, may pay for the husband's, or both husband and wife's stay in a hotel while house hunting, or get agents to send details of houses for sale in the area. Even so, for at least one wife 'the chief disadvantage is that so much money is lost over moving'. Other wives, however, welcomed the double opportunity of a salary increase at the same time as a change of house: for them moving was associated with a rise in their standard of living.

What did our managers look for in a new house? Typical of many are Mr and Mrs Dover, who moved from Cheshire to Yorkshire when he was appointed to an administrative job paying a little over £2,000. Mrs Dover said

> My husband went first and was three months in a small private hotel, coming home at weekends to visit the family. He bought the local papers and narrowed down the areas in which to look for a house and spent his evenings looking at different houses. He eventually narrowed it down to nine and I and our daughter went over and spent all day looking at these nine houses. We had decided that Churchley was the nicest district in the town and narrowed our selection down to this because of its pleasantness, convenience for buses, shopping and schools: we had heard that Churchley had a good school. We picked this particular house because we felt it had more character and a more private garden than most. It was the right price and we felt it had a good layout. We think it's important when we're changing house, that if my husband has an increase in salary, even though we want a better home, we don't want it to swallow up the salary increases. We want to benefit from it rather than plough it all into the house.

Mr and Mrs Dover are typical of many in the way in which they set about moving house – in the way, for example, that a decision is taken jointly on the basis of field-work by the husband; she is typical in her concern that their houses have a certain amount of 'character' and privacy; and she is typical too in wanting to live in a 'nice' district, and in seeing a good school as an important characteristic of a nice area. Many of the couples, in fact, start their house hunting by looking for a good school and then seek a house near it. It may be useful to consider what is not mentioned – the length of her husband's journey to work, the opportunities for work for herself, the social and cultural life of the new area. Mr and Mrs Ickham's comments also illustrate the lack of interest in the length of the journey to work. Mr Ickham earns nearly £3,000 as a management consultant and travels for one and half hours by car and train to work in London: yet when asked what they disliked most about their present home neither mentioned this journey as a drawback. Mr and Mrs Manston, too, considered a daily fifty-mile drive to work only one of many factors which encouraged them to move nearer his work:

We moved because the company were opening a new mill; we had our expenses paid for moving. We could have stayed where we were but it would have meant a fifty-mile drive to work. Anyway we get itchy feet and we'd been where we were for seven years, so it made a nice prospect to move. We discussed whether or not we should move and it was a cumulation of factors. The road where we lived was getting busy, they were putting in traffic lights and things and we felt we would like to get further out and have some fresh air.

It sometimes seems to be assumed that 'modern man' is synonymous with 'mobile man', a gadfly on wheels who buzzes indefatigably from work to home to recreation to culture centre over a wide area: for such an individual, it is suggested, 'home' is at least as big as a standard region. The accounts of their lives given by our managers do little to support this theory. When looking for a new house, for instance, though many mentioned a desire to live in a 'nice' area, this seemed to mean simply the few roads round the house or, at most, the area serving the school to which their children would go. At the other extreme some very large-scale preferences were expressed, for example, liking for 'the North' or 'the South', or dislike of London or Scotland. Mrs Kingston's comment is an example of the double concern for the very small local area, and the large national area:

Previously we lived near Liverpool, but houses had sprung up all round and we were becoming rapidly surrounded and boxed in. When my husband was promoted and had to move, I was happy to come and live in a more country area: I prefer quiet areas and don't like to be surrounded by people and houses. I think basically

I'd be happier in the North, but it wouldn't worry me if we had to go elsewhere, unless it was to London.

Mrs Manston also said, 'there's nowhere that I wouldn't particularly like to go to, although my husband would definitely not move to London'. Mr and Mrs Newington, too, agreed they would never want to live in London: when asked what they liked least about their detached suburban house in a small West Country town, Mrs Newington replied 'the prospect of a bypass being put in near by, and the smell of our neighbour's oil-fired central heating'. What does she like most? 'The house is within walking distance of the sea, the country and the shops. We're also near the primary school – schooling is always in our minds when we think about houses.' It is significant that, though Mrs Newington has a car of her own and uses it every day, it is still the very local area, within walking distance, which most concerns her. She is also typical of many in her concern about educational facilities. She, too, made a comment about her husband's journey to work: 'he is only fifteen minutes' walk from his work and I take him and fetch him sometimes. I often wish it was a bit more remote. As it is here, he pops back to the office over the weekend and then tends to meet people and talk to them so he never really gets away from his work.'

From this small sample there seems to be some indication that managers do not want to live particularly near their work. Some put up with a very long journey to work and many of the wives have never been to their husband's place of work. A comment made by Mrs Frith illustrates another aspect of this: Mr Frith earns about £5,000 as an executive in a nationalized industry; she said of her husband's employers 'they had always provided our house and we paid rent and therefore we had little choice. We decided to buy a house because my husband didn't like living among the people he worked with and he thought it would be a good investment. I didn't like the area where we were, it was a depressing area, very flat, so I was keen to move too.' It seems as though the managers from any one work-place neither want to live too near each other, nor too near their subordinates; this tendency was also found, for example, among the managers of many firms in Stevenage, who often preferred to live in the villages within a twenty-mile radius rather than in the new town.*

CONJUGAL RELATIONSHIPS AT TIMES OF CAREER CRISIS

To what extent did these managers involve their wives in decision-making about their careers? Did they discuss possible changes of job with them and, if so, at what stage in the decision-making process? We expected that the great majority, if not all, of these couples would regard their marriages as partnerships, in which decisions about the children's education, holidays, or the purchase of expensive consumer durables would be taken jointly. To what extent is the man's career seen as either a sphere involving the whole family or as a sphere in which he is autonomous?

It is difficult to evaluate the amount of discussion about a proposed job and the relative contribution of each individual to the final decision. Some of the men said that they would talk to their boss, or to their colleagues, but for many their wife was the only person whom they felt to be both discreet and interested enough to be consulted. In general, the couples can be divided into two groups, though of course each group represents a continuum within which there is great variation between individuals. In the first category the husband will talk to his wife about the proposed job *before* he feels he has made the final decision about it. Of the 16 couples who were interviewed in depth, 11 fell into this category. The wife, not being in possession of as much information as her husband, cannot take an equal share in the final decision. Nevertheless she can be very valuable as a sounding board for his ideas, and as someone who can put a different, perhaps more objective, point of view; she can raise factors which he may not have considered, or give a different weight to those which he has considered. Mr and Mrs Petham are perhaps typical of this sort of couple. Mr Petham said,

* Pahl, 1965, p. 31.

All my moves are discussed with my wife before I ever apply for a job. She has always supported my decisions and if at any point she said she didn't want to move then I wouldn't. She has encouraged me; for example, she wouldn't let me chuck in my evening classes when we were first married when I wanted to. Having a different wife would have made a great difference to me. I think I'm lucky to have an intelligent wife who can discuss things at any level I want to discuss them at. I always feel on my own making decisions and I'd feel even more so without my wife's support.

Mr and Mrs Ickham were similar: he said 'my job obviously affects everything else. We certainly discuss it, but in the final analysis I make the decision, as my wife doesn't know enough about it. But I do listen to what she does say, as an outsider is often more objective.' His wife agreed: 'we discuss practically everything, but the final decision is always my husband's'. It may or may not be significant that the wife who appears to have had the greatest influence on her husband's career is married to the highest earner in the sample. Mr Chilham earns over £7,000 a year as a general sales manager and always talked about his career decisions in terms of 'we thought', 'we wanted', 'we decided'. When asked what other factors, apart from his abilities, had influenced his career, he said,

my wife, more than anything else. She has been ambitious for us as a family and has probably made me aware of my own abilities. Also with respect to my job, she has never complained about being left, or being short of money, but has always managed well with what she had. She has definitely been the biggest influence on me. If I'd been left to my own devices I'd have loved to have been a farm labourer driving a tractor.

In the second group, numbering five out of the sixteen who were interviewed at length, the husband tended to talk to his wife about a proposed job only *after* he had made up his mind about it. He would tell her about his decision but she would not share in making it. Mr Frith, for instance, said 'I've discussed them all with my wife, although I'd already made up my mind', and Mr Bridge said,

I always talk over my future prospects with my wife and sometimes with friends at the office. I was automatically placed in the job I have now, but in all other cases I have filled in an application form and got the job in competition with other people. I discuss the applications with my wife before sending them in, but consider this to be a formality rather than any real discussion.

The majority of couples, however, do discuss a proposed job before the decision about it is taken, and though it is acknowledged to be finally the husband's decision, the wife's attitude is taken into account and, though it is rarely used, she does have the power to veto. One example of this was given by a chief engineer, now living in Essex, who wrote 'our first move to our Manchester factory was at the request of the company. There was a need at Manchester for graduate engineers and the promotion prospects were better there. The return move was made at my request. My family were unhappy living in the Manchester area and I was contemplating moving south; if need be, leaving the company.' How, then, do these wives see a move of job which also involves moving house? What seem to them to be the most important considerations? What questions do they want to ask when their husband comes home and says 'I've been offered this job'?

THE WIVES AND MOBILITY

It is perhaps significant that the 86 men themselves made few comments when asked how moving house and job might affect their families. By contrast, their wives had varied and strong views on moving. Sometimes, reading a husband's and wife's separately filled-in questionnaires, there seemed to be a lack of communication between the couple, with the wife holding strong views which her husband could not fully explain, though there were, in fact, perfectly valid reasons for these views.

One important variable in determining a wife's attitude to moving was her age. Table M shows that it is the younger wives who either like moving house, or who simply do not object if a change of job means that the family is obliged to move house. Older women are more reluctant to move, or at any rate have mixed feelings about moving.

Sociological studies in the past have demonstrated the close ties which exist between working-class women and the neighbourhood where their other kin live and where they were brought up. Table N shows that for this group of managers' wives, at least, there appears to be no correlation between lack of education and reluctance to move – or perhaps the reality is rather, as several women suggested, that once the break with the area of nurture has been made they do not mind where they live. By contrast, it is the better-educated wives who have the most doubts about moving, perhaps because of their own career aspirations.

The comments made by the wives about moving seem to fall into three broad categories. First, there is a category who actually *like* moving, who take pleasure in meeting new people, seeing new places and having a new house to arrange, who find moving stimulating, and who talk of being in a rut if they stay too long in one place. Secondly, there is a category who think more of the awkwardnesses of moving – the trouble and inconvenience of buying a new house, settling the children into new schools, making new friends, perhaps finding a new job for themselves. Most of this category, however, will move if they see that it is necessary for their husbands' careers, unlike those wives in the (small) third category who *refuse* to move if it can possibly be avoided – usually because of family ties. Mrs Tydeman is an example of this sort of wife. She was born and brought up in the industrial town in the North of England where she and her husband, her father and sister, and several aunts and uncles still live. Her husband has moved his job several times within the area, but their only house move was to a better house three miles outside the town. However, they had to move back into town, 'due to my wife's nervous illness and her desire to return to birthplace and friends'. When Mr Tydeman was asked in 1965 whether any factors prevented him from moving house he replied 'None – unless my wife's health deteriorated.' But when in 1967 a managing-director's job came up in the South of England it was refused, as Mrs Tydeman explained, mainly because I didn't want to go. . . . I feel that it isn't worth killing oneself for the thought of more money or promotion. My husband already works very hard and although he says he enjoys it I don't think it does anybody any good to live and work at top speed all the time. All I wish is for him to be happy at work and remain healthy, and if promotion means hours of work, worry and entertaining most nights people neither of us particularly like, well, our happiness and pleasure means more to me at any rate than wealth or ambitions.

For this couple then the demands of the husband's work were less important than other considerations, such as proximity to friends and relations and a relaxed and 'happy' way of life. We shall return to a consideration of this, and other, attitudes to work in the last chapter.

What concerns a wife when a change of job for her manager husband means that the family must move house? Does she think most about her husband and his new job, about her children and their schooling, or about herself and her own life? The answers to these questions may be a guide to the many different attitudes which managers' wives have to the mobility in which they are involved. Though for the majority the pay, prospects, and general character of the proposed job are of the greatest importance, other factors may play a decisive part. Table 3.5 shows the relative importance wives attached to different factors. It is striking how much stress is laid, not only on the husband's job and career, but also on the children's *educational opportunities*, particularly in comparison with the unimportance of links with family and friends and of the wife's own career and interests.

In many cases the opportunities which an area offers for children – both when at school and during their leisure time – are the deciding factor when a move is contemplated. Indeed for twenty-three of all the wives the educational facilities of an area are of *greater* concern than the characteristics of the job which her husband is thinking of taking there. Other wives describe how they have urged their husband to leave an area – and therefore the job which he did there – because the educational facilities were not of the standard which they demanded.

TABLE 3.5. The Weight Given by Wives to Different Factors when Their Husbands are Considering a New Job

Wife thinks the factor is	Educational facilities of the area*	Region where the new job is	Separation from family and friends	Husband's new work day-to-day activity	Pay, prospects and general character of new job	Fringe benefits	Wife's own work or career
	No.	No.	No.	No.	No.	No.	No.
An essential consideration	31	5	4	42	38	5	1
An important consideration	45	51	21	33	45	45	4
Not important	8	29	61	11	2	35	81
	84	85	86	86	85	85	86

* This column is analysed in detail in Table O.

The wives and mobility

Who are these families who are so concerned about education? Table O shows the great importance of the family type
and the ages of the children. This table shows that it is those
families with older, and particularly teenage, children who rate
educational facilities so highly. One wife wrote,

we have three growing children of very much school age and we
had been worried about schooling facilities for some time. Having
studied comprehensive education we decided that that was what we
wanted for our children, if for no other reason than to cut the heart-
break of eleven-plus failure. My husband's transfer offered us the
chance we needed. We found that Wetherby had just built a brand
new comprehensive school so we decided to look for a house in
Wetherby (nine miles from my husband's work). Now we are very
happy here, the children seem happy at school and have far more
opportunities.

Many others would agree with the wife who said 'we prefer
to stay put till the children have completed "A" levels . . .
after that we have no objection to moving'; only those few
whose children are at boarding school are relatively uncon-
cerned.

The nature of the region to which their husband is considering
moving is an important consideration for nearly two thirds of
the managers' wives, though often they think more of 'a
pleasant neighbourhood' than of the wider region. Wives
mention such aspects as shopping facilities, opportunities for
social life, or a preference for a small town or village as
opposed to suburbia; and there is a definite feeling against the
North of England, Scotland and Northern Ireland, a job in
these areas often being regarded as a stepping stone to another
in a 'pleasanter' neighbourhood elsewhere.

The frequency with which a couple has had to move does
not seem to bear any relationship to the wife's feelings about
the importance of the region. The distribution of their moves,
however, is significant, as Table P illustrates. This table shows
that nearly half of the more mobile wives feel that the nature
of the region is not an important consideration when yet
another move is being discussed. By contrast, those who
have lived all their married lives in one region seem more

concerned about the type of area to which they may be moving.

The wife's social origins also seem to be a guide to her evaluation of the importance of the region. Table P shows most strikingly that the daughters of manual workers attach little importance to the region when they think of moving, while the daughters of the lower-middle class are most often concerned about this aspect of a move: this deserves further investigation.

In summary, then, it seems to be those wives who have moved most, either spatially or socially, who set least store by the region in which they live – as though, having come so far, one move more makes little difference. One wife who left secondary-modern school at fifteen and who did unskilled work until her marriage said 'having moved from my home town I am quite happy to go wherever my husband's work may take him'. However, there is some suggestion that, with increasing age, women become less willing to live in an unattractive environment for the sake of their husband's career. As one said, 'when starting on a career, the region is not important, but after a certain position is reached one becomes more choosy. My husband has already reached quite a high level of responsibility and we live in an attractive spa town, so it would have to be a tempting offer.' 'Intermediate'* wives seem more concerned about the region to which they are moving, while a comparison of Tables N and P shows that wives of better education and higher social origins, though often reluctant to move at all, when they do move feel less concerned than intermediate wives about the region, perhaps because they have greater confidence that they will be able to cope with whatever environment they find themselves in.

CONCLUSIONS

There is no doubt that, compared with the working class as a whole and with people in many other middle-class occupations, our managers are highly mobile. Certainly some still live in

* For the basis of this categorization see Table 3.A, page 69.

the area in which they were brought up, but for most managers frequent mobility is an inescapable part of their way of life, particularly in the early years of their careers. Minor differences apart, mobility is the norm. We must emphasize, however, that this mobility should not be seen as synonymous with 'spiralling'. Many men move in their 'careers' without any marked change in social position. As we shall see in the next chapter, many men move through a succession of jobs which only retrospectively turn into 'careers'.*

Patterns of career and patterns of mobility are complicated and we have shown that wives are not simply passive participants in the moves in which their husbands' careers may involve them. The demands and needs of children are crucial, especially of older ones who have an established circle of friends in a locality. The limited, local neighbourhood may be of greater importance to the wives than the wider region, although a particular type of local neighbourhood is perhaps more easily found in some regions than in others. The best predictor of any given manager and his wife moving in the future is the frequency with which they have *successfully* moved in the past. In particular, once women of working-class origins have moved they may show the least antagonism to moves to any region of the country. In the next chapter we concentrate on the man himself and describe something of his own attitudes and responses to the 'career' through which he finds himself moving.

* Bell discussed the relationship between mobility and career in *Middle Class Families* (1969). He showed that, while social mobility usually requires geographical mobility, the middle-class career pattern may entail geographical mobility even for those who are not socially mobile.

APPENDIX TO CHAPTER 3

Tables

3.A Socio-economic status of managers' fathers
3.B Managers' first jobs by social origins
3.C Frequency of moves of workplace
3.D Distribution of moves of workplace
3.E Frequency of moves of workplace by managers' qualifications
3.F Managers' mobility and social origins by their age
3.G Managers' present jobs by social origins
3.H Frequency of moves of workplace by two main job types
3.I Distance of parents (still surviving) from managers' present addresses
3.J Region of nurture of the managers and the number still living there now
3.K Frequency of moves of house since marriage
3.L Distribution of moves of house since marriage
3.M Wife's attitude to moving by her age
3.N Wife's attitude to moving by her qualifications
3.O Wife's attitude to her husband taking up a new job, in relation to the educational facilities of the region in which the new job would be, by family type
3.P Wife's attitude to her husband taking up a new job in relation to the region where the new job would be, by her mobility and social origins

Appendix to chapter 3

TABLE 3.A. Socio-Economic Status of Managers' Fathers

Registrar General's Socio-Economic Group			No.	Per cent
1, 3, 4, 16	(1)	Managers in government and large-scale commerce; professional workers (probably graduates); officers in the Forces	20	23
2, 5		Managers in establishments employing less than 25 people; intermediate non-manual workers	16	19
12	(2)	Own account workers	5	6
13, 14		Farmers (large landowners in Group 1)	2	2
6		Junior non-manual workers	10	12
7		Personal-service workers	1	1
8		Foremen and supervisors	9	10
9, 16	(3)	Skilled workers; other ranks in the Forces	16	19
10, 15		Semi-skilled workers; farm labourers	4	5
11		Unskilled workers	2	2
		No information	1	1
			86	100

(1) Solid middle class
(2) Intermediate
(3) Working class
Socio-Economic Groupings (S.E.G.s) derived from the Registrar General's *Classification of Occupations*, 1960.

TABLE 3.B. Managers' First Jobs by Social Origins

	Manager's father was		
	Solid middle class	*Intermediate*	*Working class*
Manager's first job was			
Manual worker or craft apprentice	6	2	3
Junior non-manual worker	8	16	5
Intermediate non-manual worker (non-graduate)	4	1	6
Graduate entry	16	8	8
Armed Forces	2		
	36	27	22

TABLE 3.C. Frequency of Moves of Workplace

Manager has moved	No.	Per cent
Once every 2 or 3 years	19	22
Once every 4 or 5 years	28	33
Once every 6 or more years	28	33
Not at all since marriage	8	9
Other	3	3
	86	100

Appendix to chapter 3

TABLE 3.D. Distribution of Moves of Workplace

Manager has	No.	Per cent
Not moved his workplace or has stayed within the same firm	31	36
Moved between 2 firms	24	28
Moved between 3 or more firms	27	31
No information	4	5
	86	100

TABLE 3.E. Frequency of Moves of Workplace by Managers' Qualifications

	Manager has					
	'O' or 'A' level or equivalent and nothing more		Professional or technical or certificates only		At least a first degree	
	No.	Per cent	No.	Per cent	No.	Per cent
Manager has moved his workplace						
At least once every 4 years	6	46	17	44	11	32
Every 5 or 6 years on average	4	31	9	23	7	21
Less than once every 6 years or not since marriage	3	23	11	28	15	44
No information			2	5	1	3
	13	100	39	100	34	100

Managers and their mobility

TABLE 3.F. Managers' Mobility and Social Origins by Their Age

| | Manager is | | | |
| | Under 35 | | 36 and over | |
	No.	Per cent	No.	Per cent
Manager has				
Moved his work-place every 2, 3 or 4 years	15	54	19	33
Moved less frequently than once every 4 years	13	46	39	67
	28	100	58	100
Manager's father was				
Solid-middle class	17	61	19	33
Intermediate	7	25	21	36
Working class	4	14	18	31
	28	100	58	100

TABLE 3.G. Managers' Present Jobs by Social Origins

| | Manager's father was | | | |
| | 'Middle class' (includes 'intermediate') | | 'Working class' | |
Present job	No.	Per cent	No.	Per cent
Commercial/sales/ publicity	22	35	4	18
Technical/production	15	24	9	41
Other	26	41	9	41
	63	100	22	100

TABLE 3.H. Frequency of Moves of Workplace by Two Main Job Types

	Manager's job is			
	Commercial/sales/ administrative/ financial		Technical/ production	
Manager has moved	No.	Per cent	No.	Per cent
At least once every 4 years since career started	24	54	7	31
Every 5 or 6 years since career started	10	23	4	17
On average less than once every 6 years or not since marriage	10	23	12	52
	44	100	23	100

TABLE 3.I. Distance of Parents (Still Surviving) from Managers' Present Addresses

Parents live	No.	Per cent
In the same town	9	12
Not in the same town but within 20 miles or so	12	16
Between 20 and 100 miles away	17	23
Between 100 and 200	14	10
Over 200 miles away	21	29
	73	100

TABLE 3.J. Region of Nurture of the Managers and the Number Still Living There Now

Standard Region	No. nurtured there	No. still living there
Scotland	7	2
North	6	0
East and West Riding North West	16	8
Midlands	11	4
Eastern	3	1
London and South East	27	15
Southern	4	1
South West	5	1
Wales	5	1
Other	2	0
	86	33

TABLE 3.K. Frequency of Moves of House since Marriage

Manager has moved	No.	Per cent
About once a year	1	1
About every 2 years	10	12
About every 3 years	15	17
About every 4 years	12	14
About every 5 years	8	9
About every 6 years	9	10
Less than once every 6 years	22	26
No move at all since marriage	6	7
Married since 1965	2	2
No information	1	1
	86	100

Note: Time in the Forces counts as one residence

74

TABLE 3.L. Distribution of Moves of House since Marriage

Manager has had	No.	Per cent
All homes within same town	11	13
All homes within same region but not within same town	20	23
Homes within 2 regions	25	29
Homes in 3 or more regions	22	26
Has not moved since marriage or has only recently married	7	8
No information	1	1
	86	100

TABLE 3.M. Wife's Attitude to Moving by Her Age

	Wife is			
	Under 35		*36 and over*	
Wife is	No.	Per cent	No.	Per cent
Mainly favourable to moving	16	39	9	20
Mainly against moving	10	24	12	27
Mixed in her feelings about moving	11	27	14	32
No information	4	10	10	22
	41	100	45	100

TABLE 3.N. Wife's Attitude to Moving by Her Qualifications

	Wife's qualifications					
	Training of 2+ years		*'A' levels/ training*		*No qualifications or only 'O' level*	
	No.	Per cent	No.	Per cent	No.	Per cent
Wife is						
Mainly favourable to moving	7	29	8	24	10	34
Mainly against moving	10	42	9	27	6	21
Mixed in her feelings about moving	5	21	11	33	6	21
No information	2	8	5	16	7	24
	24	100	33	100	29	100

TABLE 3.O. Wife's Attitude to her Husband Taking Up a New Job, in Relation to the Educational Facilities of the Region where the New Job Would Be, by Family Type

	Family type					
	All children under 5 years		*Mixed ages 0–15 years*		*All children over 5 years*	
Wife feels educational facilities to be	No.	Per cent	No.	Per cent	No.	Per cent
An essential consideration	5	28	8	35	17	45
An important consideration	12	67	15	65	17	45
Not important	1	5			4	10
	18	100	23	100	38	100

Those without children, or for whom no information is available, are omitted.

TABLE 3.P. Wife's Attitude to Her Husband Taking Up a New Job in Relation to the Region where the New Job Would Be by Her Mobility and Social Origins

| | House moves have been in | | | | Wife's father is/was | | | | | |
| | Two or more regions | | All in the same region | | Professional/ managerial | | Junior non-manual | | Manual worker | |
Wife feels region to be	No.	Per cent	No.	Per cent	No.	Per cent	No.	Per cent	No.	Per cent
An essential or very important consideration	14	30	10	32	11	28	9	36	5	24
An important consideration	12	26	14	45	15	38	10	40	6	29
Not an important consideration	20	44	7	23	13	33	6	24	10	47
	46	100	31	100	39	100	25	100	21	100

Those cases where information is incomplete are omitted.

CHAPTER 4

The Career:
Company Schemes and Private Plans

FOR a general picture of the careers of the type of men described in this book the study by R. V. Clements, *Managers: A Study of their Careers in Industry* (1958), is still the basic starting point. There have been other studies such as that produced by the Acton Society Trust, *Management Succession* (1956), or, more recently, D. G. Clark's *The Industrial Manager: His Background and Career Pattern* (1966). However, Clements's study still appears the most thorough and the most useful for present purposes, even though his sample was taken from twenty-eight firms in a limited geographical area, concentrated chiefly upon Manchester.

As a result of detailed consideration of managers' biographies Clements constructed five 'ideal types' of career pattern. These typical patterns may be summarized as follows:

(i) *'The Crown Prince'*
Men in this type follow a particular pattern largely due to close family links with the ownership or top management of the firm.

(ii) *The Managerial Trainee*
Most of these men went to public schools and most are arts graduates. Few entered industry with any strong sense of vocation – some reacted against careers in other professions; others drifted into their careers on the advice of their fathers and many coming from universities had a vague idea that industry was simply a better-paid alternative to teaching. Few had any clear idea of any one firm being better than another. In the upshot most went into whatever was the first firm that would engage them, which might or might not be the first they applied to. 'In the words of one of them, "all looked pretty mouldy, but this one turned up"' (Clements, p. 40). Mostly they went into the sales or commercial side.

78

(iii) *Pre-Qualified Specialists*

Men who are, for example, engineering or science graduates were appointed to specific jobs in which they could exercise their specific skills. A logical series of steps provided them with promotion within the firm. Such men are likely to have come from a more mixed social background than the previous two categories and it is likely that a good proportion will come from what we have described as 'intermediate' social backgrounds. Clements finds little evidence to suggest that such men are more likely to have come from working-class origins. 'It has so far been the more favourably circumstanced men, from middle- and lower-middle-class homes, who have been able to respond most easily and effectively to the needs of industry and the challenge of new educational opportunities' (Clements, p. 47).

(iv) *Special Entrants*

These men came into industry through family links or some special arrangement. Rather more than half are on the commercial side. Their social connections are not as good as category (i) and their qualifications are not as good as (ii) and (iii). It is worth quoting part of Clements's description at some length.

'These men have a fairly good social background, but not actually the best, they have a rather good and extensive education, though not normally the best of its type; most are fairly intelligent, but not particularly academic; they have had quite a favourable introduction into industry. They are men, many of whom perhaps would do quite well but might not shine in other walks of life. Most of them probably have no special endowment of the inherent qualities that make for conspicuous success, such as application, high intelligence, or originality. What natural capacities they possess have been pretty fully developed and exploited; they are moulded thoroughly by their class, home and educational background. They are endowed with a certain self-confidence, bred by a comfortable and secure home environment, developed by a type of education that in large part makes this its aim, and confirmed by a continuous success that in part is itself due to their easy unselfconscious feeling of assurance. It is natural for them to be in leading positions. They can talk without embarrassment to their social equals or superiors who are in important posts. On the whole people from less favourable environments find it natural to be subordinate to them. They have some acquaintance with the play of ideas and have been introduced to a wide cultural background. They have many of them an ease of speech and manner which in some may be superficial, but impresses and pleases most who lack it' (Clements, pp. 57–8).

Such men were fixed up with a post through the influence of their father or they might even have replied to an advertisement. Their 'training' was rudimentary and haphazard, perhaps supplemented by vocational evening classes; many said that they doubted they would be such good salesmen if they had had more technical expertise.

(v) *Self-Made Man*

Just over half of Clements's managers rose from the bottom – that is they left school at fifteen, many without even a school-leaving certificate. These men were more likely to be older, being recruited in the 1920s and 1930s before the graduate entry boom in the 1950s. Very few indeed of such men get into the top ranks of management: 'The typical pattern of promotion then is, as one man described it, "a long tedious journey" over a good many years, up a number of small steps, all the later ones in the one firm, into lower management in the late thirties' (Clements, p. 78).

We were struck by the very close resemblance between Clements's typology and examples of specific career patterns and our own material. We were reassured that our 86 managers had very similar characteristics, controlling for age, to those Clements documents for his much larger sample of 646 managers. We saw no reason to construct our own typology since, although we would have modified Clements's classification to take into account our non-industrial managers and the wider industrial and geographical spread of our group, our cells would nevertheless have been very small and our modifications would not have been substantial. Thus, while drawing our readers' attention to Clements's more general account, we are able to complement his quantitative analysis with more detailed case studies. We could have provided very good examples for each of his categories except (i) but, in fact, we decided to concentrate on categories (iii) and (iv) for extended case studies, although we have men in categories (ii) and (v) to whom we refer in somewhat less detail later in the chapter.

Our concern is to present the job and career from the point of view of the men concerned. We are trying to portray our managers within a total social situation and to relate their careers to their homes and family background. We feel that the kind of information which we are able to present makes the whole notion of a 'career pattern' less clear-cut.

MR FRITH: THE HIGH FLYER WITH SKILLS AND TRAINING

Mr Frith was born in 1931, in a working-class home in the North East. His father, he remembers, earned £2 10s. a week and his highest-status job was that of a small shopkeeper. His mother encouraged her son towards more intellectual pursuits and to take an interest in music: his father did not read books but was good at maths and encouraged his son at sport. Given better circumstances Mr Frith felt his mother would have reached university. At home he remembers a 'voluble atmosphere of defending oneself' and, as he put it, 'I was brought up in competition with my brother and this is in everything I do. I simply had to fight for myself at home and give as good as I got. I was in competition with my parents as well as with my brother. We would simply argue for the sake of argument.' He went to six different primary schools and two grammar schools and although he says he always wanted to do something in the science line it was not until he changed schools that he 'discovered physics', which he later went on to read at university. He became very interested in a particular aspect of physics, in which he was able to do a specialist course. Half-way through his first year, when he was thinking of doing research, he was invited for an interview with the 'National Scientific Organization' (N.S.O.). Before taking his finals N.S.O. offered him a job if he got a good degree. Even in his last year at university he already felt that research would be too narrow: 'I like to persuade other people to follow my ideas and this put the idea of management into my head.' Looking back with characteristic objectivity, he remarked, 'I think I *filled the role* of undergraduate very well. For me it was an ideal one. I always had plenty of friends . . .'

At the age of twenty-two Mr Frith started with N.S.O. at a

salary of £350 p.a.: opportunities seemed relatively limited. However, such was the speed of technological change and development, and so great were the possibilities of application, that Mr Frith found himself on an escalator of advancement.

After I had been working there for a year I had the hope of earning £1,000 a year in my middle thirties. After eighteen months a major problem arose, requiring a scientist who could be a manager. The man who was works manager at this time didn't want to train managers and make them learn a new job, so he said to me, 'as from tomorrow, this is your problem'. This step came more quickly than I expected, though it had been my long-term objective. I liked controlling a lot of men, and there were lots of union problems and this human aspect took the place of scientific interest. At the age of twenty-four I was in charge of 150 men working four shifts. All this happened partly by accident.

As a section manager Mr Frith was earning £450 p.a.

The following year he was nominated for an intensive scientific training course for three months. N.S.O. was meanwhile expanding very rapidly and on his return he was nominated to do a scientific job at a regional centre. The expansion of this centre meant that N.S.O. had a struggle to find new staff. 'They had one director to look after personnel, whose job was to find people to do jobs that had never been done before.' It was decided to do this job at the regional centre and Mr Frith was promoted to Assistant Technical Manager at a salary of £750, later increased to £1,500, when he was still only twenty-six.* Then in the late fifties computers began to come in and Frith's technical expertise was needed at headquarters where he had a lot to do with their first use. He became a technical officer at £2,000 p.a. in 1960. It is somewhat difficult to explain the full significance of these moves while maintaining the necessary confidentiality. Suffice it to say that Mr Frith was on a kind of escalating see-saw. The speed of expansion of his organization was such that for a time his scientific expertise would be at a premium, and then this would be followed by an acute demand for scientists with

* At this age he married a school teacher who can be characterized as a typical *domestic* wife (see p. 226).

managerial ability to cope with the administrative problems of a rapidly expanding organization. Frith gained on both swings of the rising pendulum. In late 1963 he was moved to the financial and commercial side of the company as a senior commercial manager in London. Although a promotion, it meant, by then, a salary drop to £2,500 p.a.

The job in London was finished more quickly than had been expected: the new organization was sorted out, and the need for senior people in London diminished. Mr Frith alternated between London and the regional plant for eighteen months, before finally being put in charge of a technical group concerned with the technical and commercial problems of the latest technological advance. This was in 1965 and his job developed into one that covered the whole of the technical and policy-making areas of the organization. By the time of the interview in the summer of 1968 Mr Frith was earning £5,000 a year. He travels extensively, acting as a consultant to Japanese and Italian national organizations. Mr Frith is conscious of being where the action is:

For me it has all been more fascinating as I came in from the beginning, and it has developed so quickly from a hole in the corner operation. I have progressed differently in different jobs, and I have changed my sphere of operation, taking on things for which I am not trained. I am a sort of polymath, taking on technical, management, economic and commercial things all in the same day. I love writing projects with different aspects and I like public-speaking and giving lectures. I have had to make decisions all the way through and I think all have been right. I've had no doubts afterwards.

The tremendous confidence of this seemingly archetypal meritocrat is of great interest, since it is arguable that he exemplifies the new men of British industry. Here is a man who has taken each new development in the growth and expansion of his organization as an opportunity and has seemingly come out on top each time. Furthermore, he is a man who has thought about his career a great deal, is highly articulate and also extremely perceptive.

Throughout his career he has had an enormous interest in

what he was doing. At university he did a specialist course in radio astronomy and very nearly gave up physics for this. Later on in his career he did not hesitate to make changes:

I could have stayed at Northplace and not gone to Seatown at the same money. I had personal pressures to stay where I was, but it seemed that the longer-term prospects were better going on to a new project and I feel this is always true as long as one picks the right ones. I am motivated primarily by thinking I can do the next job up the line as well as the one I'm doing now. I have not yet met my limit. I always aim for that. It's always my prime consideration. It's always an easy decision to stay with the same money, but the project may be better, even if it means moving. I've discussed them all with my wife earlier on, although I'd already made up my mind. When we left Northplace I had a nice house, and job, a nice situation and social life, and when the chance came to do something different I still decided to leave.

Frith feels that 'now it is the time to sit tight and not to make rash decisions'. He knows that the country is short of people with his abilities. 'The sort of things that interest me are organizing large-scale scientific projects and getting them off the ground; that demands judgement and scientific ability. There are not many people who can think broadly in these areas.'

When he was asked how he would assess his career he said:

I think I've come a long way from 14 Avon Terrace where I was born. I came from a working-class home on the north-east coast with a steel works and a shipyard. My expectation at the time, if I was lucky, was that I might be a tradesman. I feel I've particularly come a long way if I meet people I was at school with. Often when I am at an international conference, deciding something important, I wonder what people in Avon Terrace are doing.

I'm used to moving rapidly and I can't bear routine. It drives me up the wall doing the same thing again and if I get the same job to handle twice I go mad . . . they know me at work and the board knows that I will serve them better with new work. I'm very adaptable, and I think N.S.O. thinks I am. I think you frequently ask yourself what are your limitations and I have only recently felt them. I object to people who won't do things they have never done before. I'm intolerant of these people. I can turn my hand to anything but other people don't like people around who want to push them ahead too fast. For example, I have thought of a new way to handle the project in Italy, and therefore beat the Yanks but the older ones don't like the risks involved. . . . I suppose in career terms I am nearly at point 100 (the top of the scale) though I rarely stop to think of it. I have people now working for me that I used to work for. . . . I have influence, and I meet people, and this is where I notice the difference. It's got nothing to do with money.

It seems to us that Mr Frith is demonstrating here a striking difference between British managers and, say, German, Soviet or American managers. Money does not seem to be an over-whelmingly important consideration. The subtle nuances of Mr Frith's social situation are noticed, understood and appre-ciated by him. Even as a measure of success money appears to be less important than the power and influence which more responsible positions give him.

When he was asked what other factors, other than his ability, had influenced his career, Mr Frith had difficulty in getting away from himself:

I am very persistent. I have gone through my career thinking that impossibilities don't exist. At the time of my first promotion most people said what I was trying to do could not be done. I follow my intuition, perhaps to excess sometimes, but I am not put off. I have tremendous enthusiasm, not for all things, but in connection with my work, and I can work hard. I was never told to do my homework, for example, at school. *I have a fire in my belly, an ambition.* If you come from a poor background, you are more motivated to do better than your contemporaries, than if you come from a comfy background. I like influencing people, and I enjoy argument. Objections don't bother me: they're a challenge. Many scientists can't communicate in our industry. There is a terrible communica-tions problem. I don't talk over my future prospects at work – I don't have people that I am friendly enough with, *as they're in the race as well you don't want to show your hand*. There are a few people, mostly older than me, who've had rapid promotion and who have big prospects, but I have found that *one's possible best friend is one's challenger as well*. I do talk to my wife about it, to some extent, but not at length.

My long-term ambition is really a pie in the sky: to be a technical director of an organization such as mine – to be really at the top, and responsible for everything. The background, etc., that I've had could lead to this, but I've no idea how long it would take. At the moment, most of the high-ups are in the mid-forties, so there will be no retirements, but if the company expands, which is a possibility, I definitely aspire to a seat on the board.

When he was asked if his present income was adequate in terms of his responsibility, he replied:

I think the most useful measure of responsibility is the cost of one's mistakes. I could easily write off £50 million at the push of the wrong button at the wrong time. Not to speak of lives. If a job fails I get no less, if it works, I get no more. There's no gearing in this way between work and achievement. I could go off on a lot of jobs, if I felt like it, and not bother, and just write a report, and the people at the other end would never know the difference, but I don't look at it that way, and in this sense the system is not working properly. I would like more money, but I don't know what I'd do with it if I had it. I have no intention to spend money on anything in particular that it grieves me not to have at the moment. It's funny, if you compare the Yanks and the Europeans who have personal acquisitions as a measuring stick of their progress, it's different from mine. Mine is how much I influence the work overall, although probably I would like a bigger house. But to the extent that I do influence the work the reward is satisfactory, and the money is better than that I was ever used to.

I have acquired skills which I can always use, no matter what the predicament of my particular environment whether hostile or not, in terms of changing places of work. I know I can always cope. If things are bad it always comes out right in the end and this has added security. I have a settled home life, though I travel away a lot. This was different to when I was not married, when I led a very odd existence of finding somewhere to sleep and·have a meal. The fact that I have a definite base to return to gives me a certain amount of security. Getting ahead in the world means influence, and the extent to which I can influence other people.

The future is not worth living, if you don't achieve something. At work obviously I hope to achieve something – that is to be the head of the organization and run it myself, and be on the board. I'd also like to be as well known in this country, as I am in some others, professionally. This is only a small aspiration. I would have also liked to have had some distinction in sport. This has now gone, and I regret it. Therefore I will pr obably work at golf, in which I have some distinction, in that I am better than most. This seems to run through my life in everything. Apart from work ones, which are obvious, I have a personal level of achievement, with nothing to do with the others. That is to do things with the utmost of my ability. When I was an undergraduate, and when I started work, I was impressed by the acquisitions of others and this made me dissatisfied. I thought I would not have a great earning power in the job I had undertaken. But my environment has changed, and I've found that this feeling died out when I found I could get happiness out of simple things. Material things mean little now, though most of my arguments for them are economic ones. For example, a bigger house appreciates faster, etc. Cars waste money, and two cars is ridiculous. We can get along with one having the car every other day [*sic* – at £5,000 p.a.]. Two is very much of a luxury. Sending the children to a particular school I rate more highly than my wife does, and this can be regarded as an acquisition, especially if you compare it to the educational problems I had when I was younger.

I plan my personal life, in that my education was planned, and getting married at a particular time was planned – I was not too young or too old. And buying my own house was planned. But ten years ago I didn't say I'd plan my work, because I couldn't because I didn't know what would exist. In work, planning is a waste of time, or one just becomes disappointed. I do plan to a certain extent in the work sense as to what would be important in the industry in a few years' time, though this is not required by the organization. I like to know what the problems will be. *I do plan in my personal life, though more recently*. I never did before. All my efforts were to work. I lead a more balanced life than I have in the past, with stress on things other than work. I do this with the children, and with sport. I am not active in politics, though I have an inclination towards it. It might come, but I have no plans for it. I'd also like to write. I would like to write hefty books. For example, I'm sure I could write better leading articles than you find in most newspapers. I have a strong interest in international affairs and economics. My wife, in fact, calls me the poor man's Alistair Cook. I am interested also in military history; I have a fair political judgement of international situations.

I have changed personally over the last fifteen years; I am much less carefree. Frustration, and endeavour to do well, and big steps are not taken without cost. They fray nerves and one's attitudes towards day-to-day things. I can't take small irritations as I used to before I saw big chances to go for. I was more carefree before marriage. I am now intolerant, and I would stress this. And this has become more evident as I have become older.

His wife appeared at this point, and agreed. He went on,

I think if you work hard you do change. It's less easy to cope with other people. I think I have deteriorated as a person. And I don't like people getting in my way. If I was a school teacher or a researcher I might be different. I might be more tolerant, but *I think work pressure has led me to what I am.*

At that point, his wife said, 'you should see him behind the wheel. He's certainly not a placid type the way he shouts at old ladies in cars.'

Seeing what happens to other people, and remembering one's own home life, if I had not had a stable home life I could not have done what I have done at work. I could not have been single-minded about being successful, and it would have had to have taken second place. *I am sensitive to upheavals caused by personality problems and these to me are greater than technical difficulties at work.* I had a stable family life, but I do not get my attitude from there. Both my father and mother were extrovertish and said what they thought regardless of other people, as compared with my wife's parents, who go out of their way to avoid friction. We, therefore, have different backgrounds, in terms of temperament.

How did Mr Frith see himself and how did he think other people saw him? He gave his own opinion of himself first:

Very modern. I know what's happening better than most people. This is probably personal conceit, but I know what will happen next in terms of work, and nationally and internationally. I hate not to know.

Then he described how his director saw him:

A bright young man, full of ideas, who can do anything but who occasionally needs bits of advice. Very trustworthy and efficient.

His parents see him as:

A person who has achieved a lot by my own efforts. They've never thought I've got above my station. I think the idea that children from working-class families leave their backgrounds is a myth. I can stand on my own achievements and can be seen to be doing it.

His colleagues see him as:

Difficult, a competitor not afraid to express his opinion. I get on well with them and mix with most sorts of people regardless. . . . I know people at work who would be friends if it wasn't for the competition. One can't afford to say you won't tread on somebody's toes as he's a friend. Apparently this diminishes as one gets on in life. I've never really given much thought to how my colleagues see me. They know I'm there. They probably see me as a high flyer. I've come on faster than them. They're probably waiting for me to crash – one or two in particular.

Finally, how did his wife see him?

No idea. Probably as someone who is extremely confident and capable in that *she only sees the result of success and never the close calls, the near misses and the trials and tribulations.* She sees the increased standard of living and thinks it is relatively easy success . . .
There've been some close calls in my job and I've nearly come a cropper but my wife never knows. I go through torture when I start a new project, about what I'm going to do with it. I don't talk to my wife about my work partly because she wouldn't understand what's going on. I think she thinks I am intolerant, and also youthfully over-enthusiastic. I do bash people down. This is a good technique, rather than a way of behaviour for me. It's a good way to win, and I often hate myself for it, but it's expedient; but it has grown to be a cult.

Inevitably Mr Frith came back to himself and his own introspection. When asked about retirement he said:

I can't imagine retirement. I will have to take on something else. I need a challenge to exist. I hope I'll become more tolerant as I mellow: to a certain extent *I will have to be.* It's regarded among aspiring executives that intolerance is bad up to a point, but intellectual arrogance is something I can't abide, and *people with it don't make progress.* If I am confident over something I will fight, but not to the extent that I fight just because I'm a scientist and therefore can be arrogant. To me this is a bad trait.

Mr Frith clearly has a high achievement motive and fits the theories of Hagen (1962) and McClelland (1961). With an unaggressive father ('he would go out of his way not to quarrel') and a more intellectually inclined and forceful mother, the socio-psychological base fits the ideal type perfectly. An expanding industry which rewards quickly and highly is again a very good setting for someone who is impatient of routine and constantly anxious to prove himself. There are hints, which we have emphasized, in his account of himself that he is tougher with himself than he would like anybody to know. Mr Frith is closer to the entrepreneur than the bureaucrat as a career type, and contrasts with the eager-to-please affability of middle-class Mr Ickham.

Inevitably Mr Frith sets too high a standard for his children and in defence his son opts out, 'he gives in, and this is completely foreign to me. I don't want him to be that way. . . . My son has no push.'

One striking aspect of this case study is how unrepresentative of our managers as a whole Mr Frith is. The account which we have given here is a very shortened version of parts of the interview material. Clearly Mr Frith enjoyed talking and has a mass of self-analysis already worked out: the objective and subjective situation combined to produce one of the most dynamic men in our sample.

MR ICKHAM: THE SELF-CONSCIOUS CAREER SEEKER

Mr Ickham was born in 1937, the son of a works manager. He left school at the age of seventeen. He had been at a fee-paying school and expected to go on to university, but then his father died and his widowed mother could not afford to keep him. For a man from a working-class background this situation would probably have been decisive and the possibility of moving into management from such a position in 1954 would not have been easy. However, the Ickhams had always been in business and Mr Ickham had always assumed that he too would have studied some relevant subject at university and followed the family tradition. At the time accountancy seemed a sensible alternative way in and so, at

the age of seventeen, he started as an articled clerk with a firm
of practising accountants in a Yorkshire town. His grand-
father, who was a friend of the senior partner of the firm,
arranged this for him and this use of well-placed kin links is,
of course, a characteristically middle-class pattern.

For five years Mr Ickham took a correspondence course,
went to night school and lived on a salary which started at £2
a week. When he qualified he had to stay on for two or three
years to pay off his debts. Then in 1962 he wanted to move to
London and one of the partners helped to put him in touch
with a firm which took him on at just over a £1,000 a year.
Two years later, and ten years after the start of his training,
he made the move he had always wanted into industry:

I had always accepted that I would spend time in a professional
office and then move into industry. There is a danger of being stuck
at a low level if you move into industry straight away, or you can
join a bad firm or have one with limited opportunities. I had to make
up my mind the type of firm that I wanted to join, but I had been
around a lot in London and got an idea of the sort of company I
wanted. I went for a lot of interviews, and had offers from some and
was turned down by others, although I had some attractive offers.
I deliberately selected an American firm as I think their techniques
and approach to business are better. I didn't just write to the firm,
I replied to an advertisement in the press. I started off with them at
£1,600 a year.

At about the same time he married a nurse he had met at a
party. She was from a solid-middle-class background, the
daughter of a G.P., who had finished her education with a
short course at the Sorbonne. They moved out from a flat in
London to a bungalow in a village in the home counties and a
year later they had their first child. This was not an easy time
for Mr Ickham, since, at this critical time in his personal life,
he became very unhappy in his work and went to the Vocational Guidance Association: 'after tests they said I shouldn't
have been an accountant at all, but a solicitor. By that time it
was too late.' Understandably he could not face another
five years of study; but it was also suggested to him that

management consultancy would suit his aptitudes and interests and so he decided to make this his long-term objective.

Thus he stayed with the firm, despite his initial unhappiness,
'to get the right experience': consultants to whom he applied
for jobs would not take him on without 'the right sort of
experience'. In 1966 he got promotion and with more money
and the opportunity for more experience he stayed on until
the end of 1967. He had been trying very hard to leave, discussing the whole issue with his wife *'ad nauseam'* – 'I spent
all the time talking about it.' Despite his enthusiasm for consultancy – 'I was itching to get into it' – he eventually decided
to get another job in industry to enlarge his experience. When
being interviewed for one job – which he didn't get – he got
on well with the interviewer and told him of his aspirations
about management consultancy. This was in February 1968:
four months later Mr Ickham received a letter from the same
man offering him a job in consultancy at £2,750, which he
took up later in the same summer.

How successful did Mr Ickham feel he had been? He felt
that he should have moved into industry earlier in his career
and moved more rapidly between jobs to get the essential
experience. When comparing himself with his father he felt he
might have done a little better, since his father had only
worked for one firm though his income progression had been
better. His brother is in marketing planning and 'has had good
experience and is well placed'; but Mr Ickham earns more.
When asked how he felt he compared with his school friends,
he again felt that he was about the same. Now, he felt, his
career was starting to level off and if the top point was a
board appointment he was over half-way there: 'I would hope
I would have a board appointment by the time I was forty.
Not necessarily, though, with the firm I'm with now.'

Undoubtedly Mr Ickham is a planner; as he put it 'I'm
ambitious, and always have been concerned about my career
and have thought about it and planned it, and I think all this
has helped.' His career is Mr Ickham's central life interest and
he is ready to discuss it with anybody. Quite readily he admitted that he had talked about his future with his friends,

with his boss, with his colleagues and with his wife. He gets a sense of security from the fact that he has had what he describes as a 'sound career', and that it will 'make sense' to a future employer that he has had an 'established career'. When asked what 'getting ahead in the world' meant to him, Mr Ickham said he wanted to be 'successful' in his career: 'I have no great ambitions to be an M.P. but I think I'd like to be sometimes. I probably have limited objectives only: just simply to get to the top [*sic*] of my career.' He clearly had some difficulty in facing up to the overwhelming importance this career success has for him. 'I have a vague ambition to be well ensconced by the time I'm forty, but nothing else.' When Mr Ickham was asked what was really important for him in his life he tried unsuccessfully to claim an alternative to his career. 'I rate my family very high and my wife and children. I put them in front of my career, if it comes down to it, but unless I'm successful in my career, I don't feel I'm doing right by them. It's not purely a selfish desire for power, it's for the security of my family.'

This ambivalence in his approach to himself and his career was characteristic of Mr Ickham: on the one hand he felt that a high salary was important as a means of assessing the 'success' of his career, but later on in the interview he claimed that he would prefer to have a job with a lower salary if he enjoyed it more. At one point he argued how essential it was to move about, but this was coupled with a professed enthusiasm to settle into the local scene. Mr Ickham's facility to switch his position was truly astonishing: despite what he said above about his limited ambition to be an M.P. and so on, he could quite easily say later in the interview 'I would like to change my career completely. If I could get a senior position in industry or commerce in the next ten years I would change, and perhaps become an M.P. or something like that. I have, perhaps, too narrow a life and would like to broaden it.' For Mr Ickham industry does not appear to form part of an attractive life style.

Mr Ickham's ambivalence is a product of his position in the 'early productive period' which we discussed in Chapter 2 (page 24). There is a certain difficulty in coming to terms with himself:

I have less choice now than before. The most choice I have ever had was about five years ago. I think you always have less as time goes on. As one's responsibilities start increasing one becomes less of a free agent, and the market for jobs decreases; therefore there are less opportunities, and at the time responsibilities are increasing. One is more careful not to make a mistake when one has a family and so forth, which makes it difficult. When I was younger I felt I had much more mobility.

Mr Ickham is torn between his career and himself, if it is possible to make this distinction:

I think I have been successful in the job at a competitive age. I think I've done better than average. I'm a well-balanced individual and so is my family, and we live a reasonable life. I have fair all round interests, a good social life and play lots of sport. *I think to have a life like this is an achievement in itself.*

Yet in his work life Mr Ickham knows that 'a consultant has to be ruthless' and understands that merit on its own is not enough. When talking about whether advancement was more likely to come from his own individual effort rather than collective action he replied:

I think one has to be *lucky* in a certain way. You might get everything you want by your own efforts, but I always feel that one needs assistance from outside, that is the right contacts to open up opportunities. For example, in my present job I got on with the bloke when I met him, so that the job was never advertised, and I think to a certain extent, *one must rely on this sort of thing.*

Mr Ickham's own self-portrait provides the best summary of the man and his career:

I'm a good mixer, I'm easy going, I'm probably gregarious as I like company, and I flourish in society rather than on my own. I am reasonably competent and intelligent, though I wouldn't think I was in any way exceptional; I'm rather average. *I'm a nice guy. I'm not ruthless*; I'm probably too easy going for the job. I'll never get right to the top. *I'm not ruthless.* I like people too much,

94

and I will make excuses for people and find the best in them. I'm
not a driver of people. I think I could have flourished in an academic background. The Vocational Guidance Association did say
I was a professional rather than a commercial man. However, I
don't think I would have been a dry-stick solicitor. The ordinary
picture of an accountant as a dull, dry, mean, finicky man I don't
think is applicable to me; in fact I tend to revolt against this image.

This emphasis on mixing easily and being thought 'a nice
guy' has come, thinks Mr Ickham, perhaps 'because I formed
a successful relationship with my wife and this has given me
confidence. I mix with a greater variety of people socially.
This is again the result of my marriage and I have found it
easier now.' Later on he said,

I'm proud of being a management consultant. It gives one a
certain amount of kudos. It's a job that is acknowledged by people
as a sign of doing well and I've always wanted a job that people
thought well of. I have a wife that I like, and whose company I
enjoy and this has given me confidence, whereas before I was
unhappy and not proud of my status. I was never proud of the
accountancy profession. I didn't feel it was useful. Now I think
I'm being more useful.

There is no doubt that a particular 'style of life' is important for Mr Ickham. He seems himself to be aiming for a particular mix of factors related to work, family and other
leisure activities. This valued style of life is seemingly more
easily obtained as a professional than in industry or commerce. This dissatisfaction with industry as a way of life is
significant. The *idea* of working hard to develop his position
so that he will be able to reach a plateau ('be well ensconced by
the time I'm forty') clearly appeals to him, and the stages of
development of a professional career would fit his expectations better. One of the themes of this book, to which we
return in the final chapter, is that paradoxically it is the *lack* of
a career which dominates the thinking of many of our managers. If they cannot control their careers they hope their
children will fare better – by being professionals. A 'professional' is to this section of the middle class a symbol of
a pattern of development and stability and carries with

it overtones of a distinctive *style*. It is this style which Mr Ickham longs for.

MR NEWINGTON: THE LOCAL JOGGER

Mr Newington was born in 1935 and was thirty-two at the time of the interview. Son of a scientific engineer, he spent most of his early life in the home counties and was educated at a well-known public school. In 1954, when he was nineteen, he left school with six 'O' levels and spent two years in the Royal Signals doing his national service. He rose to the rank of lieutenant. He then went to an agricultural college and acquired professional qualifications in land agency and chartered surveying. He needed to get a further year's practical experience to be fully qualified but certain difficulties helped to promote an early crisis in his career. First, he realized that he would get very little salary working in a land agent's firm until he could get a partnership; secondly, he had no capital with which to buy such a partnership; and, thirdly, he wanted to get married. Mr Newington wrote off to a number of firms 'off the cuff' and most had nothing to offer him. The 'Mechanical Farming Company' (M.F.C.) offered him a general traineeship in marketing and he decided to accept. At the interview he expressed interest in advertising and promotion and as, fortuitously, the advertising manager of the company was overworked, Mr Newington joined M.F.C. at the age of twenty-five in 1960 at £700 a year. His fiancée went off to the Cordon Bleu School of Cookery and in the following year, when she was nineteen and a half, they got married.

For the next eight years Mr Newington stayed with M.F.C. In the early years he got a modest rise of between £25 and £50 a year. In 1963 as a result of internal conflict he was offered the job of Marketing Officer at £1,000 p.a. A year or so later he got a further promotion 'as they eventually discovered I could do the job'. The company made much of the ceremony of 'promotion' – Mr Newington simply said 'thank you' and got another £200 a year. Each year thereafter his salary was reviewed and he received a further £100 or £150 without making an exceptional effort. When interviewed for our study in 1968 he was earning just over £2,000. He feels he should be getting more for the amount of responsibility he has. New people coming into the company led to new internal struggles and conflicts and up to now this has simply meant that Mr Newington finds himself stretched a little more. He finds he can cope; the work is interesting; so he stays on. The experience he is gaining in marketing in all its aspects is clearly valuable to him and he feels that the extra responsibility which he is being given is an indication that he is, as he puts it, 'hired on my merit and appreciated'.

When asked about his career as a whole up to now, Mr Newington made the characteristic references to luck, which we found among so many of our managers. 'Oh I think it has been a logical and smooth progression but more by chance than design. I think fortune has smiled on me.'

Mr Newington is enjoying what is to him a very pleasant domestic and community life in an attractive West Country town. The most important things in his life, in order of priority, are his wife, his children and the dog. He is treasurer of the P.T.A. at his son's school and he is a member of the Model Railway Guild. At the age of thirty-three he is not the most aggressive of British businessmen, but this is not to say that he does not do his job well. The point is that it is simply a job, however satisfying it may be while he is doing it. Being such a contrast to Mr Ickham, who seems to be always considering the present in terms of the future and re-writing the past to fit in with what is to come, Mr Newington was questioned in some detail about his ambition and plans for the future.

I know I could be earning £3,000 a year elsewhere, but I weigh this against the place and the children and the home. I know there are many high-powered people from London who would give their eye teeth to change places, therefore I think it's not so bad, though it's possibly death to all ambition – though in the end I don't think it matters. I don't take business life seriously. I'm not blasé about it, but it's not the thing that really matters. And it's imperative to have the wherewithal to do things that matter. There are so many goons in industry doing very well, but I don't envy them. There have been times when I have been frustrated, and this is usually when I have not been moving quickly enough, or perhaps it's not so much not moving quickly enough as something that's part and parcel of the team and the way the work is being done. I frequently come up against people who are worried about status and concerned with playing politics and not getting the job done. But it seems to me that the better you do the job, the more secure you are and the more you play politics the less security you have, as the times are becoming hard and it's necessary to prove one's worth in terms of profit for the company.

Mr Newington seemed to have no illusions about himself: 'I recognize myself as the person I am. I'm not particularly bright. I know I'm probably not going to get on the board; I'm a sort of middle-of-the-road guy. . . . And if I don't make the board I will find an excuse and tell myself that I have just lost interest.'

In his early thirties Mr Newington was able to say,

My career in terms of commerce is really a means to an end. I'd like to mentally turn my back on the job and get on with something worthwhile. For example, something attached to preserving natural country life, and wild life, and be able to open up to coming generations the excitement that there is in nature. I'd like them to stop and watch a duck before they shoot it down and appreciate the woods and the trees and so on. I think this is essential to balanced development of a human being.

Apart from a firm refusal to work in London Mr Newington has few fixed ideas about his future career:

I have no plans, life's not like that. You can be very limited by preconceived ideas. You refuse to see an opportunity because it doesn't fit in with your plans. And opportunities don't come in the fashion and direction you expect. To have preconceived ideas like this is almost as bad as no direction at all. So far I've been reasonably happy. I feel you've got to be flexible and exploit whatever comes up. I am not bursting with ambition, as some people are, though I probably wouldn't say it to anyone apart from you in these circumstances.

LUCK AND THE MIDDLE-CLASS WORKERS

A firm commitment to achieve 'success' is not typical of our managers, despite the example of Mr Frith. Few men were advancing along a clear and structured career line. A more likely pattern was for the men to gain in confidence as a result of a series of almost fortuitous circumstances, which teach them that they can cope with new situations. The army or other service experience was often the crucial stimulant to a managerial career. There is an overwhelming sense, when reading their complete career histories, of men being pulled up the management hierarchy, either through luck – being in the right place at the right time – or by having a patron who knew their name and suggested it at critical times.

Mr Ash, for example, came from a lower-middle-class home, left school at seventeen, and started as a warehouse supervisor. He rose to be national distribution manager in the firm in which he started, but has recently made his first change of firm in his late forties and has added over a £1,000 to his salary to bring him close to £5,000. He now expects to end his career at £7,000 or £8,000 but he never expected to get so high: 'I got much further than I expected with no qualifications. . . . I feel I have come a very long way though there has been a slight sense of unreality about each promotion . . . there was an *element of luck* – there has never been a calculated progress.' Mr Ash knows the men who pulled or pushed him up. He certainly feels more acted upon than acting.

I never set target dates etc., etc., this is partially because I am basically superstitious. I never like to talk of retirement and holidays as I am certainly or probably going to be disappointed if I plan too much ahead. As far as getting ahead in the world is concerned, to me it means nothing specific. In fact it is slightly distasteful and smacks of people with ruthless ambition. I have never taken business seriously. Others rate business success worthwhile for its own sake. I don't. Success means no more to me than my personal job satisfaction and more money. *I don't admire successful businessmen* . . .

I plan things mentally but don't like to recognize that I am planning it. I just weigh up the pros and cons. I never make any plans in terms of domestic life and family. I think about it a lot *but won't*

talk about it. This is probably because I'm superstititious as I said before....
I don't have much choice – in fact I choose not to have much choice.

Mr Bridge left school at fourteen to become a messenger boy. He was commissioned in the army which, as he put it, enabled him to lose his 'working-class mentality' – he was the son of a printer. He has now come a long way to be the head of a department with a salary of over £3,000 in his mid forties and is pleased with his progress. Each promotion led him to raise his sights. He now feels that he is at the peak point of his career on his own scale of evaluation.

In any job up to a particular point one is in command but it's very easy to overreach oneself and that probably happened when I took my last job. Taking a job like this is often a way to fall flat on your face. There's a danger at my age not of reaching a plateau but of reaching a peak and then going down on the other side. This is a definite danger. I've now got to engage in rat-race politics. I apply for promotion thinking only of my masters – there is a *need to be seen to be ambitious*. If a man is satisfied with his job he is seen by management as on the slippery slope downwards. I don't really care if I get promoted but in order to keep my present job I must make a show of being interested. . . . My future prospects don't figure much in my thinking, partly because I think I've got as far as I'm going so *I've no plan* in the positive sense *except by way of keeping myself where I am* by, to a certain extent, running on the spot.

Even those with a more conventional form of entry feel that they have had very little control over their own careers. Mr Kingston started at the age of twenty-one as a sales trainee after getting 'A' levels and doing national service. Now he is earning £3,000 in his mid thirties in his ninth position, which is as a management analyst. Most of his career was due, he thinks, to management realizing his potential and pushing him up. He has never applied for a job inside or outside the company. Success can, however, be prepared for:

You must be able to sell yourself. Part of this ability to sell oneself lies in general appearance and behaviour – lots of little things adding up as part of the total – e.g. if one is scruffy one doesn't get on in the sales side of a business. Appearance has to be watched, you have to be acceptable to the company in a number of ways – dress and the way you present yourself. It is not so much the way you talk but a matter of making a firm impression on people; without this it's an upward battle. *The other very important factor is luck.*

Mr Kingston feels his future is not so much in terms of what *he* wants to do but rather what his company wants to do with him.

This emphasis on 'luck' among middle-class managers said to be enjoying 'careers' is of great interest. Of course, realistically, they understand how little they can, in fact, plan and affect their own life chances. Mr Petham is another good case in point: his father, who was a foreman, thought he should leave school at sixteen and a half when the leaving age was fourteen and they were all hard up. He began as a bank clerk, but was called up for his national service after just over a year's work and rose to the rank of sergeant. When he came out of the Army in 1948 the wage in the bank seemed very low in comparison to what he had been getting. He discovered another clerical job at twice the pay which had the added advantage that it was near to where he lived and he could cycle home for lunch. Thus began his career in industry. The manager of his section, as Petham put it, 'Took me under his wing and thought me "a likely lad", egged me to go on to evening classes and told me I could go a long way in the company with this.' This man acted as Mr Petham's patron and got him on the trainee scheme as an apprentice and he went to evening classes at the same time. Two years later he became an estimating engineer with the company while still doing courses at the local technical college. After another two years he became a sales engineer and then after yet another two years he became, in 1954, an assistant sales manager, six years after joining the company.

At the age of thirty-one Mr Petham was champing at being responsible to a sales manager and he started to look round at advertisements for other jobs: he saw one in Newcastle advertised in the *Observer*. He moved to become a sales manager at

£1,500 a year, after eleven years with the first company. Frustration at being blocked by the managing director of his new firm forced Mr Petham to move after only a year. He bought all the papers and sent letters everywhere. He even went to be interviewed by his first firm and was offered a job. However, he preferred a smaller company in the Midlands to which he went in 1960 at the reduced salary of £1,200. Nine months after joining this, his third, company, the firm he had worked for first took it over. In 1962 he was appointed branch manager, but in 1966 a reorganization of the company led to the closure of his branch. However, he kept his job with the company and was given a bigger branch and £1,850 a year plus a ten-per-cent bonus on sales, a car and an expense account. In the autumn of 1968 he was promoted again to £2,400 p.a. with the same fringe benefits.

Mr Petham hardly feels he is enjoying 'a career':

I always have doubts if I can do a job and I often wonder if the benefits are worth it in terms of the quality of life that I have to lead as a result of the job. The financial position that we are in does not improve generally because of the increased expenses of a bigger house . . .

I don't think I've made any conscious choice about my career other than taking promotion when it was offered. I don't see it being a plan in any way. . . . I don't see my career as a logical progress apart from staying on the technical sales side. It's more a series of sharp jumps. I think I've come a very long way; I've never visualized at all what would happen. I go home and my family think I've come a long way and I'm inclined to agree with them.

Mr Petham compared himself to his father, a manual worker in a council flat who would retire on a State pension. When asked what were the determining factors in his career, Mr Petham considered the important one to be

Luck – that is defined as being in the right place at the right time. . . . I have never lobbied to get promoted. Perhaps I am a little arrogant. I always feel that if I do the job well it will be recognized. I don't think I have to butter up people and I never have . . .

I do a specific job and I have ideas about how to do that specific job, although I know if I do it well I will go on the divisional board but this is not something I have my sights on. *I don't plan as I don't want to be disappointed.* I live for the day in all things. If I do well it will be recognized. I get a tremendous amount of satisfaction from doing my job and if I didn't I would seek another one out. I don't think it's worth sacrificing all my life and my family, etc. for my work if I don't like it. In terms of my job I would not describe myself as single-minded.

Large companies may be able to plan careers for their managers with the highest potential. However, it is clear that most men, moving between moderately responsible jobs in small or moderately sized firms, simply see their life as a series of jobs of greater or less interest. Mr Dover was in the Merchant Navy until he was twenty-eight and then he went into industry. As he remarked, 'having left the sea things just happened'. He is now planning to join the R.A.F. where he may get a career but will certainly know that he can retire at fifty-two with a half pension and a gratuity of £4,000.

Typically those managers from marginal or working-class backgrounds felt that they had come a long way and were content with relatively modest salaries. How some would develop if they were given the opportunity we simply cannot tell. Inevitably their targets change as their jobs change. Mr Lenham, who also refers to the need to be in the right place at the right time, remarked

If in 1953 someone said I'd finish up as one of the top three or four executives under the board I would have thought it quite a stretch of the imagination. At that time I was just a manager. Now I'm a manager that can't be ignored.

He started his career as an office boy at fourteen and a half but gained his confidence as a pilot in the Navy. He then studied in the evening to qualify himself for the Corporation of Secretaries. For most of the early part of his career he was simply pulled up by promotions within the company, which was clearly very short of accountancy skills.

Our evidence suggests that most men's careers up to the level of middle management are simply a collection of jobs which are not necessarily defined by the men as 'successful' careers. Since luck does appear to be important many do find it difficult to have private plans or projects in the world of work which they may realistically expect to achieve. The table on page 105 provides some indication of how far the subjects of our case studies felt that they had been successful.

IS CHOOSING A JOB IMPORTANT?

The job which a man does probably determines the life style of his family more than any other single factor. The whole argument of this book is based on the assumption that job, or 'career', affect the whole nuclear family as well as just the man. And yet many times it was implied that choosing a job is not the family's most important decision. Mr Petham, who has had five different jobs and lived in five different houses in the last ten years, illustrated an attitude which seemed to be common,

> We feel that the most important decision in our life was to adopt children. We had to face up to the fact that we were not having a family of our own, and then consciously adopt first one and then the other of the children. Jobs are never difficult decisions. We don't choose if I will take a job. If it's offered and if it's a better job I take it, so this is always something that is taken lightly.

Many of the couples seemed to agree that a new job is not something to be actively planned for, sought out and discussed at length; their attitude is more passive: a job presents itself, or is offered, and the decision is about whether to accept that particular job. It is in decisions about where and how they shall live, where they should go for holidays, and, above all, about the children, that a more positive attitude is seen. Of the fifteen couples with children who were interviewed at length nine said that their most important decisions concerned their children – having them, bringing them up and educating them.

For some couples, of course, decisions about his job are taken by the husband alone, and it may be partly because questions about important decisions were asked at the joint interview of husband and wife, that the answers tend to

Is choosing a job important?

Name	Age	Present job	Salary 1968	Self-rating on career scale 0–100	Conception of what 100 would be
Ash	47	Distribution manager	£4,500	80	Board and £7,000–8,000
Bridge	47	Department head	£3,250	100	Same job
Chilham	47	General manager home sales	c. £7,000+	90	Managing director
Dover	36	Chief instructor	£2,050+	100	(if he had stayed at sea)
Eastwell	33	Company planning and development manager and on board	£5,000	85	Chairman
Frith	37	Senior commercial manager	£5,000	100?	Really the top and responsible for everything
Graveney	44	General manager	£5,250	100	Present job
Herne	34	Financial manager	£5,200	50–60	£15,000
Ickham	31	Management consultant	£2,750	50	Board appointment
Kingston	35	Management analyst	£2,900	65	Main board, £15,000 and percentage of profits
Lenham	41	Production controller	£3,400	?	Director at £5,000–10,000
Manston	41	Area sales manager	£2,500 (1967)	75	General manager £3,000–5,000
Newington	33	Sales promotion manager	c. £2,000	50	Managing director
Olantigh	48	Principal	c. £4,000	95	Assistant secretary
Bourne	42	Senior civil servant	£3,500	50	Department head, £6,000
Petham	40	Sales manager	£2,400	70	Director on main board, £4,000

emphasize domestic decisions. Nevertheless to the question 'What do you consider to be your important decisions?' only three couples out of sixteen replied in terms of job decisions. Characteristically Mr Ickham was one of them: 'my job is our most important decision. It obviously affects everything else. We certainly discuss it but in the final analysis I make the decision. All decisions concerning the family are important, for example, education, holidays and our home, and these tend to be joint decisions.'

It may be that it is because the couples feel that they have most autonomy in the private, domestic sphere that this is the sphere which they stress. The decisions made in this sphere *are* the ones in which they, as individuals, have most power. The decision to move a factory, to open up a new market, or simply to offer a man a better job, is made by others. But in the private world of home an individual may feel that he has power over his own life – and responsibility for the lives of others. Many of our couples might have agreed with Mr and Mrs Newington when they said 'the most important decisions we have to make are those concerning the children and their future – to bring them up in a certain way, to have the right job and the right home etc. All the other things, such as home and job are relatively unimportant decisions.'

Perhaps the career is not the 'supreme social reality' in the way that Dahrendorf and his followers assume, if the career is basically a *retrospective concept*, a way of structuring one's biography and making sense of the past. The 'career' is sometimes used as a convenient shorthand for a middle-class view on life which assumes that change and development are normal. But the stability and security of family life are also normal. Increasingly the middle-class 'good life' involves steering a path between the affective and particularistic ties of the family and the universalistic and achievement-oriented values imposed on the chief earner by a competitive capitalist system. In any one day the manager may behave *both* as if he really believed in the ideologies of those who want to exploit managers as a resource and *also* as if he really believed that working was only important in so far as this was related to the needs of his wife and children. We return to a more extended discussion of the ambiguities surrounding career and ambition in Chapter 9. We may conclude now by suggesting that it is the tension between the conflicting value systems of home and work, or family and 'career', which provides the dialectic of social reality for the middle class.

CHAPTER 5

The Wife's World

THE 86 couples described in our study are alike in that the husbands are all managers, earning a salary and carrying responsibilities which put them indisputably into the middle class. In the next three chapters we look at their wives, at the lives which they lead and, in particular, at the implications for a woman of being a *manager's* wife. In our society a woman tends to be categorized according to her husband's occupation, but for our managers' wives this would give a very misleading impression. The wives come from backgrounds which may vary from unskilled working class to upper middle class; they may have ended their education at any age from fourteen to twenty-four; and their work, before the children came, may have been as shop girl or secretary, as canteen worker or teacher. (See page 46 for details of their husbands' social backgrounds and educational and occupational experience.)

Though their present styles of life are now predominantly middle class, the childhood homes of the wives varied widely and some of the most delightful parts of the personal interviews were the evocative descriptions of so many different sorts of upbringing. Thirty-nine of the wives were brought up in solidly middle-class homes, their fathers holding administrative jobs in government, commerce or industry, or working as professionals.* A second group of 26 wives, which we have called 'intermediate', came from predominantly lower-middle-class homes, their fathers being junior non-manual workers, foremen and supervisors, or shopkeepers. And a third group, 21 of the 86 wives, came from working-

* This number may be slightly exaggerated and may include a few who should have been classified into the second group – it includes, for example, fathers whose occupation was given as 'company director' without further information about whether they were a director of a big firm or of their own small shop.

class homes, mainly having fathers who are or were skilled manual workers.*

The pattern of their education, too, varied widely; it was striking how very much less education the wives in our group have received than their husbands. Thus 32 of the 86 left school at fourteen or fifteen, 33 left at sixteen, and 31 stayed on to seventeen or eighteen. The great majority were educated by the state, 45 of these at schools of a grammar-school type and 23 at elementary or secondary-modern schools; 18 were educated at fee-paying schools. While only one of the men in our sample received no formal qualifications at all, 20 of the wives fall into this category; and while 34 of the husbands have received at least a university degree, some also having higher qualifications, only 5 of the wives have a degree and only 2 of these further qualifications as well. The majority of the wives have received some form of training, either in the form of short courses, such as secretarial diplomas, or over a longer period of time, as in training for nursing or teaching. In the time between ending their full-time education and bearing their first child all the wives had a job. The great majority fell either into the Registrar General's intermediate non-manual group (26 women whose jobs were as teachers, nurses, social workers or similar occupations), or the junior non-manual group (47 women whose jobs were as secretaries, typists and so on). For most of the wives, however, paid employment is now a thing of the past – or of the future: only 13 of them go out to do paid work, and for the rest the work of running a home and caring for husband and children is a full-time occupation.

When we started planning this study we had many ideas which we wanted to test, some based on professional contact with managers, some based on our reading, and some arising out of our own, and our friends' everyday experiences. One

* The first group, which we have called the 'solid-middle class', is composed of the Registrar General's categories 1, 2, 3, 4, 5, 12, 13, 14 and 16; the second, 'intermediate' group contains the Registrar General's categories 6, 7 and 8. The third group contains categories 9, 10, 11, 15, 16 and 17.

idea was that wives might be very much against the mobility which is part of the career of many managers: we explored attitudes to mobility in Chapter 3, and in later chapters we discuss some of the effects which frequent moves may have on a couple and their life style. One such effect may be to make it impossible for a wife to follow a coherent career of her own: we wanted to test the idea that wives, particularly those who had received specialized training, would be fretting at the constraints imposed by their husbands' occupations and by their roles as housewife and mother. We discuss the wives' attitudes to their many different, sometimes conflicting, roles in this and the next chapter. We also wanted to test ideas about the significance of the husband's work. One such idea was that work and home are in conflict and that, for a manager, work usually wins; we wondered whether the demands made upon managers, in terms of time and effort, might be made at the expense of their home lives and their marriages. But another idea, in many ways opposed to the previous one, was that wives might be more ambitious for their husbands than the husbands were for themselves; perhaps such phrases as 'the power behind the throne' and 'behind every great man there is a woman' had led us to expect that a husband on his way to the top must have a wife who is driving him there. We have tried to analyse the marital relationships of our couples, their attitudes to work, and their hopes and ambitions for themselves and their children in the final chapters of the book.

Our questionnaires, then, were designed to test many hypotheses, as well as simply to find out about the managers and their wives; in the personal interviews we were able to get a rounder and more complete view of the way in which the wives approached the many different roles which they had to play and the many complexities of their lives. We hope that our study may help towards an understanding, not just of our eighty-six couples, but also of the sort of people they may perhaps represent – that section of the British middle class, who do not have much capital of their own but who may be responsible for budgets running into thousands, even millions, of pounds.

How did the wives see themselves?

Most books on management do not mention the manager's wife and family,* while most books on marriage and the family give at least some attention to the occupation of the chief earner and the ways in which that occupation affects the family.† Yet the interaction between work and home cannot be simply along a one-way street, with the family at the receiving end. A man may be a manager when he is at work; when he is at home, as husband and father, different influences affect him. This is increasingly being recognized in the United States, though so far most serious work on the manager's wife and home, work which we discuss in Chapter 7, has been based on very small samples, and on samples which may not be representative of managers as a whole. The same criticisms could, of course, be made of this study; but our sample of managers, though small, is larger than many others upon which studies have been based,‡ and in addition matches husband and wife in an attempt to give a rounded picture of their lives, as individuals, and together.

HOW DID THE WIVES SEE THEMSELVES?

The wives in our sample found great difficulty in being objective about themselves and the different roles they played: many felt that it was somehow wrong to think too much about themselves. One said, for example, 'I don't like to have to

* For example, one of the few studies which attempts to give 'a general characterization' of management in Britain by McGivering, Matthews and Scott (1960) makes no reference to the manager's wife, family or community, and even in Dalton's (1959) well-known study, although there is a full chapter devoted to the managerial career ladder, there is no mention of the importance of the manager's wife or family. Considerable space is, however, devoted to such factors as being a Mason, being a member of a yacht club or being a Republican in politics.

† A recent example is *Social Class and Family Life* by McKinley (1964). Mirra Komarovsky's study of *Blue-Collar Marriage* (1962) is useful and there are some scattered studies of middle-class occupational categories, such as 'The role of the ambassador's wife: an exploratory study' by Arlie Hochschild (1969).

‡ Elizabeth Bott's widely-quoted study *Family and Social Network* (1957) was based on a sample of twenty families.

analyse myself although I've done a lot of it of late. I feel it is wrong, as I feel it is introverted.' Another said 'One of my problems in life is that I don't have any idea of what sort of person I am', and a third 'I try not to think about myself too much and I find it difficult to say how I see myself.' This inability to be objective about themselves posed great problems for the interviewer who was attempting to build up some sort of role hierarchy for each woman; thus about one interview she commented 'I had tremendous difficulty getting her to talk of herself in this way, as she said she had never thought about it and just accepted herself as a normal, ordinary woman, though other conceptions of self did emerge later on during the interview. She also found difficult the questions about how other people saw her, as she seemed to think this was something she had not considered.' All this is not to say that the women did not experience any role tension or conflict: in describing their lives it is clear that they did, particularly at weekends when two or more of their roles, for example as housewife, mother, wife, daughter or neighbour, might be in conflict. However, they found it very hard to be objective about such a situation, in contrast to their husbands who in general found little difficulty in looking objectively at the roles they played. This difference may be due simply to differences in type of training and amount of experience, or to more basic differences between the world of home and the world of work.

However, some evaluation of their different roles was obtained from a question which asked:

How do you see yourself now? Please tick one place on the scale opposite each statement. Are you someone who is:

1. providing interesting activity for your children
2. creating a comfortable and well-run home
3. a companion to your husband
4. concerned with interests of your own e.g. pottery
5. keen to do a paid job now and again
6. keen to follow a career of your own
7. active in local clubs, church, or other organizations
8. a friendly person in your neighbourhood

How did the wives see themselves?

Respondents were asked to place each possible role on a scale, which ran thus: 'essentially so, very much so, to a large extent, to a certain extent, not really'. Thus for each woman we obtained a *role profile*. A very home-centred woman, for example, gave a profile like (a), a more gregarious woman produced (b).

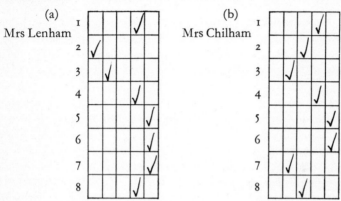

Once we had more information about the women, we often found it possible to predict what sort of pattern their chosen role profile would fall into. Some of the women used the scale as a simple one-to-five scale, while others stuck more closely to the definitions given of each position on the scale. However, the different effects of these two approaches to the use of the scale can be largely obviated by its simplification. Combining together the first three and the last two points of the scale, we get a picture of the way in which the wives see their roles (Table 5.1). The reactions to the first item, about children, were probably influenced by the wording of the statement: the result seems to underestimate the concern with children and their care, and this is probably because of the emphasis on 'providing interesting activity'. Nevertheless, this result does have a value in differentiating between those mothers for whom care of children is a matter simply of feeding, clothing and loving, and those mothers who feel they must also make a positive effort to stimulate and interest their children. The result, if mothers had been asked about the first type of child care, would probably have been similar to the answers on home care. To a certain extent the women's answers to the statement about children were influenced by the age of their children, some mothers of teenagers commenting that it was no longer necessary to provide interesting activity for their children; but even among mothers of younger children there was a contrast between those who saw this as a very important role and those who did not.

For the women in this study, as Table 5.1 shows, the roles of wife and homemaker were of overwhelming importance. How did they see these roles, and where did other roles fit in? How much was their choice of roles determined by such factors as their age, their stage in the family life cycle, their education, their life as managers' wives, or by their own personalities? For some, life seemed to be full of conflicting pressures and incompatible responsibilities: perhaps a consideration of the roles which they were trying to play might illuminate their situation?

THE HOUSEWIFE ROLE

Their roles as housewife and mother occupied more of the waking hours of most of the managers' wives than any other roles, though this does not necessarily mean that these were the two roles which they liked best or regarded as being the most important. Most of them, however, were at the stage in the family life cycle when, with young children, a busy husband, and a fair-sized house to keep, the roles of housewife and mother are at their most demanding. Of our 86 couples, 7 had no children, 12 had one child, 44 had two children, 19 had three children and 4 had four children; no couple had more than four children. Table 5.2 gives an indication of the age ranges of the children.

It seems as though it is particularly difficult to be objective when talking or writing about the housewife role. Edmund Dahlstrom in *The Changing Roles of Men and Women* (1967) offers a most useful guide through the complicated debate on the roles appropriate to each sex. He says 'the current debate

TABLE 5.1. The Importance Attached by the Wives to Some Different Roles (in numbers)

Wife sees role as being	Providing interesting activity for children	Creating a comfortable home	Companion to husband	Concerned with her own interests	Earning now and again	Keen to follow a career	Active in local clubs	Being a friendly person in the neighbourhood‡
Important*	39	78	74	30	18	9	16	47
Not really important†	41	8	11	56	67	75	70	39
It does not apply or she does not know	6		1		1	2		
	86	86	86	86	86	86	86	86

* This includes those who saw themselves in these roles 'essentially', 'very much so' or 'to a large extent', i.e. in positions 1–3 on a 5-point scale.

† This includes those who said they saw themselves in these roles 'to a certain extent' or 'not really', i.e. in positions 4 and 5 on a 5-point scale.

‡ This column is analysed in Table 6.2.

on the sex roles is no longer a controversy between women and men; it has become one between "housewives" and "working women". Both groups can find male support for their opinions. The degree of emotional involvement seems to be almost as great as when the suffragettes attacked the masculine society' (p. 173). Emotional involvement seems to be particularly in evidence when the discussion is about the

TABLE 5.2. The Ages of the Children in the Managers' Families

Children's ages fall within the range		No. of families
0–4 years:	i.e. the family has no children at full-time school yet	18
0–15 years:	i.e. at least one child is at school and at least one is still pre-school age	23
5–15 years:	i.e. all children are of school age	26
5 upwards:	i.e. all children are of school age and at least one is over the statutory school-leaving age	8
16 upwards:	i.e. all children are over the statutory school-leaving age	4
No children		7
		86

Note: the above age categories are mutually exclusive.

housewife role: perhaps some examples of particular attitudes might help to illustrate this point. On the one hand there are some, both men and women, who accept the 'traditional' view of the differentiation of sex roles, and feel that a married woman's place is in the home; another group sees a positive pleasure to be gained from such basic activities as child care, cooking and gardening, and cannot understand why anyone who is able to lead such a creative and satisfying life does not want to do so; and both of these positions gain support from those producers and advertisers of domestic consumer goods in whose interest it is that homemaking should be considered a full-time job, since stay-at-home wives may have the time and energy to equip their homes more lavishly.

But, on the other hand, there are many who disagree profoundly with such estimations of the housewife role. For example, one group may deplore the great handicap which the years of child bearing place on the woman who seeks to make a professional career for herself, or the subordinate position in which women may be placed when they are financially dependent on their husbands; secondly, many housewives experience times of profound loneliness and depression when they feel that all their work goes unnoticed and unappreciated and when the description, 'only a housewife', seems all too accurate; and a third group is composed of those experts on the labour market who seek to improve female activity rates and who see an over-indulgence in housewifery as just so many woman-hours spent unproductively.

Thus the debate is carried on at many different levels and on many different fronts, and is further complicated by the fact that some women work because they have to but would rather stay at home, while other full-time housewives yearn for a job which they cannot have because of their family commitments, the lack of nursery schools, or the shortage of suitable work. There may be disagreement about facts – for example, between those who hold that the majority of housewives are fairly content and those who hold that they are not – and disagreement about values – for example, between those who emphasize the equality of the sexes and those who emphasize their different functions in our society. Some arguments have their basic premises in considerations about equality and freedom, others in considerations about the welfare of the family, and yet others in economic considerations. The point which we are trying to make is that the whole subject is both complicated and highly emotive. Our society has an ambiguous attitude to the housewife role, which may be one reason why any individual housewife tends to have rather mixed feelings about her work. This may be particularly so among the middle class, where occupation is one of the chief signs of status, but where taking a job is less often an economic necessity than it is for the working-class woman. And uncertainty about the housewife role may be even more common among groups such as our managers' wives, where the husbands' work is unquestionably held to be important and where alternative sources of status, such as might be found in long-term involvement in the local community, tend to be absent. There is a strong desire to have the work which is most important to oneself assessed by significant others, yet it is difficult for a housewife's work to be assessed and compared with the work of other housewives in this way. This may be one reason why many housewives lack a sense of achievement: it is true that they have not been shown to be 'failures' by any comparison with others, but, more significantly, a housewife cannot easily be acknowledged as a 'success'. Success is a comparative thing and the work of a housewife does not lend itself to comparison.

Michael Fogarty and the Rapoports have written perceptively about attitudes to work, family life and domestic responsibilities among graduates in *Sex, Career and Family* (1970). Many of the couples which they studied were 'dual-career families' in which both the husband and the wife have a high commitment to work on an egalitarian basis. This type of family structure was rare among our managers, partly perhaps because of the social and educational background of the wives, and partly because the high degree of work commitment on the part of the husbands made it more difficult for their wives to take demanding work outside the home. Like the managers and their wives, the couples which Fogarty and the Rapoports studied were markedly home- and child-centred; career and family were the two chief sources of personal satisfaction. However, though they were relatively 'liberal' in their ideas about male and female roles, the division of labour within the household followed traditional patterns. Fogarty and the Rapoports discuss the development of new

work patterns for married women, emphasizing the importance of, 'engendering in woman a greater sense of vocational
commitment; engendering in men a greater acceptance of the
idea of women's vocational commitment; sanctioning for
men the legitimacy and desirability of . . . participation in
family activities; providing *excellent* facilities for delegating
child care' (page 298). They conclude 'there must continue to
be room for work and family patterns of all types . . . the aim
should be to clarify the options'.

We investigated the attitudes of the sixteen women in
our sample towards their roles by means of a series of questions which concerned the woman's feelings about her work
as a housewife, her sense, if any, of being a 'slave' to the
demands of her home and family, and her feelings about
taking a job outside the home. Several of the women pointed
out that their feelings about being a housewife varied from
day to day, even from hour to hour. However, it was possible
to divide the 16 women who were interviewed personally into
three broad categories on the basis of their attitudes: 6 of the
16 either had full-time jobs or seemed positively to dislike
being housewives; 5 women had mixed feelings; and 5
seemed, on the whole, positively to enjoy being housewives.

Feelings of boredom, loneliness, and inferiority were
described by some of the women. Mrs Eastwell, a graduate
and mother of three young children was perhaps the most
negative in her attitude. She said,

there is nothing really about the house that gives me any sense of
pride at all as I'm not really interested in the house. For me it is
just somewhere to be in. I'm even averse to choosing the curtains
– homemaking is definitely not my strong point. Children irritate
me, even my own, and I will be glad when they grow up and leave
home. I would say I am reasonably intelligent, and frustrated, not
finding an outlet for my intelligence. I have a dreadful inferiority
complex and this has been more so since I married. I have suffered
from serious depression and still feel a total lack of self-confidence.
I have the car all the time as my husband can't drive, and I would
die without it as I would be so cut off. I never do any gardening
and I have a washing machine, a spin drier, a fridge and all the

gadgets and don't now feel too much of a slave, though I definitely did when the first two were very small, when I had no help. The only way in which I do feel a slave is in being tied to the children's timetable. Now I have a woman in two days a week to do the housework. More than anything I feel like a tidying-up machine – small children are so untidy.

Mrs Eastwell is a reminder that attitudes to being a housewife are not necessarily related to the amount of work which has to be done, but are part of a wider complex of attitudes in which the need for freedom and autonomy in one's own life are important. Other women mentioned loneliness, which is especially common when the family has recently moved house, and boredom as unwelcome aspects of the housewife's life.*

For several, the heavy demands of their husband's work meant that they were responsible for more of the household chores than are wives of junior white-collar workers, for example, whose husbands might be free to spend evenings and weekends on joint activity around the home. Many of our managers expected to spend some evenings and at least part of the weekend doing office work: one regularly works all Sunday while his wife 'potters around in the house and garden'.

Blood and Wolfe in *Husbands and Wives: the Dynamics of Married Living* (1960) describe a similar situation in the United States. They say:

The evidence . . . is unmistakable: high-income husbands do less work around the house. It is important to remember that this is not

* Gans in *The Levittowners* (1967) presents evidence about boredom, loneliness and depression among the inhabitants of an American suburb. He found that women with poor marriages, and those whose husbands were on the road or who were long-distance commuters, tended to complain of low morale and loneliness. About boredom he says 'forty per cent (about a third of the women and more than half the men) are never bored, and only a few women are constantly so. Boredom does not seem to be a serious problem in Levittown. . . . About a third of the bored women attributed it to the menstrual period, poor health or a periodic bad mood. But two other reasons are mentioned more often: housework and being "stuck".'

just because wealthy men hire gardeners to mow the lawn. Since this is the *relative* division of labor between husband and wife, for everything the successful man does less of, his wife does correspondingly more. She, too, of course, may have more servants and more labor-saving devices to cut down on her own household tasks. But the rise in her index of task performance shows that the housework as a whole becomes increasingly her responsibility because her husband is so absorbed in his career. (p. 60)

This is particularly so for the self-made, occupationally oriented man. 'The man who struggles to get ahead does so at the expense of family participation. But the man who has a secure position in the community, because of family background and higher education, can afford to orient himself more towards the enjoyment of life in family activities' (p. 61). It was difficult for us to test this thesis since the majority of our managers do not consider that they have reached the top of their particular ladders (see page 105).

It would be wrong, however, to suggest that all the managers' wives were unhappy in the housewife role. Few said that they felt themselves to be 'a slave to the home', and some found a great deal to enjoy in being a housewife, and felt it to be a satisfying life, particularly while they had young children. Mrs Dover said 'I don't really want to go back to work as I like being at home. It's not that I'm lazy; I don't stop [work] at home, but I enjoy it; I'm never bored. There's always something I can find to do and I'll enjoy doing it. I'm very sorry for people who say they are bored in the house.' Mrs Newington seemed to speak for many when she described how she saw herself and her life (she is a full-time housewife with two young children, her husband is described on pages 96–8).

What sort of person am I? Fairly ordinary, I suppose. Relatively uncomplicated. Words fail me, really. I like people, am quite friendly, but I wouldn't be able to go to Blackpool and sit on a beach or anything like that. I think I'm of average intelligence and common sense. I'm probably an average British female, in other words, very much a wife and mother. . . . Being married and having children has given me more self-confidence. As far as having a life of my own, yes I do, insofar as I want it to be my own, but I don't particularly want it to be my own. I've never been ambitious. From a child I've never wanted anything but a home and a family. I never really feel bound by housework, though there are times when I think I do nothing but feed and clean and get depressed about it.

Mrs Newington then accepts her role, regarding it as the norm ('an average British female . . . very much a wife and mother'), not expecting or wanting a high degree of autonomy, and only occasionally feeling depressed about the monotony of housework.

It is difficult to write about depression since its causes are many and very different. For Mrs Newington, her occasional depression seems to be chiefly the result of the monotonous nature of housework; but for others their depression may have a physical or psychological cause (Mrs Eastwell (page 119) has had treatment from a doctor for her depression). And the responses to depression may vary too: thus Mrs Bourne, who has two school-age children and a job as a nurse, said 'My depression gets so bad at times, and it's when I'm not working, that I simply can't cope with it. My husband is so helpful that we cope very well in the house, as I don't have any home help. I don't think I would be able to do the work I do if my husband wasn't so helpful. My job is my hobby, in a way, and I don't feel that there is any tension between that and my home life.' This illustrates one way in which the demands of a man's work affect his wife's own particular adaptation to the role of housewife, in this case by making it possible for his wife to take a job outside the home. But taking a job is not necessarily a response to dissatisfaction with the housewife role. Several wives foresaw a time when the lessening of family responsibilities would leave them under-employed at home; thus Mrs Olantigh, a full-time teacher, said,

I prefer to be at home with the children and with my family. I take my teaching seriously and will end up with a teaching career, but in many ways I would rather have stayed at home, but there's not really enough to do with the children off my hands. I would prefer more children, and for my husband to do a lot of entertaining, rather than to go out to teach, though I do like teaching very much. But I'm the sort of person who likes making curtains and cushions, and painting and decorating, and arranging flowers.

She does not like everything about being a full-time housewife, however, or else her feelings are exceptionally vacillating, for later in the interview she said, 'I like to have a lot of household gadgets as I feel they are essential to doing a job and running a home at the same time. I very much feel tied down by the housework as I hate it. It's the sort of job one has to do one day and then do again the next day and in this way I do feel a slave to the house.' Perhaps the point about the apparent discrepancy in Mrs Olantigh's statement is that it is not in fact a discrepancy; the role of housewife includes many parts and some of these she finds satisfying – those concerned with child care, with entertaining and with creative activities – but other parts are seen as boring, or as having an inferior status.* It is also a role which is different at different stages in the family life cycle. For example, a woman may enjoy being a housewife when her children are young, but may feel under-valued and under-employed as they grow older; when the children are young she may say that she intends to take a paid job when they are older, but by this she may mean either that she is eager to get a job as soon as she can, or that she may be forced to get a job by the diminishing of her roles at home.

All this might be illuminated by being considered in terms of the concept of reference groups. A brief definition of this term was given by Kemper (1968): 'In general a reference group is a group, collectivity or person which the actor takes into account in some manner in the course of selecting a behaviour from among a set of alternatives, or in making a judgement about a problematic issue. A reference group helps to orient the actor in a certain course, whether of action or attitude.' Three main types of reference group are described by Kemper. The first is the *normative group*, the group from which a person takes his standards or from which he derives his norms. Normative groups may include one's family, one's religion, one's nation, or individuals such as one's parent or one's spouse. An individual may conform with the norms put

* See Fogarty, Rapoport and Rapoport (1971).

forward, or may purposefully act in exactly the opposite way from that which the normative group requires. What is important is that in some way or other the norms of the group are affecting his behaviour. A second type of reference group is the *comparative group*, the group whose situation or attributes a person compares with his own. If such a group is deprived in some way, by comparison with himself, an individual may feel a comforting sense of well-being; but if a comparative group is in some significant way better off, this may give rise to feelings of relative deprivation.* An important type of comparative reference group is the role model from whom an individual learns how he should play his part. Thus a married woman may adopt her mother as a role model, the student his professor, the new factory worker his bench mate. A third type of reference group is the *audience group*. This is a more passive type of group in that it is one to which an individual attributes certain values and then attempts to behave in accordance with those values. The audience group may or may not express its values; its significance lies rather in what the individual believes its values to be and the way in which he allows them to affect his behaviour.

Any one individual is likely to take into account reference groups of several different types, and perhaps will be a reference group or part of a reference group for others. For a reference group to affect an individual's behaviour or attitudes it is not necessary for it to be in existence in the present: a reference group which has been highly significant for an individual in the past, or which he can see is going to be significant in the future, may also be taken into account by him. Thus the product of a certain school may continue to behave as she feels the school expected, even though her personal links with the school have long since been severed and the school itself now in fact expects different patterns of behaviour of its pupils. Similarly a man who expects and hopes to attain to a higher level of management at work may begin to behave in the ways which he considers such managers are expected to behave. As Shibutani (1962, p. 130) says 'The

* See W. G. Runciman (1966).

environment in which men live is an order of things remembered and expected as well as of things actually perceived.' Shibutani analyses the different sorts of reference groups and the ways in which they affect the individual. He emphasizes their subjective nature: 'To understand what a man does we must have some appreciation of his definition of the situation, and this requires knowing something of what he takes for granted. This is especially true in a pluralistic society, where different people approach the same situation from diverse standpoints and where the same individual utilizes dissimilar perspectives in different transactions. Being able to identify the audience for whom a man is performing, therefore, becomes a task of decisive importance.' He describes the stress which may arise when an individual is responding to conflicting reference groups, or when the members of a group, supposedly all in the same situation, are in fact responding to different reference groups. Thus, for example, dissent may arise in a P.T.A. between the head-mistress, whose reference groups are the education authority and the association of head teachers, the teachers, whose reference groups include their fellow students at college and an image of 'teacher' as put forward by the mass media, and the parents, with a multitude of reference groups varying from their own parents, the members of other organizations of which they are also members and so on. The members of the P.T.A. may agree that it is 'the good of the children' which concerns them; but it would be impossible to understand their different views of what represents that 'good' and how it should be achieved, without some knowledge of their reference groups.

The concept of the reference group seems to be useful, too, in our attempt to understand different attitudes to the housewife role, especially since, as we have seen, there are many different parts to that role and a woman may have different attitudes about each part. As an example of this, let us take the activity of shopping. In an interesting analysis Stone (1954) has shown that shopping may be regarded in many different ways; for one woman, shopping is a functional activity and her criteria of behaviour are economic; for another, shopping is a social activity, and even though it is more wasteful of time, she shops frequently in order to have more opportunity of social contact; for a third, shopping represents the putting into practice of values and ideals and she takes pains to shop in the smaller concerns because she believes that the small tradesman should be supported. If the three meet in the high street there is a possibility that each may misunderstand what the others are doing, even though they are all shopping.

To understand what a woman feels about being a housewife, it is necessary to know what her definition of that situation is. Her definition of the situation is partly a product of her reference groups. Thus a woman may tend to feel dissatisfied with the housewife role if her reference group is the graduates with whom she was at university, all of whom seemed to look forward to interesting careers, or a group of friends all of whom combine being a housewife with having a job, or perhaps her mother, against whose cosy domesticity she is still reacting. On the other hand, she may be perfectly satisfied as a housewife if she compares her lot with that of the girls who still work in the noisy, dirty factory where she was once employed, or with her mother whose lot as a working-class housewife in the Depression was so much less enviable than her own. If her reference groups include her manager husband this, too, may affect her attitudes. She may feel fortunate in not having to take responsibility, work long hours and travel hectically about the world; on the other hand she may envy the interest and variety of his life and yearn for a job or a career of her own.

HOUSEWIFE OR CAREER WOMAN?

A striking result of the questions designed to evaluate different roles was the relative unimportance to the women of a job or career for themselves. In spite of one current view of housewives as the reluctant victims of a patriarchal and exploitative society, longing to get back to the 'real' stimulat-

ing world of work, these women were to a large extent content to stay at home, at any rate for the time being. They
found it hard to see themselves objectively, or to envisage
life very far into the future. Out of the 86, 3 were working
full-time when the questionnaire was filled in, and 10 were
working part-time. Between filling in the postal questionnaire
and being personally interviewed, at least one more woman
took up full-time work as a nurse – an example of the way in
which the opportunity to take a paid job depends on the
stage in the family life cycle. The low rate of employment
among these women must be due in part to the fact that most
have young children, and probably many more will take a job
when their children are older. Another group of women,
though not employed, was engaged in training, which varied
from full-time nursing or teacher-training courses to a rather
desultory taking of the odd 'O' level at the local tech. Those
women who are engaged on full-time education face the same
difficulties as those with jobs.

Much has been written about the problems married women
face when they attempt to combine the work of a housewife
with paid work in a job. (The way the choice is sometimes
presented 'Are you just a housewife or do you work?' must
have insulted many a hard-working housewife!) But in spite
of the problems an increasing number of married women do
take paid employment. Viola Klein (1965) showed that 31
per cent of all married women, and 28 per cent of women in
the top social classes, had either full- or part-time employment
in 1957.

Alva Myrdal and Viola Klein in *Women's Two Roles* (1968)
consider some of the dilemmas which face the woman who has
both a job and a home to run, describing the employment
situation in France, Great Britain, Sweden and the United
States. However, it should be remembered that Myrdal and
Klein write in a particular cultural tradition and from a particular point of view (as they acknowledge in their introduction). *Women's Two Roles* was written in answer to a request
by the International Federation of University Women for a
study of female employment, which would help to make it

127

'easier for women to pull their weight in the economic life of their country'. Thus their concern that women 'should' take paid employment may have led them into a certain unbalance, an overstressing of the advantages and importance of paid employment in comparison with work as a housewife: they assert, for example, that 'the years that women spend at home looking after their families need not be regarded as a loss to the rest of society provided women endeavoured at the same time to keep their professional skill alive' (p. 158). In a different cultural context, for instance, in a less materialistic and work-oriented society, or in one which held the role of mother in greater esteem, it would be unthinkable that time spent looking after children should be regarded as 'a loss to the rest of society'. In addition, their concern with the 'employee' role leads Myrdal and Klein to oversimplify the role conflicts involved: the day-to-day life of married women with children involves a perpetual juggling of many more than two roles, and even for those in employment, the role of employee is rarely the most important one.

Hannah Gavron's *The Captive Wife* (1966) also emphasizes the conflicts between the roles of housewife and career woman and the frustrations of the housewife role. A very high percentage of women in her sample intended to go back to work (92 per cent) and 37 per cent of the middle-class women in her survey continued to take paid work even when they had children under five – an unusually high proportion. One suspects that the questionnaire may have suggested to the respondents the sorts of answers they were expected to give:

> Did you work before you were married?
> Did you enjoy it?
> Did you work after you were married?
> Did you enjoy it?
> Why did you stop work?
> Did you find yourself bored at home?

Studies such as *The Captive Wife* are valuable in that they describe and analyse the loneliness, boredom and frustration which many housewives experience. But, on the other hand, there may be a danger that they help to create the very problems which they seek to alleviate: by accepting the definition of the housewife's role as an inferior one, by defining it implicitly as 'non-work', they help to make it so.

A more rounded study is *Britain's Married Women Workers* by Viola Klein (1965) which was based on a representative sample of 1,068 women, living in all parts of Britain. Fifteen per cent of these women had full-time jobs and another 16 per cent did part-time work. Three out of every 4 women gave money as the chief incentive for going out to work, though other motives, such as interest in their work, boredom in staying at home and pleasure in meeting people were also important, particularly among middle-class women. Of the full-time housewives, half had no desire to have any job, but most of the others would have liked a part-time job and were prevented from taking one; the chief reasons for staying at home were the needs of their children, their own health, or their husbands' disapproval of married women going out to work. (Nineteen per cent of employed women also had husbands who disapproved.) Dr Klein concludes,

The outstanding impression gained from this survey is that women's lives, today as much as ever, are dominated by their role – actual or expected – as wives and mothers. Home and family are the central point of their interests and are regarded, by themselves as well as by others, as their responsibility. All other occupations are subordinated to this central function. The continuous and general increase in the 'extra-mural' activities of married women during recent years is a corollary of the reduction in domestic responsibilities.

It tends to be the case that women who write books about married women with jobs are themselves employed; however objective they may try to be, they tend to feel some bias towards holding a job, as opposed to staying at home and being a housewife. This may in part account for the disparity between the tone of the literature about married women workers and the comments of the managers' wives, for the great majority of whom following a career, or having a job,

The wife's world

seemed to be of small importance. For most of them, at the time of the interview, a discussion about the conflict involved in 'women's two roles' would be a discussion about the wife and mother roles, and about the conflicts which may arise between being a good wife and being a good mother. Even for those women who do hold jobs, their domestic roles take priority.

It may be that it is because most of them have children living at home that jobs and careers have so little importance and that the situation will change when the children leave home. Certainly a proportion do intend to take a job when they are able to, and others plan to undertake further training. But more than half the women in our group do not have a job now and have no plans to have one in the future as Table 5.3 shows. It is possible that when the time comes more women will take jobs than now plan to do so: we showed elsewhere (pages 99–104) that planning ahead is not a characteristic of their husbands either. Nevertheless Table 5.3 does not support the idea of married women longing to get back to work. Is it because the difficulties that face them are so great, or because the attractions are not great enough, that so many seem content to stay at home?

The reasons which the wives gave for taking a job were similar to those given by the wives in Dr Klein's survey (1965) though the greater affluence of our sample is reflected in the fact that money is for them a less important incentive.

TABLE 5.3. Future Plans for Work Outside the Home

The Wife	No. of women
Plans to take a job in the future	21
Has plans for further training towards a job	4
Has plans for voluntary work only	3
Is working full- or part-time at present	13
Has no plans for work outside the home	45
	86

Table 5.4 shows that a woman's attitude to taking a job was related to her social background and her qualifications, so that

women from middle-class backgrounds, or with professional training, were most likely to have plans for a job outside the home. This pattern seems to be consistent with some other hypotheses. For example, it supports the idea that a woman whose reference groups include a working-class family background is more likely than her middle-class counterpart to feel that she is fortunate in being able to stay at home and in having no financial need to take a job. Among our couples, at any rate at this stage in their family life cycle, there was not usually any pressing financial need for the wife to go out to work; indeed tax arrangements are such that a wife may find herself with no financial gain at all if she has to pay domestic help to take over her responsibilities at home. The table illustrates what happens when the interest of the work itself takes over from financial necessity as the main motive for taking a job: thus women who have had extensive training may take a job because the work itself interests them, because they feel it to be useful, or because their identity as a nurse or teacher is a salient part of their own identity. But none of these motives may apply to an unqualified woman, who seems both less likely to take a job and likely to do so for different reasons, such as for the social contacts which she makes at work.*

By far the most frequently mentioned reason for going out to work was the opportunity it might provide for making new friends and developing wider interests.

One woman, at present training to be a teacher, said 'I do it because I'm interested in it. I've got more to do for the

* Celia Fremlin put it all in another way in 'The Wider Life' (reprinted in J. M. Cohen *Yet More Comic and Curious Verse*, Penguin Books 1959).

> I once was a dull, narrow housewife
>   With nothing to talk of at all
> But the loves, the frustrations,
> The rows, the relations
>   Of the woman from over the wall.
> But now I've a job I'm quite different
>   I can talk with a sparkle like wine
> Of the loves, the frustrations,
> The rows, the relations,
>   Of the girl at the desk next to mine.

TABLE 5.4. The Wives' Attitudes to Taking Jobs Outside the Home by their Social Backgrounds and Qualifications (per cent)

	Wife's social background†			Wife's qualifications			Total
	Middle class	Intermediate	Working class	Training for 2 years or longer	Some training but for less than 2 years	No higher education	
The Wife							
Has a job now or plans to have a job*	56	54	24	73	48	21	48
Has no plans to take a job outside the home	44	46	76	27	52	69	52
	100 = 39	100 = 26	100 = 21	100 = 22	100 = 33	100 = 29	100 = 86

* This category is further subdivided in Table 5.3.
† For definitions of these categories see Table 3.A.

next thirty years than just cleaning a home.' Another woman, in the process of training to be a nurse, said,

I just wanted a job I could do while the kids were at school, and then I wanted a job that was interesting. I go in six days a week and this follows along with school hours, so it's convenient, and I'm also enjoying it. I couldn't possibly stay at home all day as I get depressed sitting around here doing nothing. And when I say depressed I mean really depressed. I get practically neurotic about it. My husband is quite happy that I'm doing it as he knows it makes me happy.

Several wives mentioned that their husbands had encouraged them to work and Mrs Olantigh, a full-time teacher, commented on the change in their married relationship:

I think I felt for a long time that I wasn't enough a part of my husband's life. He didn't want me to give the things I wanted to give him, and funnily enough in achieving a certain amount of independence I feel more a part of his life. He didn't tell me about things and now he does since I have had a job. Perhaps it's because I've shown I can do more than just dusting and sweeping. Perhaps it's also because I'm important to other people and I feel useful to them, so a little more confidence is given in what I offer in the house.

In spite of all this over half of the wives in our study did not have a job outside the home and had no plans for doing so. One deterrent, which was mentioned mainly by those women who did intend to work, was the difficulty of finding satisfying work. We have already seen that the main motive for taking a job was the interest and stimulus which would be gained from it. Yet for most their job would have to come second to the demands of home and family, and might also have to be part-time. The problem was to find a job which was sufficiently satisfying to make it worth going out to work, but which would not affect other commitments. A new attitude to the *content* of part-time jobs by employers might encourage more women of this sort to take work outside the home. Mrs Olantigh explained,

I'd like to try several types of teaching and one day have a specialization. I've thought of handicapped children, but it's difficult to follow a career and run a home at the same time. I have tried part-time teaching which gives me time for other things, but if there's no particular job with a particular set of children, I really feel it's half a job. I'm thinking of work like child guidance because, although hours are short, you do a complete job, being assigned to two or three children.

The same problem faces women without qualifications even more acutely: one woman who did not plan to go out to work gave as her reason 'after being housebound for the last four-teen years and having no qualifications to offer, I could not expect to be employed doing an interesting and well-paid job'. One reason, then, why relatively few of the women had a job or were considering a job, seems to be that the employment market is not designed to fit their needs and demands. Talent and energy may be wasted because the work to be done is not arranged in a way that makes it both satisfying enough and feasible for the woman whose home and family also need her.

As we have seen, a chief problem of the married woman is that of reconciling her many roles, and to take paid employment outside the home is to take on a role which is popularly supposed to diminish her ability to carry out all her other roles; in fact the adding of the mother role to the wife role may produce more marital tension than the adding of the employee role to the two former. But when a married woman takes a job, her employers may suspect that she will not be fully committed to them, while neighbours may await the first signs of delinquency in her children.* As Mrs Olantigh

* Several studies have been done on the effect of a mother going out to work and they are described in *Working Mothers and Their Children* by Simon Yudkin and Anthea Holme (1963). In general there seemed to be no relationship at all between delinquency and mothers being at work; there seems to be agreement that it is neglect, and not a mother's employ-ment, which harms children and that most working mothers make ade-quate arrangements for their children's care. They quote an American study: 'If a mother remains at home but does not keep track of where her child is and what he is doing, he is far more likely to become a delinquent than if he is closely watched. Furthermore, if a mother who works does arrange adequate care for her child in her absence he is no more likely to be a delinquent than the adequately supervised child of a mother who does not go to work' (p. 98).

said 'Some of my friends and neighbours think I can't be completely competent as a housewife as I go out to work. . . . I don't know if they envy me because I teach and have a career outside the home, or pity me and think I must be un-successful at home and therefore need to go out to work.' (Another wife commented 'because I'm jealous of other women going off to work and looking as though they are having a marvellously interesting time, I always tend to look for faults in the children of these women as a sort of proof that I'm doing the right thing in staying at home'.) All the women with jobs as well as home responsibilities emphasized the extra work and organization which this involved. Other studies have shown that the actual number of hours worked by housewives with and without jobs are not very different.* This must mean that the housework was speeded up, and indeed several women mentioned that having a job made them more efficient at home. Nevertheless the extra work involved can be formidable: Mrs Olantigh described how,

At the weekends I'm cleaning, cooking, shopping, or preparing meals and I have no time to do much else. During the week it doesn't make so much difference. My husband works in the evenings anyway and I prepare my lessons after the kids have had their meal. I go to work because I want to – we don't need the money and my husband doesn't help with the housework at all. It seems too that even if I have someone in to help, I still have no time at weekends.

It seems as though if a wife works because the family needs the extra money then her husband shares some of the responsi-bility for the housework; but if she works 'because she wants to' then he has no such responsibility. Mr Manston used this area of interaction for showing his disapproval of his wife's employment: she described how 'in general my husband doesn't help at all in the house except if something is wrong, when he will get out the Hoover; this is more of a

* Jean Stoetzel (1948) showed that the more than eighty-hour working week of the average married woman with children and a full-time job, exceeded the working week of a full-time housewife with children by only six to eight hours per week, or about one hour per day.

demonstration of his annoyance. When I react because my husband doesn't help me in the house, he says I am doing it because I want to and if I don't want to then I can always give up.'

Several of the wives mentioned that their husbands did not allow them to take a job outside the home or did not approve of their doing so (though this last did not always mean that wives did not take a job). Traditional attitudes about women's place being in the home seemed to linger on, as one said 'My husband likes to feel that everything is organized and waiting for him when he returns from work.' Men whose mothers had not had a job seemed more likely to expect their wives, in turn, always to be at home when they themselves were.

But more crucial factors preventing wives from following a career stemmed from the demands of their husbands' own careers. Frequent moves mean that a wife has no opportunity of getting really experienced in one job and one area, and it severely limits the type of employment which she can take up; one wife wrote 'What is the point of a wife settling down and making a life of her own (i.e. my own Marriage Guidance counselling) when if her husband is offered promotion she must put that first and go?' A university lecturer wrote 'The problem with our recent move within the London area was the fantastic toll on my own professional time exerted by choosing of furnishings etc. If my husband was moved out of the London area this would probably involve my relinquishing my own job.' Both such commitment to work, and such strong reactions were rare; more pervasive was a general feeling that the husband's career must come first, that even the smallest demands of his work take precedence over any aspect of his wife's career. And on the whole husbands and wives concurred in this: a committed teacher, who does not plan to have children of her own, said 'Although I should like to continue teaching I would attach far more importance to my husband's job and happiness.' For some husbands, it seemed that it would alter the way they felt about their own job, if their wife were also to work. The wife of the general manager of a company, who left school at seventeen to become a junior clerk and advanced his position by dint of years of study in the evening and early morning, said, 'My husband would object to me going out to work. It's something in the same way as his respect for the dead. It goes very deep. I suppose it would be undermining his position if I went out. I know that if I had worked at the beginning of our marriage he wouldn't have studied as he wouldn't have thought it was worth it if we were both earning.'

The fact that her husband is a manager may have other, indirect effects on a wife's attitudes to work. For many managers their work is interesting and challenging and their career provides a crucial framework for their lives. They are used to the assumption that one job leads on to another, and that there is some logic in the sequence of jobs, even if it is a retrospective logic. The close conjugal relationship may lead the wife to share this attitude to work – an attitude which it is almost impossible for her personally to put into practice, since any 'career' will be drastically interrupted by child rearing, and her ability to do a challenging and interesting job will be reduced by the demands of her other roles.

Faced with such problems – the difficulty of finding interesting part-time work, the organizing needed to cope with the extra demands of paid employment, the constraints imposed by the husband's career, and so on – it is understandable that so few of the wives take jobs outside the home. Some, of course, are quite content with this: they enjoy using the skills of the housewife and feel that it is a wife's duty and pleasure to provide a peaceful, well-ordered home for her husband to return to after his long day in the more aggressive and demanding world of work. But for a wife who wants a job too, so many other things tend to take precedence, that the problems are immense. Mrs Newington spoke for many others when she said,

When one has young children one's place is definitely with the children. However, I do have this fear of becoming a cabbage and I don't think that going out to tea and coffee, and chit chat over garden fences is really enough. So *if* a woman has no children, and *providing* it's O.K. with her husband, and *if* the marriage does not suffer, *then* she should go out to work.

The whole question throws light on so many aspects of women's life today and of the marriage relationship. So much of what has been discussed is a matter of definition. If being a housewife were defined as 'work' and as 'a job' then perhaps a choice could more easily be made. But somehow a different, more emotive value is put on being a housewife, which also affects the value of any job she does. The housewife role is not thought to be greatly esteemed by society, but she is expected to be totally committed to it. A housewife – as most of the women in our study took for granted – is expected to subordinate her own interests to the interests of her husband, children and home. Most do this gladly most of the time; but it makes the problem of taking a job more difficult, when a wife is quite unused, both to taking initiative for herself rather than adapting herself to the daily routines of others, and also to doing things solely because *she* wants to. For a chief earner a job is defined as being exhausting and demanding and the doing of it is an unselfish act; but for a middle-class married woman a job (perhaps the same job) must be fitted in round her other commitments and she is expected to do it because she is interested in it (a most uncharacteristically selfish reason). Perhaps this is one of the many reasons why jobs such as teaching and nursing, which are clearly seen to be helping others, are so popular, because they provide a more adequate justification and compensation for all the hard work, organization and sacrifice which going out to work actually entails for a married woman. The present system of taxation exacerbates the problem for women whose husbands earn the sort of salaries our managers earn: it means that the financial reward is small and they cannot so easily justify having a job, as a working-class woman can, by the material benefits it brings to their family. Perhaps this is one reason that they sometimes find justification in such reasons as 'a job makes me a more interesting wife', or 'I'm a better mother because when I am at home I give the children more attention because I feel guilty about having left them.' It seems as

138

though society places a heavy burden of guilt on these women: though many enjoyed being housewives, they felt when their children had all started at school that this role alone was not really enough and that they had to make excuses for being so 'lazy'. On the other hand, those who did take a job felt that they had to make excuses for their presumed neglect of other roles.

CHAPTER 6

Family and Community

ON KNITTING THE SOCIAL NETWORK

Patterns of social behaviour can be formal – as in committee meetings or in structured work situations – or they can be informal, as in the chats at the shops or at the canteen. Sometimes the formal intrudes into the informal, when conflicts over work decisions intrude into and affect out-of-work activities, while sometimes informal behaviour intrudes into the most formal work situation, often through jokes or the influence of the opposite sex. Sociologists have documented this intermeshing of the formal and informal in a variety of contexts. Such is the stuff of social life. At one extreme participant observers such as Roy (1960) have joined a work group on the shop floor, or like Harrington (1964) have joined in the social life of a group of working-class housewives so as almost to be one of them. At the other extreme sociologists have simply analysed the frequency of attendance at clubs and associations and noticed variations between different categories of the population and between societies. More ambitiously, sociologists such as Homans (1961) or Blau (1964) have sought the basic principles that govern *all* social behaviour. The former stresses that people engage in activities only insofar as such activities provide them with rewards, and the latter stresses 'the norm of reciprocity', that is, that human behaviour is basically a form of exchange, so that where relationships are free from external constraints men will typically seek social interaction with more or less social equals so that situations of subordination and superordination are less likely to arise.

We are concerned in this chapter with the way middle-class women form clusters of social relationships in the localities in which they live. We are less concerned to show that middle-

class women join more clubs than their working-class counterparts in Britain or fewer than their middle-class counterparts
in the United States. The energetic social life of the American
middle class has been described in many studies (for example,
Axelrod, 1954; Hausknecht, 1962; Seeley, Sim and Loosley,
1963). There has been much documentation of the great
importance attached to friendly, neighbourly and community-
centred attitudes, as they express themselves, for example, in
morning coffee clubs, afternoon card-playing sessions, and
neighbourhood barbecues, and in the many activities associated
with the school, the church, the company and the profession,
or with the commercial, political and cultural life of a town.
By contrast the British seem to lead a very subdued social life
and to be content to do so (indeed British managers tend to
speak with some horror about the frenetic social life of their
American colleagues). Bracey attempted to compare the
situation in the two countries in *Neighbours* (1964); unfortunately he did not sub-divide his two national categories by
socio-economic group, but his book does give a vivid, impres-
sionistic account of the differences in attitudes. Bracey was
somewhat critical of British patterns of social life: 'English
husbands and wives are unenterprising stay-at-homes compared with their American counterparts' (p. 163); and he
concludes 'the most noticeable contrast between the two
countries to emerge from the inquiry is the greater neighbour-
liness existing on American subdivisions contrasted with
the aloofness, if not actual chilliness, which passes for neigh-
bourliness on English estates, both council and private enterprise' (p. 181). However, this stress on differences may mask a
similarity of need which is satisfied in different ways, so that,
for example, feelings of insecurity may in one group produce a
characteristic retreat into the family, while another group
characteristically responds to similar feelings of insecurity by
increased social activity in a search for meaningful relationships outside the family. We are also sensitive to the dangers
of implying that those who, for example, do not join associations, have qualitatively less satisfying lives than those who do.
There is an argument in political sociology that intermediate

Family and community

associations and institutions between the family and the state are essential for a democratic society, but this argument need not detain us here (Kornhauser, 1959).

Patterns of social behaviour vary within and between societies and the processes involved are complicated. There is no reason for the same social need to produce the same behaviour, since a specific need can be met in many different ways. Nor, on the other hand, do similar patterns of behaviour follow from similar needs. And both the needs which people feel, and the patterns of social behaviour which they consider to be appropriate responses, are to a certain extent determined by the wider social situation. Thus church-going may in one society be an expression of faith, but in another may be an expression of community solidarity; and belief may in one society be expressed by attendance at May Day parades, but in another by going on pilgrimages to holy places.

Our present problem is to understand and, if possible, explain the significance of everyday behaviour, which, to those accustomed to it may appear commonplace, but which to a complete stranger to our culture might appear bizarre. A Mediterranean peasant, for example, might find the rituals of a middle-class drinks party in London both confusing and alarming. But, on the other hand, a member of the English middle class might be completely insensitive to the subtle nuances of social interaction in a Mediterranean village, where a simple action, such as the way a girl walks, can constitute a major attack on a man's much-prized honour. Conceptions of honour and shame – particularly related to the preservation of virginity – are deeply embedded in parts of Mediterranean society and it is necessary to make an imaginative leap to get inside the social world that takes them for granted. Even within our society the range of social worlds is wide, and the *Room at the Top–Lucky Jim* syndrome illustrates some of the strain, or even cultural shock, which can be engendered by rapid social mobility (Luckmann and Berger, 1964).

There is a danger that the sociology of the middle class concentrates on the man's career and the wife's patterns of child rearing and formal community involvement; in some ways it seems easier to explain the functions of behaviour which takes place in more institutionalized structures (the firm, the school and so on) than the functions of informal patterns of behaviour, patterns which are not directly tied to the functions of formal structures. Thus it may be easier to explain the behaviour of a man who is trying to sell a product than to understand the behaviour of the same man at leisure: as an example, the act of joining the local rugby club meant a variety of things to our managers – one joined because he likes to think of himself as athletic, another joined solely in order to enjoy the social life, while a third pays an annual subscription because he feels that there 'ought' to be such a local community focus. The more structured the situation, the easier it is to 'explain' what people are doing in it; the less structured the situation the more what people do depends on their private plans, ideals and assumptions, so that the understanding of their actions requires a more flexible and sensitive approach.

But if it is in their informal life, in the interstices between institutions, that people are most free, while yet social pressures are still felt at these times, then it is in informal life that certain sorts of social realities are most clearly revealed. We may be able to analyse the formal work situation, but how would we analyse the need for relationships with people who are called 'friends' but who must not be unduly imposed on and who are not expected to be too demanding? The creation of such relationships often gives rise to anxiety; their continuation can involve the individuals concerned in a demanding ping-pong match of obligations and expectations. And how do we explain the nervousness which arises out of everyday sociability? People worry about their impact on each other, tensely finger their hair or their jewellery and put themselves through various ordeals when they could be sowing beans or reading a book. What are the positive functions of superficial friend-making, and the like?

The cliques and cabals and other informal activities related to the men's working lives have been analysed and interpreted in relation to the overall functioning of the organization

(Burns, 1956). But to what framework, goal or purpose does one relate the informal behaviour of their wives? Perhaps seemingly unimportant behaviour may provide us with a clue to the fundamental nature of the social situation of the manager's wife. Some of the greatest insights of science have arisen from such humdrum activities as apples falling from trees or kettles boiling. We have no pretensions to being a Newton or a Watt. However, we do have a commitment to consider all aspects of social behaviour as of potential equal interest. With that extended apology for what all our readers would take for granted if this were a book about the Australian aborigines, we return to our theme.

Before we turn to consider the patterns of the relationships which our managers' wives had with people outside their immediate family, it might be valuable to look at some of the tools which sociologists have developed for use in such pattern-building. An individual does not simply associate at random with others, nor does he relate in the same way to all, but different relationships are developed according to the nature both of the individuals involved and of the situations in which they find themselves; all acquaintances do not become friends, nor are all friends the same sort of friends. It is in order to analyse the complexities of these relationships between people that sociologists have developed the concept of *social network*. The use of the term 'network' to describe a set of social relationships has been defined:

> Each person is, as it were, in touch with a number of people, some of whom are directly in touch with each other and some of whom are not. . . . I find it convenient to talk of a social field of this kind as a *network*. The image I have is of a set of points some of which are joined by lines. The points of the image are people, or sometimes groups, and the lines indicate which people interact with each other. (Barnes, 1954, p. 43)

The concept of the network is a way of putting system into the complicated patterns of people's social relationships. It is perhaps particularly useful in the study of modern industrial society, where people do not often live in established social groups in which each member knows all the other members, but rather where each individual has a unique pattern of social relationships, a pattern of which he or she is the centre. Thus, for example, a woman (X) may maintain relationships with A (her oldest friend), B (her neighbour, who is also a friend), C (a good neighbour but not really a friend), D (a relative), E (a local tradesman) and so on. Some of these individuals may know each other (perhaps B, C and E); some may know only X and no other member of her network; but it is quite likely that only X knows every individual in X's network.

The notion of social network has been refined and developed by many sociologists,* as they have explored the patterning of the links in the network, and the nature of the links themselves. Thus Mitchell says,

> From the work that has already been done on social networks, however, there appear to be several morphological and several interactional characteristics which are likely to be apposite in any attempt to describe social behaviour adequately. The morphological characteristics of a network refer to the relationship or patterning of the links in the network in respect to one another. They are *anchorage, density, reachability* and *range*. The interactional criteria on the other hand refer to the nature of the links themselves and are the *content, directedness, durability, intensity* and *frequency* of the interaction in the links. (Mitchell, 1969, p. 12)

The discussion about the patterning of the links, then, is concerned with the centre, or anchorage point of the network (whether it be an individual, a couple, or a group), with the links by which one person in the network can reach another or by which attitudes, information and so on can flow from one part of the network to another, with the density or extent to which individuals in a network already know each other, and with the range of the network in terms of the number of persons in direct contact with its anchorage point. The

* The essays in *Social Networks in Urban Situations*, edited by J. Clyde Mitchell (1969), are a valuable recent addition to the literature, containing discussion both of theoretical aspects of the concept of social network and of its practical application in interpreting the behaviour of African townsmen in social situations.

discussion about the nature of the links is concerned with their content, whether it be economic help, kinship obligation, friendship or whatever, with their directedness since a relationship between two individuals may be perceived differently by each one of the two, with their durability over time, with the intensity of the ties which bind the individuals to each other, and with the frequency of contact between them.

Perhaps this point might be more clearly brought home to the reader by imagining all the people to whom he or she sends Christmas cards gathered together in one room. The reader, as anchorage point, will have many different sorts of links with the others in the room, that is, in his social network. To some he will be linked by economic ties as employer or employee; some links will be relatively new; others will be the long-established links of kinship or childhood friendship, some of them intensely valued, others shallow despite their continuity over time; a few of the people in the room the reader will not have seen for years, yet he may have a richer relationship with them than with some of the people who live so near that they delivered their cards by hand. One relationship may be valued by the reader but not by the other, who may not even have troubled to send a Christmas card in return. Some of the people in the room might know each other well, perhaps so well that they exchange Christmas presents with each other but only cards with the reader; others might appear isolated, since few members of their own personal network are present.

The concept of social network, then, is a useful tool which can help in the analysis of the complicated patterns of social relationships. Other useful tools are the concepts of role and reference group, which was discussed in a previous chapter (page 123). We are acutely conscious of the fact that we have not made as much use as we might have of these tools. Our problem was that we were examining a relatively unexplored field of human experience and were unsure as to what parts of it would prove most interesting. If we had known what areas we most wanted to analyse we could have used a more rigid and more methodologically correct questionnaire – but by so doing we might have missed certain crucial areas of our managers' lives altogether. In this sense every study is two studies: one study is tentative, exploratory, and makes use of the talents of the novelist as much as those of the scientist; the second investigates the complexities revealed by the first, using the tools of the social scientist to abstract meaningful patterns out of the complexity of reality. Thus we hope that this study will lead on to a more comprehensive work on more senior men in industry.* However, it seems only possible to make full use of the conceptual tools if one either knows exactly what data one wants to gather or if one knows in great depth about the people one is studying, as a social anthropologist studying a small community might be expected to do.† It was impossible to make a detailed study of the social networks and reference groups of our managers and their wives, partly because of the limited resources at our disposal and partly because concentration on one such area might mean that another, more significant area would be neglected. Nevertheless, it is important to bear in mind that these different approaches all provide valuable, but different, insights into the complexity which is reality. We hope that our explanations are valid in terms of the data which we gathered.

FRIENDS AND NEIGHBOURS

We have found that attempts to be objective about the nature of relationships between friends and neighbours are particularly likely to arouse scepticism and hostility. This may be because it is part of the essential nature of friendship that it be spontaneous and unselfconscious. However, it was clear that for most of our managers' wives their friends were important – but of varying importance: relationships between

* This is to be financed by the Institute of Directors and directed by R. E. Pahl.

† The painstaking method of finding out in great depth about the kinship patterns of the families they studied was used by Raymond Firth, Jane Hubert and Anthony Forge in *Families and Their Relatives: Kinship in a Middle-Class Sector of London* (1970).

friends took many different forms. Thus the answer to the question 'Why do you have friends?' may superficially be 'Because I like them . . . because I enjoy their company . . . because I like to have someone to share my interests'. But if friendship is looked at sociologically it is clear that it serves many different functions for any individual. One of these functions, and one which we feel may be particularly relevant in this study, is the way in which friends can help to confirm an individual in her identity and reassure her about her position in her social network.

The wives were asked where their friends lived and those who were personally interviewed were asked for more detailed information about their friendship patterns, in particular about how they had met and kept up with their three best friends; in this way at least three key points of their social network were identified.

Most made a clear distinction between friends and neighbours. A 'good neighbour', it was generally agreed, was someone who was ready to help if help were needed, but who did not otherwise obtrude into a family's privacy. A successful relationship between neighbours then might be described as being mainly instrumental. Relationships between friends, however, seem far more subtle and complex, involving as they do both instrumental and expressive dimensions of personal experience. At one extreme best friends may also be 'good neighbours', giving and receiving help, rather in the way that sisters did for each other in the stable, working-class community of Bethnal Green (Young and Willmott, 1957). The help may be practical – a packet of tea or an evening's baby-sitting – or it may be more expressive and emotional – comfort in times of trouble and worry, or sharing in the preparation of children's birthday parties and other festivities. It seems as though this pattern, of finding one's best friends among one's neighbours, is more common among women who come from a working-class background or who have not themselves had a salient occupational identity or have not been mobile. For them their identity as a housewife is of greatest significance, and so perhaps it is only to be expected that friendship patterns, too, should centre on and confirm them in this identity.

At the other extreme best friends may rarely be seen, but their friendship may still represent to an individual a valued part of her identity, thus functioning as an important reference group for her.* Particularly among those who have been highly mobile, such continuity of relationships with friends may help to give them a sense, almost, of the reality of their own autobiography. Thus one individual, for example, may say of her friends: 'There's A; we were at school together and our parents are still friends; and B and I were at college together though I haven't seen her for years; and then we used to live next door to C and she and I were always in and out of each other's houses and though we moved away we still keep up with each other.' It was striking how many women described a friendship pattern like this, and it may be significant that one such woman added 'my husband thinks of them as being necessary for me, and is friendly with them, but tends to sigh when I suggest we go and see them or he is informed that they are coming to visit us'. This same husband, very ambitious and successful in his career, says that he has no one he would call a best friend and does not seem to experience this as a deprivation; he gets his identity through his career and might choose other terms to describe what his wife calls friendship. This couple, then, illustrate the idea that friends are more important as givers and confirmers of an identity to housewives. They are also characteristic in that both come from solidly middle-class backgrounds and both continued their full-time education into their twenties.

In asking people about their three 'best friends', it became clear that the term has many meanings. Those who claimed that they had no best friends may have meant that they felt genuinely isolated, or they may have meant that among their many friends no three could be chosen out, or their interpretation of the term may have been such that a relationship would have to be exceptionally close before it could be put into

* For a wider discussion of 'identity' as we have used it see McCall and Simmons (1966).

this category. And for those who did describe their 'best friends', each of such friends may have significance for them in one, or more than one way, as reference-group theory has suggested. Thus a friend may fill an instrumental or an expressive role, and may be expressive of one or more aspects of the past, present or even future identity, or self-concept, of an individual.

TABLE 6.I. The Distribution of Their Friends by the Mobility of The Couples

	Couples have been				
	Mobile*		Not mobile†		No information
Friends live mainly	No.	Per cent	No.	Per cent	No.
At a distance	17	37	8	22	
Locally	4	9	5	13	
Some locally and some at a distance	25	54	24	65	
	46	100	37	100	3

* 'Mobile' is defined as having moved house on average every 5 years or more often: our average 'mobile' couple has moved house every 3 years.

† 'Not Mobile' is defined as having moved house on average less often than once every 5 years, or not having moved house at all since marriage.

A majority of our couples, as Table 6.1 shows, had friends both locally and living at greater distances. As might be expected, those who had been more mobile were also more likely to have most of their friends scattered about the country and only a small proportion of such people had mainly local friends. More surprising is the category of non-mobile people, most of whom had lived at their present address for many years, who still felt that their friends lived mainly at a distance. They illustrate the continuing nature of some friendships, maintained over many years, not by frequent contact, but by letters, telephone calls and occasional visits. It may be that such continuing friendships are a characteristic of the middle class, being made possible by the possession of telephone, car, spare room and letter-writing skills, and necessary by the need for a continuing sense of identity, such as a man might find by looking back at his career.

Another aspect of friendship is illustrated by the very great anxiety which many women felt about making new relationships, an activity which may involve the development of new conceptions of herself; this anxiety often expressed itself in a passive attitude to the making of friends. When moving to a new place many made no positive effort to make friends, waiting to make friends, for example, with the mothers of their children's friends. Many said, as Mrs Ickham, an ex-nurse, did,

I'm never in a hurry to make friends when we move to a new area. I like to take my time. I would invite the neighbours in the new area, but I'd be very careful about this. It's not that I'd want to keep ourselves to ourselves, but if you push yourself too quickly you sometimes get saddled with people you don't like. For example, there's a widow next door to the house we're moving into, and I feel that if I get to know her too quickly, she may be round every minute of the day. If I thought she was lonely or needed help, then I wouldn't hesitate, though.

This comment illustrates well the delicate balance of rights and obligations inherent in a social relationship, which we referred to at the beginning of the chapter. Others regretted, as one wife did, past initiatives towards friendship:

I used to make an effort to track down children of the same age for my children. This proved to be very unsatisfactory as I became over-friendly with the mothers, then found I didn't particularly like them and it was difficult to get out of the situation. Now I never look for friends for the children. I do, however, invite the neighbours in for coffee quite frequently and this has grown to the extent that there is never any peace at all.

Some of the problems a housewife meets in making new friends may be illuminated by comparing her situation with that of her husband. A man going into a new job faces the problem of getting to know a range of new people in the office or organization. He must learn to find his way about their social world, discover the relevant points of conflict and the relative importance of different positions. One of his problems will be to avoid getting entangled in alliances which he might later regret. However, the work situation is such that before long the power struggles and the areas of conflict begin to be revealed, giving some clues to our new manager as to the behaviour which will be most rewarding for him. His wife, however, carries out her work as a housewife by herself; her social interaction must be limited to times of leisure or semi-leisure. If she feels that she needs friends, but yet does not find that all potential friends are equally acceptable, she is faced with the problem of differentiating those who will be her friends, from those who will be merely acquaintances, or less. As we have seen (page 111) many housewives have no very clear view of themselves and feel that they lack a clear identity. (Indeed many have been conditioned to see a wife and mother as someone who should be able to adapt herself to fit in with the needs of others.) In the context of making friends, how-ever, the situation may be one in which a woman, not knowing exactly what sort of person she ought to be, sets out to make a relationship, the warmth and depth of which she does not yet know, with another woman, about whom she possesses little information and who is probably equally unsure about what sort of person she is.

Problems about 'making friends' are compounded by mobility. For those who need to have friends who live near them and whom they see reasonably often, each move brings with it the need to take the initiative in seeking out new friends. Some women do not look for new friends, either because they find their roles of wife and mother perfectly satisfying, or because they feel they cannot take such initiative because they feel too shy, or lack the necessary social skills or for some other reason. But for many moving house means making new friends, an operation which may be associated with anxiety or anticipation or satisfaction, as old conceptions of herself are confirmed or found unacceptable, new ones revealed, and new patterns of relationships worked out. Some of the conflicts which this may involve for the individual are revealed in the self-aware words of one graduate wife, Mrs Eastwell:

When my husband moves I lose friends, thus I am very wary of getting involved. I don't keep up with school or college friends. My neighbours are madly busy – never there and always rushing around, and I don't like staying in and playing with the children. So I take them out for walks and do things where I can take the children with me and therefore I suppose the neighbours see me as being very active and busy myself. I reckon too they often hear me screaming at the children and possibly think I'm not a very good mother. I have a friend who is madly efficient, who lays concrete and does the garden and I feel this my husband's idea of the ideal woman. But when I mentioned this to the woman concerned she said that she always thought I was like that. I'm a member of the Young Wives and the vicar's wife always used to rely on me to talk to new people who had problems but this indicates the sort of person the vicar's wife thought I was. I was on the committee of the Young Wives till I had a row with the new vicar's wife. I was a bad committee member as I couldn't stand people fiddling around and not getting things done. The other members of the committee were very wary of me in case I got upset. I'm also a member of the local church choir and think the choir members see a very different side of me because the choir master is a riot and there's always a lot of joking. I'd say they see me as an extrovert and very good humoured. But I'm bored stiff at home and get very irritable and unpleasant, especially to my husband and the children.

This woman was exceptional in her ability to be objective about herself, and her comments may illustrate the identity-giving function of friends and acquaintances, the conflicts she experienced in containing such varied versions of herself and the different value she placed on some of the many reference groups in her life. As she said, 'one of my problems in life is that I don't have any idea of what sort of person I am. I hope it won't be too late when the children are grown up to become more independent and concentrate on finding the real "me".' It may not be a coincidence that this couple are also exceptional in their high rate of mobility, their high level of education, and the husband's great success so far in his career.

The different rates of mobility among different categories of the population have the effect of limiting the number of potential friends available to the mobile category. People who have lived for a long time in one area tend to have a settled local social network, with most of their friends and perhaps their relatives living near by.* A newcomer may be added to their circle of friends, but might have to be more than averagely acceptable. For them there is not the same urgency about making new friends as is experienced by people moving into the area for the first time. Some of our more mobile couples mentioned this difficulty and gave this as one reason for liking a house on a new housing estate where 'we're all new together'. Another reason for choosing to live on a housing estate might be the greater likelihood of finding neighbours of similar social status, among whom it would be easier to find friends and to build up a local social network. Mobility can also affect the sort of friends a couple make and the way in which they make them. One wife, who had had three moves in six years, said 'When one moves about with the job, one learns not to try to make real friends, just acquaintances.' And a husband wrote about the social skills which highly mobile wives need,

When you hear these couples talk it is obvious that when moving like this the wife's place is all important. One's job tends to be all-embracing with only time at weekends, but the wife is faced with settling in with the house and place in town or village. If she is not prepared to smile or speak first, then you can remain silent within a community. In fact, an acquaintance with a tobacco firm who moved to live on a new housing estate did just this. All the couples moved in almost together but did not speak and sort of hid from neighbours. Except when the men combined to put up a communal fence at the rear of the gardens; then they all chatted and some even went off to the pub, but when the job was completed all went their separate ways. In fact the wife is becoming neurotic without any children and having no conversation all day.

* Bell (1968) demonstrated the importance of geographical mobility for friendship patterns among the inhabitants of two Swansea housing estates.

This comment illustrates the important role of the wife in making local friends for the couple.

Some women then seemed content to be primarily wife and mother; others felt a need to seek out, or to keep up with, friends. Are there, we wondered, any other differences, which might suggest reasons for these different attitudes to friends and neighbours? Is it simply a matter of chance, of inherited personality differences, which make some more friend-oriented than others? Or are there circumstances in a woman's past or present situation which influence her behaviour? We attempted to answer some of these questions by asking each woman to what extent she saw herself as 'a friendly person in your neighbourhood', by asking about the clubs and other associations to which she belonged and then by analysing the answers.

Two groups were differentiated, one containing those who felt that to a large or very large extent they did see themselves as a friendly person in their neighbourhood, and one containing those to whom such relationships were less important. There were no differences between the two groups when the age, the number of children, or the ages of the children were considered. However, a consistent pattern of differences began to emerge when we looked at social background and educational experience (see Table 6.2). It seemed that the most friend-oriented came from the middle class, and particularly from the lower middle class; they had received at least two years of full-time further education (mainly as nurses and teachers) and their husbands had been to university. In addition, wives of men working on the sales side of industry seemed to be more gregarious than those whose husbands worked in other spheres – but as was shown on page 50 the sales side tends to be recruited from the middle class. Those who were least friend-oriented, on the other hand, tended to come from working-class backgrounds and to have received no higher education. Some women in this category clearly felt the lack of close friendships and regretted their shyness and feelings of inadequacy: for them, perhaps, their husband's leap into the middle class had left them behind and

TABLE 6.2. Importance Attached by the Wives to 'Being a Friendly Person in the Neighbourhood', by the Wife's Social Background and Qualifications and by the Husband's Qualifications and Job Type (per cent)

	Wife's social background			Wife's qualifications			Husband's qualifications			Husband's job type			Total
	Middle class	Inter-mediate	Working class	Training for 2 years or longer	Some training, but for less than 2 years	No higher educa-tion	Univer-sity	Other higher educa-tion	No higher educa-tion	Sales	Produc-tion	Admin-istration	
Wife regards 'being a friendly person' as													
Important	51	73	38	62	58	45	71	41	54	69	50	47	55
Less important	49	27	62	38	42	55	29	59	46	31	50	53	45
	100 = 39	100 = 26	100 = 21	100 = 24	100 = 33	100 = 29	100 = 34	100 = 39	100 = 13	100 = 26	100 = 24	100 = 36	100 = 86

feeling uncomfortably unsure of themselves. But others in this category found plenty of satisfaction in their relationships with husband, children and perhaps with other kin.

The friend-oriented, too, could be sub-divided. Some really seemed to *need* friends and to feel that a lack of them would mean a genuine diminishment in their lives: for such women moving to a new area, for example, would mean urgently seeking out new friends at clubs, evening classes and coffee mornings. Others found their chief sources of satisfaction at home, or sometimes at a job, but it was part of their life style to give and go to dinner parties, to take part in local activities, and to pursue interests outside their home.

By contrast, friends did not appear to be nearly so important to the men as they were to their wives. Most mentioned local friends, often those they had made at a local sports club; but they would add that they went to the sports club in order to keep fit, or because they enjoyed that particular sport – their wives would have been more likely to say that they went because they liked the people they met there. This difference between the men and women does not, surely, reflect any innate difference between the sexes: in some societies it is the men who spend the day gossiping and sipping while the women are at work. Rather the different significance placed upon friends must reflect the different social worlds in which husband and wife live. However, though a man might spend the greater part of his waking hours at work, he often did not seem to find any close friends among his work colleagues. A chief reason for this must be the hierarchical nature of many organizations, which means that colleagues are divided into those who are senior to oneself, those who are junior, and those who are potentially in competition for promotion. As an example of this we could take Mr Frith (see page 81 for an extended discussion of Mr Frith's career). He said,

My colleagues see me as difficult, a competitor not afraid to express his opinion. I get on well with them and mix with most sorts of people regardless. I used to have the reputation of being good humoured and a story teller, but this has soured as I have got older. I think I fitted the role of undergraduate very well; I always had plenty of friends. I know people at work who would be friends, if it wasn't for the competition. One can't afford to say you won't tread on somebody's toes as he's a friend.

Mr Frith's comments illustrate the way in which the work situation can inhibit the development of friendships.

Only one of our sixteen managers talked at length about his friends and the value he placed on his relationships with them, though all were asked about their friends. This was Mr Eastwell, one of the most successful men of our sample, in terms of his achievements at work, already on the board of directors of his firm in his mid thirties. He said,

> I have a number of people with whom I am on intimate terms, for example, the person who was best man at our wedding whom I have known since school when I was ten. I also have one or two friends from university whom I haven't seen since, but I feel I could always pick up the ends with them if I met them again. There are twelve to fifteen people with whom I work that I know well in terms of their character, domestic life, values and so forth; these people know my soft centre better than most others. I am generally seen in professional circles as a driver, though a fair one, but hard; this hardness is not my native disposition, though I'm told I take it home with me. For example, I enjoy playing with my children, which would surprise a lot of people, except my intimate friends. Most of these friends are geographically scattered, but I will go to enormous trouble to see them.

Mr Eastwell, then, values his friends because they make him feel that he is not only the aggressive, ruthless man which his work has made him; they reassure him of the continued existence of his gentler side, confirm his view of himself as a man who enjoys playing with his children as well as being a member of the board of directors. For Mr Eastwell, friends seem to have the same sort of identity-confirming function which we have suggested they may have for many women, and in the same way he has retained many friends from his past who represent important parts of his identity.

Nevertheless, it remains true that for most of the men in our sample friends did not have the same importance as they did for the women. The men's comments were very low key: thus they said, that they 'got on alright' with their colleagues or neighbours, and that they thought their friends would see them as being 'a pleasant enough sort of chap', or 'a nice guy'. Few talked at any length about their friends and few seemed to have really close friends. We were puzzled as to why the men in our sample seemed to have a different attitude to friendship from their wives. This seems a possible subject for further study, but with the information available to us we can only put forward a few hypotheses. It may be that managers are simply too busy to make and keep close friends; they work for long hours, frequently take work home, and have heavy family responsibilities at this stage in their life cycle. It may be that they do not need the emotional props which are often the function of friends; success at work has given them self-reliance and self-confidence. It may be that some do have close friends but that they are of a type not readily acknowledged to an interviewer – none of our managers admitted having a mistress. Or it may be that even they do not realize that their secretary may in fact be their best friend, if friendship is measured in day-to-day contact, mutual need for and understanding of each other. It is a little hard, too, to see what form conventional friendship would take for such men. As we have seen, the work situation inhibits friendship between equals. For many men the weekends are fully occupied in gardening, taking the children out, helping their wives with the shopping, visiting their parents, or catching up on office work. Friendship cannot flourish unless some time and interest are invested in it; yet many of the managers have little time and few interests apart from their work. For those men who play sport the common activity might lead to close friendships. Yet it seems as though it is often the activity, rather than the relationships, which is valued.

CLUBS AND COMMUNITY

About half the managers' wives whom we studied belonged to a club or clubs of one sort or another – the Townswomen's

Guild, the P.T.A., the Young Wives and the tennis club were perhaps the most commonly mentioned. For most club members a chief reason for joining was to meet other people, to make new friends.* However, compared with the relatively simple, person-to-person activity of making friends, participation in voluntary associations may be a much more complicated activity, one which will certainly mean interacting with a group, and which may also involve taking responsibility as a committee member, the commitment of further time and energy, and the identification of oneself with the public image of the association. Sociologists have devoted considerable effort to the study of voluntary associations, partly because, being both 'social' and 'voluntary' activities, they can be a valuable guide to social structure and social behaviour, and partly perhaps because they are easy to study. Thus there has been much discussion of the nature, extent and significance of participation in voluntary associations, particularly in relation to age, sex, social class, level of education, nationality and other variables.

Hausknecht in *The Joiners* (1962) provides good summaries of the literature as well as describing two surveys of voluntary-association membership. Like many American sociologists, he lays stress on the part voluntary associations can play in contemporary democratic societies, since it is asserted that they provide a means by which power can be diffused and individuals integrated into society. It seems doubtful whether voluntary associations serve this function to any very great extent in Britain; at least, the democratic function seems less important than that of bringing people of similar interests and social characteristics together. Hausknecht describes the membership of voluntary associations, showing how participation bears a direct relationship to social and economic status, as measured by income, education and occupation. This link between high social status and high

* Margaret Stacey in *Tradition and Change: A Study of Banbury* (1960) discusses the prime importance of social contact as a reason for joining clubs: 'Banbury people do not engage in sport as an exercise in competitive athleticism but as an occasion for social intercourse' (page 88).

levels of participation in voluntary associations has been documented by many studies.*

Hausknecht also reports a consistent link between participation and age, with the middle-aged having the highest rates of participation, but there is some dispute about whether there is a relationship between sex and membership of voluntary associations. Stacey, writing of Banbury, and Axelrod (1954), writing about Detroit, show how, on the whole, women were less involved with voluntary associations than were men, and were involved in different sorts of associations.

Axelrod says,

The roles and functions of woman as wife and mother are concentrated within the family. Their participation will be with groups which are more proximate, both spatially and functionally, for example, with neighbors or relatives, or informal organizations such as P.T.A. and church groups ... the woman's role as an adjunct to the spouse in achieving his social and occupational goals has not gone unremarked. Belonging to the right clubs and entertaining the right people become important. Because her functions are clustered in the family and the home, the female is more likely to achieve participation in neighborhood and kinship groups. Neighborhood association probably serves the same function for women that the informal work group does for men.

Among our managers it seemed as though voluntary associations were more important for the women than for the men, a difference which may reflect the dominant position of his work in the man's life, and the woman's need to build up social networks of her own. In addition, men and women seemed to prefer different types of clubs. Thus the men mentioned being members of sports clubs far more frequently than other sorts of clubs; tennis, badminton, golf and rugby football were particularly popular. On the other hand, their wives were more likely to belong to social clubs or to go to educational classes in the afternoon or evening.

* In Britain, for example, it was confirmed by Willmott and Young in *Family and Class in a London Suburb* (1960), by Stacey in *Tradition and Change* (1960) and by Bottomore, in Glass's *Social Mobility in Britain* (1954).

It seems, however, that the American middle class is much more club-minded than its British counterpart. It is difficult to make exact comparisons, but a few examples might serve as illustrations of this point. Of the lower-middle-class inhabitants of Levittown in Pennsylvania, described by Gans (1967), only 27 per cent of those interviewed did not belong to any voluntary association; by contrast in the London suburb of Woodford, described by Willmott and Young (1960), 45 per cent of the middle class and 66 per cent of the working class did not belong to any club, though it is claimed that Woodford is particularly rich in its clubs and active in its social life. Again, of the American executives' wives studied by Helfrich (1965), 32 per cent reported that they spent over fifteen hours a week on social affairs, and 30 per cent reported spending over fifteen hours per week on civic affairs (presumably some respondents come into both categories); by contrast, of the British managers' wives who are the subject of this book only 20 per cent reported attending once a week, or more frequently, at any social or civic association, or church service.

We approached participation in group activities among the women in our survey rather as we had approached attitudes to 'being a friendly person', differentiating categories with different rates of participation and then exploring the differences between these categories. We included church-going as attendance at a voluntary association, and defined 'frequent' attendance as attendance more than once a month at any church service, club or other voluntary association. Even with such very undemanding qualifications only 45 per cent of the managers' wives fell into the participant category, 17 per cent were occasional attenders at church or club and 37 per cent claimed to have links with no voluntary association at all.*

This pattern is reflected in the answers to the question 'To what extent do you see yourself as being active in local clubs, church or other organizations?' Only 16 per cent saw such a role in the community as being at all important to them;

* These proportions are similar to those found among the middle class of Woodford by Willmott and Young (1960).

50 per cent said that it was not important at all, and the rest felt that it was important to a certain extent.

An analysis of the differences between the 'frequent' attenders and those who belonged to no associations at all may help towards an understanding of the social processes involved. We had wondered whether wives who had been particularly mobile during their married life might be more likely to participate than those who had been more settled, in order to give themselves a feeling of belonging – or less likely to participate, since their personal reference group is elsewhere? However, there did not seem to be any significant correlation between rates of participation and mobility. When we turned to comparing the groups in terms of social background and educational experience, however, differences in rates of participation were revealed. Those who participated most in voluntary associations were likely to come from middle-class or lower-middle-class backgrounds and to have had at least some further education – the ex-secretary was particularly likely to be a frequent attender. Women from working-class backgrounds, or with no higher education, were the most likely to belong to no clubs at all. Thus far the pattern is similar to that which had emerged when we explored the importance to the individual of being a friendly person. But when we considered the ages of the individuals concerned we found that this is a significant factor in determining rates of participation (see Table 6.3). It seemed that women over thirty-five, and those less tied by children, found it easier to participate in voluntary activities, a difference which may be due to having more opportunities, or to greater need, or to the involvement in organizations such as P.T.A.s or Brownies, which having school-age children can imply.

Mere documentation of rates of participation, however, does not tell us why people join clubs and what it is they are seeking when they go to meetings. One reason for attendance is to make friends, an activity which, as we have shown, is characteristic of the middle class, but which might seem extremely unusual to other social or cultural groups. Thus Mrs Eastwell said, 'Before marriage I was not a great joiner of

TABLE 6.3. Attendance at Clubs, Church and Other Voluntary Associations by the Wife's Social Background, Qualifications, Family Type and Age (per cent)

	Wife's social background‡			Wife's qualifications			Family type			Wife's age		Total
	Middle class	Inter-mediate	Working Class	Training for 2 years or longer	Some training, but for less than 2 years	No higher education	At least one child under 5	All children over 5	No children	35 or under	36 or over	
Wife attends												
Frequently*	49	50	33	42	58	35	40	47	67	36	53	45
Occasionally†	20	15	14	25	12	17	17	21	0	20	16	17
Never	31	35	53	33	30	48	43	32	33	44	31	37
	100 = 39	100 = 26	100 = 21	100 = 24	100 = 33	100 = 29	100 = 42	100 = 38	100 = 6	100 = 41	100 = 45	100 = 86

* 'Frequent' attendance is defined as attendance at a church or club more often than once a month.
† 'Occasional' attendance is defined as attendance once a month or less often.
‡ For definitions of these categories see Table 3.A.

organizations, but now I feel it's the only way to meet people';
and her choice of marriage as the turning point emphasizes the
personal isolation which many middle-class housewives
experience. This isolation is likely to be more acute when a
family has recently moved house, and Mrs Dover commented,
'I think that on moving that joining something like the
Young Wives is a good idea as people ask you to come round,
and you can then ask them, and when people know you are a
new person in the area they make a special effort. I think this
is one reason why it is important to live in a nice area as one
meets a nicer type of people.' Whatever their overt purposes,
then, many clubs serve chiefly as places where people can meet
each other; and for people like our managers and their wives,
whose kin often live far away, and who have not lived for
long enough in one area to have become part of long-
established, local friendship patterns, but yet who want to
have friends, clubs serve a useful purpose.

In the United States, as Whyte (1951), Helfrich (1965) and
Axelrod (1954) showed, a wife may sometimes be expected to
join certain clubs because of her husband's position in the
firm. This does not seem to be expected of our managers'
wives, though it is possible that the wives of prominent local
tradesmen, for example, may be encouraged to take part in the
Inner Wheel or local charitable activities. However, our
managers' work lives are carried on by and large in the setting
of national or regional companies, while their wives live
mainly in a local setting: thus there is no need, and indeed it
would not be possible, for them to reflect and enhance their
husband's work status by their own status in local voluntary
associations. We return to this topic in the next chapter. Our
managers' wives did, however, have a variety of attitudes to
charitable and community work, the sort of voluntary work
which might be said to be 'doing good', whether by helping
in the local hospital or clinic, by joining pressure groups such
as Shelter or the local Association for the Advancement of
State Education, or by serving on the local council.

Six out of the sixteen personally interviewed expressed
doubts about such charitable activity, describing, for example,

a reluctance to appear to be a 'do-gooder' or a 'busybody' or to be conspicuous in local politics. When asked whether they felt they had a part to play in the local community, many women answered negatively. Mrs Ash replied 'I have no sense of community at all. In some ways I suppose it's a good healthy thing to have a communal spirit, but I can't see myself as part of the set-up. It seems a little trivial, though I realize you've got to have people doing things like council work.' Mrs Bourne said 'I don't feel I have a role in the community. I think it means feeling you are important in the community and I definitely don't. I've no community feeling at all. I know there are people who feel they have to go and do voluntary work, but I don't feel I do.' Mrs Frith defined a role in the community as 'more of a busybody type than anything else – people who try to organize things and work for organizations'. Mrs Petham described some of the paradoxes which she felt in this area of her life:

I have no idea of having a role in the community. I'm not the sort of person who would be a council representative, but there are people in the area who are the obvious people to do this, and that's what they think they're there for. I'm not the organizing type, but I will help. I am a member of the things that I'm a member of for pleasure; I don't feel I ought to take part in anything. The main reason for joining things is that it enables me to meet people. This is also so with the tennis club; it's not only for exercise. However, I do feel I ought to do other things. For example, when I was in the Midlands I met an elderly lady by chance and visited her every weekend because she was housebound. In the end it became so that if I had to miss a week it was a terrible thing: I enjoyed visiting her and got very involved with her. But I wouldn't like to do something arranged by the council, because then I'd look like a do-gooder.

Mrs Petham seems to speak for many in her dislike of taking a conspicuous community role, either on the council or in organized charitable work, and in feeling that other people are more suited to such roles. The implications for democracy may be disquieting. More light was cast on attitudes to these types of activity by Clements in *Local Notables and the City*

Council (1969). He analysed the reluctance of many people to become involved in the disputes and conflicts of public political life; they prefer, by contrast, the relative consensus about aims and means which is found in voluntary charitable work.

A few women (four out of the sixteen) felt that they had a duty to do some sort of community service. Thus Mrs Bridge said,

I'm mainly interested in being a member of a club as a means of making friends and also as giving me a place to go to. I feel I don't do enough in this way, but don't know what more I could or should do. I used to do voluntary work at the hospital. Recently the vicar asked me to be a Brownie captain, but I didn't accept and I have consequently felt very guilty about this. But I didn't feel that I had any qualifications for doing that sort of thing. I very much feel a duty to do something to help people who are either poor or old or ill, but I don't quite know where to start finding out about opportunities.

This comment illustrates some of the difficulties felt by women wanting to do voluntary work – reticence, inexperience, a lack of self-confidence. Mrs Dover pointed out another difficulty: 'If we were settled in one place long enough to know it really well I would be much more interested in community affairs. As it is, when we move around so much, we just start to get to know an area and then we move again.' (The Dovers had three homes, in three different regions of Britain, between 1964 and 1968.)

Other difficulties arose out of the demands of the husband and of his work: on the whole our managers had long working days; they arrived home comparatively late and expected to have a meal and to spend some time with their wives. A wife who frequently had to spend the evening out of the home might find that she met disapproval from a husband who felt that, both as a housewife and as a wife in a close conjugal relationship, she should stay at home when he was at home. Thus Mrs Olantigh said 'My husband doesn't allow me to go out in the evening more than about once a month. He likes me to be at home when he's at home, even if he is working.

I'd like to be a member of more things and to go to evening classes for painting and "arty-crafty" things like pottery or dressmaking, but I don't go because my husband doesn't like me being out.' Mrs Graveney said 'I go to day classes; I can't join evening classes as my husband would object. I did at one time when I was secretary of the Women's Institute, but my husband wanted to go to night school on the same night. This made it all very complicated and he said his job came first. Therefore, in general, I prefer to do things in the day now.' Mr Ickham's attitude may cast light on his idea that marriage should be a partnership of equals: Mrs Ickham said,

He's not too keen on me going out in the evenings, unless it's to something more intellectual, such as evening classes. I've done night classes once a week for two or three years: I did German for the first year, with my husband, and French last year, and this year I've been taking the dog to obedience classes. There was an attempt to drag me into the Young Wives, but I'd rather have outside interests more on my husband's level, so I don't become bogged down with a family, kids and domesticity.

Here once again are illustrations of the importance to our managers and their wives of their marriages, and of the way in which the role of 'wife' is separated from the role of 'housewife'. If a couple's style of life is inseparably bound up with having a close conjugal relationship, and if the only time on a weekday which they can spend together is in the evening, it is unlikely that they will be willing to give up this time to voluntary activities on more than perhaps one night a week.

TWO CASE STUDIES

It seemed, then, that attitudes towards friendship and club-going were part of a whole *style of life*. Perhaps two examples might illustrate this point: both the women described have two children, live in three-bedroomed houses in the south of England and are in their mid thirties. The first, Mrs Lenham, left elementary school at fourteen; her father is a skilled manual worker, and her husband is a production controller at £3,400 a year. Of her natal home she said,

My parents didn't go out much on their own; they never left the house really because of us. We used to go out to the country once or twice in the summer. And Mother's relations would visit a couple of times a year. My parents had one or two close friends whom they are still in touch with and they used to occasionally come round and the men would sometimes play cards. We usually spent the evenings in the home with Dad reading, and Mother sewing and knitting and we kids would read a lot or play games.

Mr Lenham's parents, similarly, never spent an evening or a night away from home, though they were very much more gregarious, having 'an ever-open door' for numerous friends and relations. Mr Lenham's father was a north-country smallholder; he described his childhood home:

We lived on the outskirts of a small town and our back garden backed onto the fields which made up the farm. The family as a whole made its own entertainment. My mother played the piano and my father played the violin. My sister sang and one of my brothers played the violin also. We played cards as a family and welcomed visitors, in fact we had an ever-open door. My wife would throw a fit if a family suddenly descended on us in the way mine used to descend on my mother. However, we had a large old home, which made a difference. I spent a lot of time on the farm, riding horses and thinking, and enjoying nature – or simply helping my father. I have always been a dreamer. Our family culture extended to brass bands and music festivals. Our holidays consisted of day trips to the seaside. But there were never family outings to the cinema and there was no theatre or anything like that in the area.

(Interviewer: 'What are the differences between your childhood home and your present home?')

[Mr Lenham] There is no puritanism now. But we lack the conversation we had in my home and we have allowed television to play too great a part. We are well blessed for transport and now the kids take a lot of things for granted and don't enjoy the things we would expect them to, for example, car rides in the country. I was brought up in the 1930s and saw kids with no soles to their shoes and patched clothes. This acted as a driving force to me. And the lacking of this experience in my children may result in there being a failure on my son's part to apply himself to his career in the way I have done to mine.

Family and community

The Lenhams present home is quietly domestic, centred round the family itself, the house and garden and the television. Mrs Lenham described a typical weekend:

We frequently spend it decorating the house, though we just finished a batch of that three weeks ago. On Saturday morning nobody gets up early. My husband goes out and has a haircut and does odd bits of shopping for himself, and the children just play around. I spend most of the time in the kitchen cooking the dinner and tidying. In the afternoon we may all go into town. If not my husband watches the television and I get cross as I don't like television, so I'll get work to do, such as knitting or odd jobs around the house. I don't like television on a Saturday afternoon because my husband watches sport and I don't like to. On Saturday evening all the family watch the television. On Sunday morning again nobody gets up early. My little girl goes to Sunday School and my husband does odd jobs around the house, such as cutting the lawn, and I cook. The last few Sunday afternoons we have all been out on picnics. If not we stay in and watch television again. In the evenings we basically sit around the fire watching the television and chat. It's pretty much the same during the week, though sometimes my husband helps our son with his homework.

(Interviewer: 'Is there anything you'd particularly like to do which you can't do?')

[Mrs Lenham] Not really. My mother comes to stay every third weekend and then we go up to town on our own and have a field day and that tides me over till the next third weekend. Me and my mother go window shopping and shopping in the town and enjoy it very much. If I go without my mother I have to take the children and that's boring for them, so I store it all up till my mother comes and the two of us go off on our own.

Mrs Lenham has two good friends living near by with whom she frequently has a cup of tea, but she belongs to no clubs, only rarely goes out in the evening, and in her description of family weekends, friends are not mentioned at all. She says 'I am quite content and happy with my lot. My husband wishes I would get out and mix more, but it doesn't really worry him if he knows I am happy as I am, and it doesn't worry me.' She wrote,

I am a very shy person and have rather an inferiority complex and so feel very ill at ease with people, unless they are very close friends. Therefore I refuse to attend social gatherings and parties, etc. with my husband, although I don't mind how many he attends. There are times when I feel I am a failure to him in this aspect and wonder whether it will ever affect him, indirectly, in his career.

Both stressed, however, that their marriage was a very happy one, Mr Lenham becoming quite lyrical: 'sometimes I feel as though I'm still on my honeymoon'.

The other contrasting couple also felt themselves to be particularly happily married. Mr Newington (see pages 96–8) is a sales manager earning just over £2,000 a year. Mrs Newington's father was a publisher and she ended her full-time education at eighteen; her childhood home life was that of the traditional middle class. She said,

I had a very comfortable home life. It wasn't stately-home wealth, but we didn't want for anything. We were allowed to have friends home to play and we went to the theatre a lot. We always had family holidays. My parents didn't go out a lot, not as much as we do, though they had friends over at weekends and occasional cocktail parties or dinners.

Mr Newington's father was an engineer and his family life must have been as full and active as a wartime childhood could be:

We had a dog and went out for lots of walks together. I was encouraged to do model making. My uncle and father used to go sledging at midnight - we were known as the mad Newingtons in that area. It was a full and lively life with lots of people joining in. I was never bored. I played cricket and my father and uncle did too, and we went bell ringing together. My parents never went out or had people in for dinner, so as far as social life was concerned I didn't know anything about it. I was very *gauche*.

It is interesting that both in the case of the Newingtons and of the Lenhams the present friendship patterns of the family resemble those of the mother's family more closely than those of the father's family. The Newingtons lead a busy social life – Mrs Newington sees friends for tea and coffee during the day,

and as a couple they go to and give dinner parties, visit the
theatre and take part in many local activities. Mrs Newington
described a typical weekend:

On Saturday morning we get up very late, about nine to nine-
thirty, and have a leisurely breakfast. If it's nice we go for a walk
on the beach or a swim. We only occasionally go into town as my
husband hates shopping. Sometimes I go to the hairdressers and
then my husband does the garden with the children, or goes to see
his parents. We have our main meal at one or one-thirty. In the
afternoon, depending on the weather, we do gardening or decorating or take the children and the dog for a walk. We have a tea-
supper at five-thirty or six o'clock; in the evening we quite often
go out to dinner with friends, or to our parents, or to the local
theatre: we do this about every two to three weeks. If not I might
do some dressmaking, and my husband does his model railway
out in the garage. Then we have coffee and cheese at about ten-
thirty and go to bed about eleven.

Sunday morning is usually pretty much the same as Saturday
morning: a walk on the beach or gardening with the children, then
we go for coffee with my husband's parents, or have a drink
before lunch with my parents. We might do this if they have friends
in. The children usually come with us and we expect them to
behave for that amount of time [children aged five and three].
We have a traditional Sunday lunch and in the afternoon we go to
a public garden or for a walk in the country. We again have a tea-
supper. In the evening we watch television, or listen to the radio
or records, and do the accounts and generally get depressed as a
result of this. We go to bed about ten-thirty.

Some weekends we spend the day with friends, or friends come
to us. We both feel that there are lots of things we will do when the
children are older. My husband would like to play golf and cricket
more than he does. I would love to ice skate, but there's nowhere here
to do it. And we both like to go out for the day and have a nice
lunch somewhere. We like to go to a hotel, rather than worry about
picnics, but that is expensive and not practical with young children
and a dog.

Of the clubs he belongs to Mr Newington said 'they're a bit
of a drag, apart from the good social events they have, and
the people I meet through them'. People and friends are important
in the Newingtons' life. Mrs Newington wrote,

Conclusion

I have a lot of local friends, but as I come from London and my husband from Hertfordshire and we both made a good many friends at boarding school, college, national service, etc., we have friends in many far-flung places. Most of these we contact at Christmas and meet as and when the opportunity arises. Both sets of parents have houses locally which means that other relations visit fairly frequently for weekends, etc. All my relatives live in or near London so we keep in contact fairly regularly by the telephone and visits, etc.

It might be interesting to look more closely at the Newingtons' social network, especially in the light of Elizabeth Bott's comment (1957, p. 105) that 'connectedness does depend, in part, on the husband's occupation. If he is engaged in an occupation in which his colleagues are also his neighbours, his network will tend to be localized and its connectedness will tend to be high. If he is engaged in an occupation in which his colleagues are not his neighbours, his network will tend to become loose-knit.'

Mr Newington works in the small town in which he lives. Five of his colleagues live in the same road as he does and his wife meets their wives 'at coffee mornings, at school, on the beach, and in the town generally'. Nevertheless the Newingtons continue to maintain their large and scattered network of friends, even though they have lived in the same place for eight years and might have been expected to have a mainly local network. Thus in Bott's terms they have both a local, tight-knit network *and* a loose-knit network.

CONCLUSION

Why are friends so very much more important for some people than for others? Certainly it is not simply a matter of income: Mr Lenham, for example, earns at least a thousand pounds more annually than Mr Newington. Nor are the patterns simple – there are many exceptions and each one of the number of variables associated with a certain pattern of behaviour does not apply to each individual who shows such behaviour. Friends are valued partly because they provide the individual with an opportunity to express different sides of his identity, or to try out new identities. Thus one woman may 'be', and want to be, at different times and to different friends, an amusing companion at the keep-fit class, a dog lover, Johnny's mother, someone with whom one can have an intelligent conversation, or a friendly person in the neighbourhood. Friends are also valued because of the help and support both material and emotional, which they can give. In a sense most people, those who have spent all their lives in the same area, take their friends for granted. There will be certain people, those whom they particularly liked at school, at work, or in the immediate neighbourhood, to whom they turn and whom they would call their friends. But friends only become a problem when they cannot be taken for granted, as for example when mobility breaks the bonds of taken-for-granted friendship. A man may make new friends at work. But a married woman at home has no ready-made way of making new friends. She may respond by contenting herself with her home and her relationships with her nuclear family: this is often the response of women, such as Mrs Lenham, who come from a working-class background. For those women who remember childhood hardship, it is satisfaction enough to be able to create a comfortable home, and they are content to be able to be a 'good wife and mother'. In addition, women from working-class backgrounds may feel socially insecure and so be afraid of unfamiliar people or unfamiliar situations.

But for women who come from a middle-class background, or who have had educational or occupational experience of a middle-class type, attitudes to friends may be different. For those who come from a solid-middle-class background only one, or at most two, generations separate them from the time when cheap and plentiful domestic help made possible the leisure to cultivate friends, develop cultural and artistic interests, and pursue a wide range of activities outside the home. Friends would be an intrinsic part of such a way of life, as companions with whom interests could be shared and as significant others, confirming the individual in her identity. In addition, a large proportion of the middle class have experienced several years of boarding-school education, an

Conclusion

experience which may have led to anxiety about acceptance by a peer group and so to an increased stress on the importance of having friends. For those women who have in the past achieved roles outside the home in which they felt themselves to be valued – as teachers or nurses, for example – personal relationships outside the home may be a valued source of identity. If mobility means that long-established friendship ties are broken, there may be responses such as we have described – the cherishing of old friends even though they are rarely seen, anxiety about making new friends, the seeking out of friends at clubs and coffee mornings. From this point of view friends are often more important for a woman than for a man; for him his career provides his chief identity, but she must look elsewhere, if she does not find that the roles of wife, mother (as long as it lasts) and housewife are enough. For the woman who wants to have some sort of role outside the home, but whose family commitments prevent her taking paid employment, friends and clubs can provide alternative sources of companionship, interest and status.

CHAPTER 7

The Wife and Her Husband's World

IN this chapter we are concerned with the wife's involvement with, and her attitude to, the company which employs her husband, and with those times when the two worlds, of the wife-at-home and the husband-at-work, actually meet. For though our theme may be the interaction between home and work, these two worlds rarely do meet, but rather are mediated to each other through the person of the husband. We have discussed some of the tensions and conflicts between the two worlds (and will explore others in subsequent chapters), so it might be expected that the occasions when the wife and the company meet each other, in person as it were, might be times of anxiety and stress. On the surface, of course, such occasions are often trivial – the firm's annual dinner dance, the informal entertaining of customers – but some of the most important clues to the understanding of social behaviour have come from taken-for-granted, trivial aspects of social life. By looking at how the wives of managers react to involvement with their husbands' firms we have hoped to illuminate both some aspects of middle-class conjugal relationships and some of the tensions which can arise out of one of the few occasions when home and work actually meet.

Much company folklore is attached to the ways in which a wife can help or hinder her manager husband. The typical manager's wife, it is said, is gregarious, confident and extro-verted; she is greedy for material goods and ambitious for her husband, fostering his career in whatever way she can, from entertaining his colleagues and clients at candle-lit dinners to playing bridge with their wives. She can ruin his career, it is said, in any number of ways, from drinking too much, or dressing outlandishly, to pushing him too much – or not enough.

Yet for all the informal, gossip-type importance which she

is accorded, very little is known about the manager's wife, in
the sense of formal, objective study: the popular interest does
not appear to be shared by most sociologists. What little work
has been done on the manager's wife *per se*, and on the
manager at home, has been done in the United States; thus
not only may much of the common myth be based on American soap operas, but most of the serious literature, which we
discuss below, is also American. There may perhaps be
significant differences between the American and British
situations about which we can only guess.

THE MANAGER'S WIFE IN THE
UNITED STATES

The American study which is perhaps most relevant here is
The Social Role of the Executive's Wife by Margaret L. Helfrich
(1965). In answer to the question 'Why has the wife of an
executive become so important?', Helfrich discusses the shift
in emphasis in American society from production to con-
sumption, the greater importance of business entertaining,
and the demand of industry that their executives work long
hours and move more frequently than they used to. She concludes 'In general then, it can be said that because of the change
in the status of women, and the changing native character
and structure of business, corporations are increasingly
interested in the wives of their executives.'

Helfrich's study was based on the questionnaires filled in
by 50 wives (a response rate of only 34 per cent to the 145
questionnaires sent out). The 50 wives lived in 11 different
states, with 30 living in Pennsylvania; some of them were
reached through their husbands, who were attending a course
on management problems, and others were approached
because they 'were known to meet the sampling specifica-
tions'. Forty of the wives had worked before marriage,
typically as teachers, secretaries and saleswomen. Their
husbands were top- or middle-level executives earning between
$10,000 and $50,000 a year. When asked the question 'What
do you consider to be the basic duties and responsibilities of

the executive's wife?', wives, regardless of the specific role they choose, gave the following answers,

1. to take care of the house and children
2. to manage so that her husband gets some of her time
3. to keep the home running smoothly and to be able to entertain
4. to participate to some extent in civic and social affairs

The wives, particularly those of middle-level executives, felt that it was important to conform: 'she must conduct herself properly at all times', 'she must reflect her husband's position', and all agreed that in every aspect of her life, extremes, both good and bad, should be avoided. Helfrich divided her wives accordingly to the major role which each chose as important to her, and thus defined six different categories. These categories were the family-centred wife (23 wives), the community-centred wife (11), the creative wife (6), the consultant wife (5), the career wife (3) and the student (2).

The *family-centred wives* differed from those in other groups by having, on the whole, husbands at lower levels of management and earning lower salaries, and by being more recently married and more likely to have young children. They were. however, similar to other groups in their degree of social and civic participation: 7 of the 23 family-centred wives spent fifteen hours or more each week participating in social organizations, especially in bridge playing, bowling, garden clubs; the P.T.A. and the Scouts were important civic activities. This was considered to be rather a small amount of participation: one wife said 'I guess I will probably be more active in community and civic affairs in the future as our daughter grows up'; another said 'my husband encourages me to join organizations because there I meet prospective customers and wives of other executives. It is good public relations.' (This group is probably the one most similar to our group of British managers in income, age and life-cycle stages but the contrast between the two groups is striking, both in their attitudes to their own involvement in their husbands' work lives and in the extent of their activity outside the home.

The *community-centred wives* still put their husband, children and home first, but in addition they took an even larger part in social and civic organizations. Characteristically these wives have husbands who have reached higher levels of management; on average their husbands' salaries are greater and they themselves are older than wives in other groups and they are less likely to have young children. Six of the 11 community-centred wives spent more than fifteen hours a week in participation in social affairs, and 8 spent more than fifteen hours a week participating in civic affairs.

How did the family-centred women in Helfrich's study see the job of being an executive's wife? In the words of one wife 'my basic duty as the wife of an executive is to run the home as independently as possible'. The stress is on the *independence* of the wife: there was no talk of a partnership between husband and wife in their homemaking or care of the children. Instead their roles were highly segregated, with the wife taking responsibility for home, children and often the family's financial affairs, and allowing the husband to concentrate on his work – or his leisure: one wife said 'I must assume many responsibilities to assure more leisure time for my husband.' Wives must accept frequent moves as the price their husband pays for promotion in his career. Most wives accept this as part of the way of life, though one recalled a wife 'who was always complaining about moving so they don't do it any more and it looks as though her husband will not get the promotion he was after'.

Entertaining the husband's business associates is also seen as being part of the role of an executive's wife. One wife said 'I feel an executive's wife can be important to him in entertaining. She can do much to create a favourable impression for both him and herself.' Dr Helfrich comments,

The wife of an executive and his home must reflect his position and socio-economic status, but give some indication of his ambitious nature. Her clothes, hair style, manners, perfume and jewelry are all conspicuous objects for the observers. The home, its furnishings, paintings, music, literature, china, silverware and linens are further evidence of their 'life style'. Granted, some of these things are more important than others, each is nevertheless important.

Participation in social and civic affairs is also seen as being a basic duty of the executive's wife: all but 4 of the 50 wives in Dr Helfrich's sample were involved in both social and civic affairs. This they did for several reasons: on behalf of their husbands: 'my husband expects me to represent the family in the community. He is busy with his work, therefore I joined some civic organizations in the community'; on behalf of their children: 'the wife of an executive should be active in community and church affairs. If she has children she must be interested in and take part in their organizations'; and on behalf of their husbands' employers: 'One has the feeling that the company expects this of you – to participate in civic and social affairs and, if possible, to be a leader in the community; they don't come right out and say this in so many words, but you just know it is what they want you to do.'

In her conclusion Dr Helfrich discusses the sequential role-pattern characteristics of the executive's wife – first as an economic partner, then as a housewife and mother, and finally as a companion to her husband. She says,

> Most wives of executives in the sample have an understanding of their roles; they consider their activities important to their husband's career whether they engage in civic or social affairs or stay at home. Only a few executives were interviewed for the study. It would be interesting to interview more executives to obtain their thoughts about the roles of their wives, and to compare the wife's conception of her role and her husband's conception to obtain a more comprehensive analysis.

She might have added that it would be interesting to compare the American situation with that in other countries – certainly, by contrast with the American executive's wife, the British wife is hardly conscious of having a special role as *an executive's* wife, and both sees such a role and acts it out in a very different way from her American counterpart.

William H. Whyte, in his study of *The Wives of Management* (1951) confirms the picture of America drawn by Helfrich.

His study was based on 230 interviews with corporation officials, management consultants and psychologists, and with managers and their wives. The wives he interviewed were those of the coming generation of management, with husbands aged between twenty-five and forty and in junior or middle management. Whyte says,

> With a remarkable uniformity of phrasing, corporation officials all over the country sketch the ideal. In her simplest terms, she is a wife who is: (1) highly adaptable, (2) highly gregarious, (3) realizes her husband belongs to the corporation. Is the corporation asking the impossible? It would appear not. For the significant fact that emerges from any study of the question is not that corporations are trying to get this kind of wife. The significant fact is that they *are* getting her.

How do the wives that Whyte interviewed see their role and how do they evaluate the different roles they must play? The striking thing that emerged from the wives' comments is the negativeness of their role as wives: 'a good wife is good by *not* doing things – by not complaining when her husband works late; by *not* fussing when a transfer is coming up; by *not* engaging in any controversial activity'. Consistently anti-feminist, slipper-warmers to a woman, the wives saw themselves as 'stabilizers', 'good listeners' or 'sounding boards' for their husbands. As one said 'A man gets so frustrated at the office – it's such a rat race – he should be able to come home to calmness.'

But the wives also emphasized another aspect of their role, that of being gregarious, popular and highly adaptable 'mixers'. One executive said 'She should do enough reading to be a good conversationalist . . . even if she doesn't like opera she should know something about it, so if the conversation goes that way she can hold her own. She has to go with you if you're going to make a speech or get an award, and not be ill at ease.' The women described the many different social situations in which they had to be able to be at ease, and seemed to accept without demur the frantic juggling of social roles which their lives involved. One woman might have to entertain her husband's boss and his wife, welcome junior colleagues to the firm, provide a weekend stopping place for touring top-brass of the company, be a responsible member of P.T.A. or other local organization, and be acknowledged a 'real person' by the girls in her street. For a wife must not only *do* the sort of things expected of her, she must also *be* the sort of person expected by the group of which she is a member. Whyte says,

> One rule transcends all others: *don't be too good*. Keeping up with the Joneses is still important; but where in pushier and more primitive times it implied going substantially ahead of the Joneses, today keeping up means just that: keeping up . . . neither must one be too outstanding in personal ways. The good corporation wife does not make her friends uncomfortable by clothes too blatantly chic, references to illustrious forbears, or excessive good breeding, and intellectual pretensions she avoids like the plague.

As one wife said, 'it's a very worthwhile bunch we have here. Edith Sampson down on Follansbee Road is sort of the intellectual type, but most of the gang are real people.'

If it is difficult to generalize about national characteristics, it is even more difficult to generalize about differences between cultures. However, from studies such as those discussed above, a certain image of the American executive's wife begins to emerge. It seems as though she is a wife who, on the whole, expects to have a part to play in her husband's work life, as she expects to take part in the social and civic life of her community. Compared with her British counterpart, she appears more out-going, more gregarious, perhaps more 'other-directed'.* To a certain extent this may be because the average executive's wife in America is better educated, a higher proportion of such women being graduates than would be the case in Britain. It may also be true that the world of the American executive is one in which there are fairly clear norms, which are widely shared and upon which there is to a large extent agreement: for example, it seems probable that British managers' wives would find difficulty in defining a good executive's wife, and that there would be a plurality of different 'good' types, while their American

* Riesman, 1961.

counterparts may find both definition and agreement much easier. Differences between Britain and the United States may also be due to different attitudes within the companies employing the managers. It seems sometimes as though the American company is in league with the wife in a joint endeavour to make a man work harder.* By contrast, British managers prize, and British firms respect, the privacy of the home and the clear separation of home and work – even though they may affect each other the two worlds do not often meet. Where there is a demand that links between home and work should be multiplied, it is, as we shall show, often from the wives themselves that such a demand comes.

In informal discussion most British managers deplore the sort of situation which Helfrich and Whyte describe – yet at the same time most will acknowledge the importance of the wife's attitudes to her husband's work and the difference which she can make to his career. Discussions with managers about the extent to which wives should be involved in their work life tend to become emotional or tense. Those who believe in the psychological significance of jokes may see the tension revealed in a joke which was told during a company's internal training course. The managers on the course were divided into groups in order to discuss the interaction of career and family life. One man started his report on his group's discussion with the following story:

A manager's wife had looked forward to the firm's annual dinner with great pleasure. She bought herself a new dress, had an expensive session at the hairdresser and took great pains to have all the right accessories, scent, and so on. On the day itself the children got to bed in good time, her mother arrived to baby sit and she had every expectation of a marvellous evening. The final touch came when she found she was sitting next to one of the most senior men in the company, a man who could do much to further her husband's career.

She felt confident and pretty and chattered away gaily and intelligently. It was in the midst of a particularly witty piece of

* Thus William H. Whyte in *Is Anybody Listening?* (1948) wrote 'As an economic lever on the salesman, companies have learned, there is no stimulus quite so effective as the wife if properly handled.'

conversation that she suddenly realized that she had just leant across and cut her companion's dinner up into small pieces for him.

The joke was well received: the whole course roared. It seemed to relate to some subconscious nightmare.

ATTITUDES TO INVOLVEMENT WITH
THE COMPANY

Most of the 86 couples we studied could go to some sort of social function arranged by the firm which employed the husband. These functions varied from the minimal annual office party to a wide range of dinner dances, children's sports days, luncheon clubs, car rallies, incentive trips abroad, and so on. Twenty-six of the wives said that their husbands' firms arranged social occasions more than once a year, and 38 said that such occasions occurred at least once a year; only 22 of the wives could not, or did not, go to any function arranged by the firm.

Why do so many firms feel it necessary to involve their employees' wives and families in this way? There seem to be contradictions between the manifest functions of these occasions and their latent functions – that is, between the purposes which they are said to fulfil and other, often unacknowledged, purposes which they are in fact fulfilling.

These contradictions may be one reason for the anxiety such occasions sometimes seem to cause. Thus, while it is said that social occasions are arranged for the enjoyment of all concerned, the firms themselves may see them – sometimes explicitly but more often implicitly – as an opportunity to vet wives whose husbands are in the running for a top executive position or a tricky overseas post, or as a way of increasing the loyalty of wives to the firm so that they will be more tolerant of the demands made on their husbands.

When managers themselves are asked whether they think that firms should interview wives, very strong reactions are aroused. Logically they are prepared to accept that a man's career should be planned by his firm and that this should be

based on extensive information; they also, in a rather confused way, believe in some right to privacy and a personal life.
We discussed this subject with 36 managers of an international oil company, apart from our 86 couples. Of these
managers, 26 considered that informal social functions should
be arranged for managers' wives, and 16 thought that a wife's
behaviour at these functions should be taken into account
when her husband was being considered for promotion. But
30 out of the 36 were against giving the wives a formal interview – it was considered 'less embarrassing' if the firm vetted
the wives at an informal occasion. Thus one man wrote 'I feel
that if informal social functions are provided this will help the
wife who needs social guidance. On the other hand, in many
cases where the wife is unsuitable as a key executive's wife,
she will realize this after attending the social functions and the
decision required will then be realized by husband and wife as
a family without the embarrassment of company inter-
ference.' And another wrote 'This is a problem which will
grow rapidly – action is needed urgently. There is little logic
in training husbands for advancement without keeping wives
abreast of his progress.' A number of the oil men, however,
felt that a wife should not be too involved in her husband's
work life and stressed the importance of protecting the
family's privacy: 'My general feeling is that the family is a
separate entity and the company cannot assess and use the
family environment without being responsible for its development. This can best be ensured by providing contacts and,
most importantly, by ensuring that the husband has the
leisure time to maintain family links.' These short quotations
point up yet again two of the dominant theses of our study:
first, there is the tension which arises between the ideal of a
close conjugal relationship and the reality of the separateness
of the lives of husband and wife; and, secondly, there is the
tension between the ideal of the privacy and autonomy of the
family at home and the reality of the ways in which the worlds
of work and home interrelate.

Thus what appears to be a simple social occasion may have
very different meanings for those involved in it. Wives and

husbands can either support or betray each other, and this creates both confidence and vulnerability. So one husband may see it as an opportunity to show off his intelligent and pretty wife; a second as an occasion when his shy, home-centred wife could let him down badly; and a third as a time when the separate threads of his life (as husband, boss, employee, convivial drinking companion and so on) all come together to produce a tangled web of social anxiety.

One wife may experience an occasion ostensibly arranged for her benefit as an act of exclusion, emphasizing her non-membership of her husband's work world. Another woman, with many interests of her own, may feel that she is being depersonalized by being labelled 'so and so's wife'. A wife who is proud of her skills as a housewife may feel she herself, as well as her skills, is being undervalued.

Knowing that these and other tensions are felt by some of those who attend such social occasions, we asked the wives in our survey to tell us how they felt and what their experiences had been. Of those who attended once a year or less often, half had favourable feelings towards the firm's social occasions, and half had either mixed or unfavourable feelings. But of those whose firms arranged more frequent social occasions three quarters said that their feelings were favourable. It seems, then, that if a firm wants wives to enjoy the company's social occasions, it should arrange them fairly often. It should also try to make it possible for wives to make genuine relationships with each other, for it was clear that enjoyment of the firm's social occasions had a direct relationship with the number of other wives a woman knew well.

From this point of view, some large firms – particularly those which tend to move their managers from one branch to another – almost serve as a community. Thus one woman spoke enthusiastically about the firm's dinner dance: 'It is an opportunity of meeting old friends and acquaintances, as we have moved about the country so much and know a great number of people in the company.' This woman has moved nine times since she married twenty years ago. Another reason given by several women for enjoying the firm's social occasions was that, in relatively dull lives, these are exciting events. One wrote: 'The dinner dance is looked forward to. It provides a "dress-up" occasion and I receive a feeling of well-being accompanying my husband.' This woman left school at fourteen and was a typist before she married; she is a housewife, belonging to no clubs and having no desire to have a job outside the home.

A third, and large, group of women welcomed an opportunity to meet the people their husbands worked with: for them it was important to be able to take an intelligent interest in their husbands' activities, and for them a good wife had a part to play in relation to her husband-at-work as well as to her husband-at-home. One such woman regretted the lack of social occasions: 'It would help a lot to know some of his work colleagues as more than the names and characters they are to me. Discussion over problems concerning them would then be easier and more beneficial to us both.' This sort of woman is more interested in meeting her husband's colleagues than their wives and does not thank the organizers of a social event if a purdah-like segregation occurs; for her the firm's social occasions are chiefly important because of their importance to her marriage.

However, there were those wives who did not enjoy the social occasions arranged by their husband's firms, finding them unnatural and unsatisfactory occasions. These are some typical comments:

I don't like them because I just feel awkward and I don't have a wide enough knowledge to talk to people and consequently I dry up. As far as mixing work and home entertaining is concerned, I think it would be very embarrassing if there were differences of opinion at work and one was meeting them at home as well; wives could be very nasty about this. So I think it's wise not to get to know the wives; and as well I feel that the other wives would look at me and say, 'Whatever did he see in her to marry her?' as most of the others are much better educated than me. [This woman left elementary school at fourteen to become a hairdresser.]

I loathe the annual dinner dance. The band plays so loudly that the women cannot talk to each other. Inevitably the men buttonhole each other and talk shop. We don't do any duty entertaining at home – I resent the fact that people often seem to find nothing else to talk to me about except children; I think they regard me as a moron and I find it insulting that they think the only basis of communication with me is as a mother. [University graduate.]

It [the annual dinner] is very unsatisfactory. Everyone is at their most unnatural, the wives on the whole unable to talk 'shop' with real knowledge and unable in the short time to make real contact in any other way. [Woman with art-school training to age twenty-two.]

These comments not only illustrate some of the reasons for disliking a firm's social occasions, but also show how impossible it is to lump 'managers' wives' together as though they were all exactly the same sort of people.

The first woman is like many who come from a working-class background, in her shyness, lack of self-confidence and anxiety about playing unfamiliar roles: she feels overstretched by the role of 'manager's wife'. The other two women, by contrast, feel understretched in the role of 'manager's wife'. Their success educationally and their experience of work have given them a feeling of personal significance, and they feel diminished by being defined by who they are rather than by what they have done.

Some women, we found, had not been to any social occasions arranged by the firm. In some cases this was simply because none was ever arranged. This was more often a cause of regret than otherwise. In several cases a husband chose to keep his home and work lives separate, though his wife would have welcomed closer links with his work. Six out of the 16 couples who had extended interviews fell into this category. Interviewed on her own, one wife said:

My husband doesn't approve of mixing social things with work, although it seems to work with other companies, and I don't quite understand this. I wish that my husband had to do more duty entertaining; I find that most of my friends have to do a certain amount of entertaining of this sort, and I resent that I don't have to. On the other hand, if I had to do it I might not like it as I'd probably be hopeless at it.

Attitudes to involvement with the company

By contrast, her husband, interviewed on *his* own, said:

I don't do much duty entertaining and I don't have any business people to the house. I think it's hard luck on a wife if this happens and she has to be nice to people simply because they are her husband's business acquaintances. It must be awful to have to butter up a chap's wife if you don't like her. I'd prefer to keep business and social life apart.

Another wife said: 'We do not often attend as my husband does not enjoy these occasions. He prefers to spend his leisure time away from any office contacts. Not being an extrovert myself, this makes it difficult to make new friends when we move.' This wife had been a typist before marriage. It may be that this kind of background tends to develop sympathy towards the culture of the company, or to make a wife feel that she should have a part to play in her husband's work life. Another ex-secretary, however, claimed that by spending leisure time with her husband's colleagues she would have a rather narrow outlook on life. She quite enjoys the activities which the firm arranges, particularly the sports day for the children, but she resents being too closely held to the firm in her social life.

Entertaining for business purposes did not seem to play a very large part in the lives of our managers and their wives. Two thirds of the wives said that they had entertained their husband's colleagues and their wives, but this was mainly entertaining of equals on a basis of friendship. Entertaining for business purposes, or to further a man's career, seems very much less frequent than in the United States. It seems as though this separation between the worlds of work and home is more often encouraged by a husband than his wife, since several wives complained that there was so little entertaining to be done and no husband complained about his wife's unwillingness to entertain. This may throw light both on a husband's attitude to his work and on a wife's attitude to her role as a wife: it seemed that many of the men wanted to keep work and home separate, perhaps in order to have a place of escape from the tensions of each, and in particular to be able to spend at least part of their time away from their work identity. Wives, on the other hand, anxious to play a role as partners to their husbands, might feel it necessary to bring some part of the work world into the home in order that they might familiarize themselves with it.

In firms where the entertaining of customers and clients at home is encouraged, this often seems to be the result of the policy of a particular individual, rather than being associated with the nature of the work; that is to say, while men working on the sales side are more likely to have to entertain than men on the technical and scientific side, whether their wives are involved or not in the entertaining is likely to depend on individual policy. Mr Kingston explained, 'there was a period when I had a boss who believed that wives should join in as many functions as possible and the wives became semi-hostesses to a large number of customers. This is no longer required.' Mrs Kingston added,

> The company has cut down on the number of functions involving wives. But I still feel I should be, and am, an asset to my husband just by going to functions and hearing remarks let drop by others. For example, the wife of one of my husband's friends wasn't any help to her husband because she is quiet, timid, withdrawn and frightened. If the wife 'comes out well' it will affect what colleagues think, and is important from the promotion point of view – in some companies.

Thus, by drawing the wife into her husband's work world, the life style of the family may be subtly affected – and the work which the husband is considered able to do may be affected by his home life style. Mr Graveney, a general manager, said,

> Obviously having a different wife would have made a difference to me. It might have been possible for me to have a wife who would have been all at sea mixing with the sort of people we mix with now. For example, I know one wife who chose her house in a particular place because it was within walking distance of Woolworths. If I'd had a wife like that I don't think things would have gone so well. It's necessary to have a wife who can adapt to your way of life and do such things as business entertaining. If I hadn't a job with this sort of earnings [about £5,000 a year] I would not have been able to lead the same sort of life and meet the same sort of

people. Most people who live in this close are professionals. If I didn't earn the money I do earn I would not have been able to live with such people.

PATTERNS OF INVOLVEMENT IN COMPANY ACTIVITIES

We tried to seek out the characteristics which differentiate those wives who welcome involvement in their husbands' firms from those who do not. Some of the variables which we expected to matter did not seem to make any difference. For example, a young wife is just as likely to enjoy the firm's activities as an older one, and a woman with many children just as likely as the woman with few or none. And though several wives had worked in the same firm as their husbands this experience did not seem to make any difference to the wife's attitude to the firm's social activities.

When we turned to look at the wives' social origins and educational and occupational experience, patterns began to emerge (see Table 7.1). We must stress that with such small numbers any hypothesis must be tentative; but within the limits of the survey, a very consistent pattern was found.

Characteristically, a wife who both enjoyed going to the firm's social occasions and also enjoyed entertaining her husband's colleagues from work came from a lower-middle-class background, had attended grammar school, and had followed a short course of training, typically becoming a secretary. This group consistently had more positive attitudes towards involvement with their husbands' firms. Only in the case of entertaining colleagues at home did the products of fee-paying schools have more favourable attitudes, perhaps because of greater confidence in their social skills.

Closer analysis of the results seemed to indicate that differences did exist between the 'upper-middle-class background and longer training' category and the 'working-class background and no training' category. Members of the former category tended to go to the firms' social occasions and do some entertaining at home, but did not particularly

TABLE 7.1. The Wife's Attitude to Company Social Occasions and to Entertaining Her Husband's Colleagues, by Her Social Background Qualifications and Type of School (per cent)

	Wife's social background			Wife's qualifications			Type of school			Total
	Middle class	Inter-mediate	Working class	Training for 2 years or longer	Some training but for less than 2 years	No higher education	Fee-paying	Grammar/high	elementary/secondary modern	
Wife's attitude towards company social occasions:										
Favourable	44	62	43	42	61	41	33	58	43	49
Other*	56	38	57	58	39	59	67	42	57	51
	100 = 39	100 = 26	100 = 21	100 = 24	100 = 33	100 = 29	100 = 18	100 = 45	100 = 23	100 = 86
Wife's attitude towards entertaining colleagues:										
Favourable	46	58	29	38	55	41	56	44	39	45
Other†	54	42	71	62	45	59	44	56	61	55
	100 = 39	100 = 26	100 = 21	100 = 24	100 = 33	100 = 29	100 = 18	100 = 45	100 = 23	100 = 86

* 'Other' includes women who attend social occasions but dislike them, and those who do not or cannot.
† 'Other' includes women who do entertaining, but dislike it, as well as those who do not entertain colleagues.

enjoy it; members of the latter group, by contrast, seemed reluctant to become involved with their husbands' work at all. Wives from lower-middle-class backgrounds, or with experience of working in an office, seem more interested in office life. They are also more interested in talking to their husbands about their work, and are more likely to give them practical help with it.

Many reasons could be suggested to explain why women from lower-middle-class backgrounds, or with secretarial experience, are most interested in, and most enjoy involvement with their husbands' firms. It may be that the annual dinner dance, or whatever, has a lower-middle-class atmosphere, being arranged by the junior office staff, whose idea of a 'manager's wife' is a sort of grown-up secretary. It may be that women from this background have aspirations to leading the gregarious social life traditional in the solid middle class, and that they welcome the ready-made sociable occasion which relieves them of the financial and emotional burden of arranging their social life for themselves. It may be that there is a pressure from society – expressed, for example, in certain advertisements and women's magazines – which emphasizes a certain sort of wifely role, in which the dinner she cooks for the boss and the annual office party are seen as important testing grounds.

Nevertheless it must be remembered that, for most of the wives in our study, entertaining for, and being entertained by, their husbands' firms was a relatively small part of their lives. For most of them the firms' social occasions were fairly infrequent events and, though they might entertain colleagues or friends from work, there was little business entertaining to be done. As we have shown, the situation in the United States seems very different. Thus Margaret Helfrich's study of *The Social Role of the Executive's Wife* (1965, p. 44) describes the increasing encroachment of the business world into the home. One wife she studied said: 'One must be flexible and ready to act as hostess when business requires it', and another said: 'Entertaining customers and associates and seeing that they enjoy it is especially important in sales work.'

The wife and her husband's world

As Helfrich says:

In the business world of today, which transcends the office and enters the home, one must know whom to invite to dinner and whom not to invite; one must know when to decline invitations and the proper way to do so; one must know what to do and say, and perhaps more important, when to remain silent . . . the wife of an executive entertains and is entertained by her husband's associates, clients, potential clients and superiors. Each may require a different pattern of behaviour.

But though this may be the pattern in the United States, it does look as if the situation in Britain is still very different. It seems, for example, that there is a greater resistance on the part of both husband and wife to encroachment by the company into their private lives, and a greater resistance to the type of incentive which gives an increased standard of living in exchange for increased commitment to the company. The firm's social occasions are definitely used to vet certain wives, but it is doubtful whether this is the fairest or most effective way to do it and it is clear that the practice arouses resentment. Certainly there seem to be some legitimate moral arguments for defending personal family life from the 'impersonal' demands of the organization. And even if such surveillance is considered legitimate it is doubtful whether a company function, with all its strains and tensions, is the most appropriate setting.

There does seem to be a welcome, however, for the genuine give-away social occasion with no obvious strings attached. Firms which attempt to arrange such occasions might remember that they give more enjoyment if they occur fairly frequently and if they provide opportunities for wives to meet and talk, both with other wives and with their husbands' colleagues. It seems as though such occasions are most likely to be appreciated by wives who come from the lower middle class; if a company wants to give pleasure and amusement to a wider cross-section of its managers' wives, then more varied functions must be arranged, perhaps of a more cultural nature to attract more educated wives.

ATTITUDES TO COMPANY FRINGE BENEFITS

One way in which a company can affect its managers' families, and may influence family decisions about a manager's career, is through the fringe benefits which it offers. Wives were asked 'If there is a question of your husband taking up a new job, how much weight would you yourself give to the following aspects of the new job?' (See pages 63–6 for a discussion of their answers.) One of the aspects of a new job which we asked about was the fringe benefits which might be attached to it. Fifty of the wives felt fringe benefits to be an important consideration, the rest feeling them to be unimportant or something about which they do not mind. This means that fringe benefits were seen as a less important consideration than the present and future nature of the job itself, than the educational facilities of the area, and than the region in which the proposed job was situated; fringe benefits were seen as being a more important consideration than separation from family and friends or the demands of a wife's own work or career.

Many different types of fringe benefit were mentioned, such as the provision of a firm's car or telephone, or insurance for private hospital treatment (sometimes for the whole family, sometimes for the husband alone); many benefits were attached to moving house, such as financial help with removal costs or with refurnishing the new home, or the provision of hotel accommodation while house hunting. A wife's past experience of moving did not seem to affect her attitude to fringe benefits. More significant were the ages of her children, those with young children setting greater store by fringe benefits than those with older families, and her own social origins, wives from lower-middle- and working-class backgrounds valuing fringe benefits more than wives from the solid, professional middle class. So it seems that it is those families who are still in the early, financially less secure, stages of family life, or those with fewer financial resources available among their near kin, who are most likely to be influenced by the fringe benefits which a job offers. Conversely those from solid, professional, middle-class backgrounds are able to be more independent, both in their choice of a job and in their relationship with the husband's employers, since they often have an alternative source of financial help towards the costs of furnishing a house, buying a car, and so on.

We also found that the husband's job type affects his wife's evaluation of fringe benefits. The wives of men working in sales or in administration laid very much more stress on the value of fringe benefits than did wives of technical or production managers, possibly because fringe benefits are more common in these types of job and so become a more significant part of a family's standard of living.

However, fringe benefits may be valued as much for what they represent as for their monetary value: Mrs Ash, the wife of the national distribution manager of a large company, said 'As far as fringe benefits are concerned my husband gets expenses and a company car; running a car definitely does make a difference to one's income. Then there's a good insurance scheme which is separate from the pension scheme – and as this rates high with management it cannot be discounted.'

CONCLUSION

During our interviews we had the impression that many wives were not really very interested in the organizations which employed their husbands. That is to say, a typical wife was not interested in the work situation in general, but rather in *her husband's* work situation as *he* experienced it – and as she experienced it, in terms of the financial rewards and status the job brought to the family and in terms of the external demands the job imposed on family living patterns, demands, for example, that the husband should work long hours or frequently be away from home. Many a wife felt a degree of antagonism towards her husband's firm, resenting the demands of the work and the inevitable conflicts between her husband's occupational and family roles, yet welcoming the material advantages the work brought to her family and the satisfactions it gave her husband. In the final chapter we shall discuss more extensively the conflicting attitudes which many wives had towards their husbands' work.

Direct contact with the husband's firm, or with his colleagues, seemed to be valued largely because of the insights this contact would give into his work life. Of course, once colleagues and their wives became valued as friends the relationship changed. But a wife's initial attitude to involvement with her husband's firm might well be like that of Mrs Ickham: 'It would help a lot to know some of his work colleagues as more than the names and characters I imagine them to be. Discussion over problems concerning them would be easier and more beneficial to us both.' The wife's focus, that is, is not on the work situation itself but rather on her relationship with her husband, a relationship which is the subject of the next chapter.

CHAPTER 8

Man and Wife

All the people in our sample were married at the time we met them and most had children living at home. Thus their marriage, and their family life, provided an important framework for their lives. For many their marriage was intensely important: this was particularly so for the women in our sample, but even the most ambitious and work-oriented of the men was likely to claim, 'I do it all for my wife and children.'

The majority of the couples (54 in all) had met in the course of leisure-time activities, having been introduced by mutual friends, for example, or meeting at a party or club. Fourteen couples had met at work, usually in a situation in which the woman was employed at a lower level than the man. Ten couples had met because they were neighbours, 2 couples had met as students, and the remaining 7 had met in other ways. In most cases the husband was slightly older than his wife and this difference is reflected in Table 8.1. Table 8.2 shows that to a large extent each partner had chosen to marry someone from a similar social background to his or her own. This pattern has been documented by many other researchers, who have shown that on the whole people marry someone who lives reasonably near them, who is near their own age, whose family status is not too different from their own and whose educational level is similar to theirs.

SOME THEORETICAL APPROACHES TO MARRIAGE

There is a very large American literature on marriage and it would be impossible, and inappropriate, for us to attempt an exhaustive treatment of it here. In addition, it seems likely that there are differences between British and American patterns of marriage, even when similar socio-economic groups are

Some theoretical approaches to marriage

TABLE 8.1. Age at Time of Marriage to Present Partner

Age	No. of husbands	No. of wives
Under 21	9	28
22 to 25	45	42
26 to 29	21	13
30 and over	11	3
Total	86	86

compared, which means that American findings are not always applicable to Britain. By comparison, the British sociological literature on marriage, and in particular on middle-class marriage, is slight.* Some community studies may include a discussion of working-class marriage, but there has been little serious investigation of middle-class marriage patterns, even were it possible to generalize about so varied a category as the middle class. Such investigation as there has been has tended to approach the marriage through the family, both extended and nuclear, to the neglect of other dimensions, for

TABLE 8.2. The Relationship between the Social Backgrounds of the Managers and Their Wives

Husband's social background is	Wife's social background		
	'Intermediate' or working class	Middle class	Total
'Intermediate' or working class	35	14	49
Middle class	11	25	36
Do not know	1		1
	47	39	86

* Some of these studies are summarized in Josephine Klein's *Samples from English Cultures*, Vol. 1 (1965).

example those associated with career, or with personal identity.*

A less academic, but yet valuable book is *The English Marriage* by Drusilla Beyfus (1968), who uses edited interviews to illuminate some aspects of marriage. In her Introduction she says,

> Wives I found to be almost obsessively interested both in their own marriage and in the dilemmas common to all married couples. Men tended to be bored with the idea of discussing the minutiae of married life and to wonder who on earth would be interested in it. But amongst younger husbands and wives I found an increased awareness of themselves in relation to the state of being married.

To a certain extent we found the same problem with our managers and their wives. In addition our interviews covered slightly different ground for husband and wife; thus a husband usually had more to say about his career and his attitudes to his work, while his wife's interview was more concerned than his with their marriage and home life, though she too was asked about her experience of jobs outside the home. This imbalance, probably inevitable because of their different patterns of day-to-day life, may have introduced some bias into our findings about marriage. Our most challenging problem was Drusilla Beyfus' conclusion: 'My conclusion is that there are no rounded, global generalizations which wrap up the state of modern marriage. I find it encouraging that the marital tie remains the most personal, volatile and unclassifiable of human bonds. No marriage can be tidied away into definitive pigeon holes, or completely explained away by neat sociological, economic, or psychological labelling' (p. 162). We too were often daunted by the richness and complexity of the information we had gathered about our managers and their wives, especially since we knew that the information must often be but a pale or inaccurate reflection of reality. Nevertheless, we thought it important to try to understand how our couples felt about their marriages,

* See Margaret Stacey's *Tradition and Change* (1960), Willmott and Young *Family and Class in a London Suburb* (1960), and Elizabeth Bott's *Family and Social Network* (1957) to which we return later in this section.

which for most of them are a crucial part of their lives, and how the marriage reflects and affects the whole life situation of the two people involved.

Before we return to our managers and their marriages, it might be helpful to consider three theoretical approaches to the subject, so that our factual material can be considered in the light of more general theory. The first of these approaches sees *marriage as a power relationship*. Blood and Wolfe in *Husbands and Wives* (1960) say,

> Power may be defined as the potential ability of one partner to influence the other's behavior. Power is manifested in the ability to make decisions affecting the life of the family. Authority is closely related to power. Authority is legitimate power, i.e., power held by one partner because both partners feel it is proper for him to do so. The family authority pattern is prescribed by the society at large in such forms as: 'the man should be the head of the house' – or 'husbands should not dictate to their wives'. Power, on the other hand, refers to the ways in which husbands and wives actually deal with each other. (p. 11)

Blood and Wolfe conclude that,

> The balance of power in particular families and in whole categories of families is determined by the comparative resourcefulness of the two partners and by the life circumstances within which they live. Husbands can no longer take for granted the *authority* held by older generations of men. No longer is the husband able to exercise power just because he is 'the man of the house'. Rather he must prove his right to power, or win power by virtue of his own skills and accomplishments in competition with his wife. (p. 29)

Blood and Wolfe measured the relative power of husband and wife by finding out which of them was responsible for each one of eight decisions affecting their family life. The greater a partner's decision-making responsibility, the greater his or her power was said to be. The average marriage was comparatively egalitarian, with a slight balance of power in favour of the husband. This balance of power is affected, as we have seen, by the contribution which each partner can bring to the marriage, the contribution itself being rated according to the values of the society or of the individual couple. Blood and Wolfe show that the higher the husband's social status, income and level of education, the greater will be his power within the marriage; a wife can redress the balance to some extent if her own level of education, earning capacity or involvement in the local community mean that she can contribute more to the marriage.

Looked at in terms of relative power and in terms of the contribution which each makes to the marriage, it is clear that most of our couples are husband-dominated. On average most of the husbands have received considerably more education than their wives; they hold relatively high-status jobs, and earn good incomes, which are in most cases the family's only source of financial support. Blood and Wolfe emphasize that a husband-dominated marriage is not necessarily an unhappy marriage; indeed marital dissatisfaction is most often associated with wife-dominance, since wife-dominance in American society is usually a response to an inadequate or incapacitated husband. Certainly the majority of the sixteen couples whom we interviewed personally seemed content with their marriages and, as we shall see, the husband was likely to be the chief decision-maker. It must be remembered, though, that the value put upon an individual's contribution depends upon how such things as social status, income, education, and so on are themselves valued. In a society which particularly valued artistic talents, or fecundity, or skill in personal relationships, for example, quite other contributions to the relationship might become valuable and so the balance of power might shift. As we show in the last chapter there is considerable confusion among our couples about values, in particular among the women in our sample.

A second approach sees *marriage as a set of roles*, or as a set of rights and duties. In this sense all individuals are being socialized into the married state from their earliest years, as their ideas about what it is to be a husband or a wife are formed. Ideas about the rights and duties appropriate to each partner may continue to change throughout married life as other circumstances of couples' lives alter: as a husband becomes more and more involved with his work life, his wife may be forced to take over some of his domestic responsibilities; or if a wife takes employment outside the home her husband is likely to have to do more in the home. Blood (1962, p. 270) says,

The division of labor in the home is concerned with the division of responsibility between husband and wife for the tasks involved in running a home. Marriage is also profoundly affected by the nature of the couple's participation in the division of labor outside the home, that is in the occupational system. Most conspicuously, the wife's choice whether to work at all outside the home affects family living. Less obviously, the nature and extent of the husband's work affects it too.*

Blood and Wolfe measured the division of labour within the home in the same way as they measured decision-making, that is, by finding out who is responsible for each of eight household tasks. They found that the more successful the husband and the greater his income and social status, the less help he gives in the home: 'Not that successful husbands disdain household tasks – they are just too busy being successful to have the time.' We have already seen in an earlier chapter that the demanding nature of their husbands' work is one of the reasons why many of the wives in our sample did not take a job outside the home; we shall also show how it affects their attitudes to other roles, and in particular the role of wife. The demands of the husband's work may also affect the relationship of the couple with the world outside the home and work situations: a busy husband, with an ideal of task-sharing in the home, simply may not have time for other activities. That is to say, the roles of manager and husband may so dominate his life that other roles are squeezed out.

Elizabeth Bott also approached the relationship between husband and wife in terms of their role-relationship in *Family and Social Network* (1957). She classified the organization of household tasks and used her classification to form a scale

* This is probably the best guide through, and discussion of, the literature on marriage. Also useful is J. R. Udry, *The Social Context of Marriage* (1966). The ways in which the couple adjust to each other and to their roles is discussed by Jessie Bernard in 'The Adjustments of Married Mates' in Christensen (1964, pp. 675–739).

Man and wife

ranging from a *segregated* role relationship, in which there was a clear differentiation of tasks, to a *joint* role-relationship in which husband and wife shared as many tasks and activities as possible. She concluded,

> *The degree of segregation in the role-relationship of husband and wife varies directly with the connectedness of the family's social network.* The more connected the network, the greater the degree of segregation between the roles of husband and wife. The less connected the network, the smaller the degree of segregation between the roles of husband and wife. . . . If husband and wife come to marriage with such loose-knit networks or if conditions are such that their networks become loose-knit after marriage, they must seek in each other some of the emotional satisfactions and help with familial tasks that couples in close-knit networks can get from outsiders. (p. 60)

Bott's hypothesis, though a useful jumping-off point and one which makes sure that any study of marriage and the family takes account of their social environment, has received much criticism and modification. As we have mentioned (page 144), the concept of social network has been refined and developed.* Certainly we found it impossible to say of each individual in our sample that he or she lived only in a close-knit, or only in a loose-knit, network: rather each lived in a number of more or less close- or loose-knit networks with which he or she interacted with varying degrees of intensity, frequency, ease and so on. Several writers† have criticized Bott for her lack of conceptual clarity, for example, in not making it clear whether she was referring to the network of each spouse separately, or of both together. Certainly in considering our managers and their wives we found it necessary to take the husband's social network, with its implications for his expectations about their married relationship, separately from his wife's social network and marital expectations, and we presume that the fact that husband and wife lived in such very different social worlds was one of the chief causes of marital tension. As Blood (1962, p. 198) says,

* In particular see J. Clyde Mitchell (1969).
† See Turner (1967) and Harris (1969).

There is good reason to believe that both types of adaptation – of role behaviour and of role expectations – are made more extensively by wives than by husbands. Even though ideal husbands are just as willing to be adaptable, the roles of women impose more changes on them than men. . . . When role conflict occurs, wives also make the chief concessions. The very fact that marriage is their chief role in life gives them a greater stake in its success and more concern to make it work.

A third approach sees marriage as an agent of *identity formation*: it is perhaps in the spirit of this approach that people place photos of themselves and their children in the living room ('mum and dad') and of themselves on their wedding day in the bedroom ('husband and wife'). This approach was discussed by Peter Berger and Hansfried Kellner in 'Marriage and the construction of reality' in *Diogenes* (1964). They describe the process by which every individual has his identity confirmed (or, disturbingly, not confirmed) by those with whom he comes in contact:

Every morning the newspaper boy validates the widest coordinates of my world and the mailman bears tangible validation of my own location within these coordinates. However, some validations are more significant than others. Every individual requires the on-going validation of his world, including crucially the validation of his identity and place in this world, by those few who are his truly significant others. (p. 4)

They argue that in modern western society marriage is a crucial agent of identity formation:

The private sphere includes a variety of social relationships. Among these, however, the relationships of the family occupy a central position and, in fact, serve as a focus for most of the other relationships (such as those with friends, neighbours, fellow members of religious and other voluntary associations). Since, as the ethnologists keep reminding us, the family in our society is of the conjugal type, the central relationship in this whole area is the marital one. *It is on the basis of marriage that, for most adults in our society existence in the private sphere is built up.* (p. 8; our italics)

From this point of view, it is clear that marriage is usually more important for a wife than for her husband: when he gives his occupation as 'sales manager' or 'chief accountant', she may say 'married woman' or 'wife and mother'. He finds confirmation of his work identity every day in his interaction with his colleagues, his secretary, his boss, and so on, and for our managers their work identity is often their prime identity. If her husband does not confirm for her the importance of her identity, a wife may feel dissatisfaction, not only with her marriage, but with her whole life. Children can be givers of identity too, and a wife who is dissatisfied with her relationship with her husband may turn to her children, or may have more children, as an attempt to increase her sense of being valued and needed.

ATTITUDES TO MARRIAGE AMONG THE MANAGERS AND THEIR WIVES

When we turn to consider the marital relationships of the managers and their wives, we feel it is important that this relationship be seen in terms of the whole pattern of their lives. The centrality of the relationship means that it is affected by, and affects, large parts of the lives of both of the partners. In previous chapters we have attempted to describe and analyse the life experiences of the men and women in our sample by means both of specific examples and also of more general discussion. Thus in thinking about their marital relationship it might be helpful to remember:

our couples' experience of mobility, and the ways in which husband and wife approached a change of job for the husband (Chapter 3);

the personal work experience of the men in our sample, as exemplified by Mr Frith ('the high flyer'), Mr Ickham ('the careerist') and Mr Newington ('the local jogger') (Chapter 4);

the random nature of the men's work lives, which made them to a large extent acted upon, rather than acting (Chapter 4);

the home-centred, domestic lives of the majority of the wives, their self-effacing commitment to home and children and their inability to be objective about themselves (Chapter 5);

the importance of friends for the wives, both for help and for identity formation (Chapter 6);

two characteristic weekends, as illustrated by Mr and Mrs Lenham and Mr and Mrs Newington (Chapter 6);

the very different day-to-day experience of the husband-at-work and the wife-at-home, which means that wives are not as socialized as their husbands into the ideologies of the work world (Chapter 7).

Our postal questionnaire was only concerned with the marital relationship of the couples in our sample in the most superficial way; we felt that so involved, emotionally charged and intimate a subject could only be dealt with in any depth at a personal interview. Accordingly we asked the sixteen couples who were interviewed at length a series of open-ended questions relating to their view of themselves as individuals and as married couples. We asked husband and wife, at separate interviews, from what source each got his or her sense of security and how their own home differed from that of their parents; we asked them together about decision-making in the family and about how their marriage compared with that of both sets of parents; we asked each wife about the expectations she had of marriage when she was single and about her experience of it; and we attempted to find how important his marriage was to each husband by asking what he considered to be his greatest achievement and what the most important thing in his life.

In a way the questions we asked were banal. Yet they served two purposes: the first was to enable us to build up some understanding of how each couple experienced their marriage and some knowledge about the patterns of their married life; the second was to provide a basis for broad generalizations about the marriages of our managers, and in particular about the way in which the husband's work affected the relationship.

One theme which emerged clearly was the difference in marital relationships between many of our couples and their parents. This difference was most marked in couples who had been socially mobile, whose parents might have a marriage characteristic of the working class of the interwar period, while they themselves felt that they had a more egalitarian conjugal relationship. The trend towards a more egalitarian pattern of marriage has been documented elsewhere. It may be that the trend has gone further among people such as our managers than among other sections of the population, since their relative affluence has freed them from material dependence on their kin and their mobility means that they have often been separated, physically at least, from their parents and from the friends of their childhood.* Certainly in comparing themselves with their parents many of our managers emphasized their greater affluence. Thus one described his childhood home,

My mother came from a working-class background, and my father gave her regular money, but she was a poor manager. She was always running up debts, and pawning our clothes. This was the way of life in many working-class homes at that time, but it's an expensive one. I had an ordinary working-class sort of life, though I did get to grammar school. I went to the club at nights and to the cinema. Otherwise I would play cards and gamble on Saturdays with my friends. I really have a shocking background. My father also was a big cards player, as were all my brothers. At home we never did any entertaining, and my parents never went out much.

(Interviewer: 'How did your childhood compare with the life your daughter has now?')

It's another world entirely. When she was nine she had already been abroad on four holidays: I never went ten miles outside of the town when I was her age. She goes riding and belongs to the Guides, and goes to judo and swimming, things that we were never allowed to do, nor indeed was there the money for.

Many couples mentioned how their present home, and indeed their marital relationship, was to a large extent centred on their children. Mr Herne compared his childhood with that of his own children,

We lived in a very small semi-detached council house with a quiet, friendly, though uninspiring atmosphere. My parents did nothing very positive in the evenings. They didn't, for example, go out to pubs and drink and they only had guests in about once a month. My mother was one of seven children and her sisters and their husbands used to come around to play cards. My father loved

* See, for example, Fogarty, Rapoport and Rapoport, *Sex, Career and Family* (1971).

Attitudes to marriage

to play the piano, though he played it badly. The most obvious difference between the two homes is that my wife and I have a positive interest in teaching the children. I was 'allowed' to grow up and learned very much by picking things up for myself. I now feel I like to 'expose' my children to such things as opera, ballet and theatre, and I like them to read the right sort of books, including bad ones as well as good.

Mr and Mrs Olantigh also described the contrast between the way they were brought up and the way they are bringing up their children. Mrs Olantigh said,

I was brought up in a village on the Essex-Suffolk border; my mother still lives there now. We did a lot of visiting as a family to friends and relatives and a lot of them visited us. My parents didn't go out much on their own: we did things as a family. In the evenings we mainly read. My father was a craftsman with wood and did a lot of painting and carving. Mother was very religious and did everything connected with the church, but we never went to museums or to cinemas or theatres or anything like that. We went to the cinema once when I was twelve and it was *Bluebeard* and I cried and they didn't let me go again for a number of years.

(Interviewer: 'What differences would you describe between your childhood home and your present home with your children now?')

I hope my husband and I are aware of all the needs, and they are many, of the children. [Mr and Mrs Olantigh have two children, aged eleven and nine at the time of the interview.] My mother was aware of my physical needs and emotional needs and I was well looked after in this way. Intellectually she wasn't aware of any need. We try to be aware of needs, particularly in talking to them about topical items from newspapers and T.V. We take them to museums and we never pass a castle or an old home without a visit. The same applies to gardens and houses. They have a fair knowledge of the age of houses; they can recognize Georgian houses and so on. They like to look at new ones and have very definite ideas of what they like.

I hope both of them will go to university and choose some career. They are at the moment at the local primary school and being carefully educated. My parents thought that if you gained a place at university, 'Well, that's very nice, dear, hope you enjoy it', and

209

didn't push and help in the way we hope to be able to help if our children want it. My parents weren't educated so they couldn't, even if they had wanted to. We do help the children, and if they want to know something we go to the public library if we can't find it in the books with which we've provided them. My husband teaches them about money matters and how to buy a house, mortgages, insurance, banking and so on, and will do this much more as they get older.

In talking about her children Mrs Olantigh touched on ideas about child rearing which were characteristic of many of our managers – such as her emphasis on making positive efforts to educate her children at home, the value she placed on cultural education, and her long-term view of child rearing, with university and a chosen career as the goals at which to aim. We shall return to a discussion of these and other aspects of such a life style in our last chapter; a point which should be made now is that for this, as for all of our couples, child rearing was the concern of both father and mother. When they were asked what they wanted for their children both father and mother characteristically had a great deal to say about the sort of education, career, life style and pattern of personal relationships which they hoped their children would have.

Our couples then, on the whole, felt that their marital relationship was more egalitarian, more 'close' was the word usually used, than that of their parents. Of the sixteen couples who were personally interviewed only three felt that they were less close than either of their own parents had been. It is possible that this 'closeness' which our couples described, and which to quite a large extent is expressed through their joint task of child rearing, is a product of their particular stage in the life cycle. It may be that when their children grow up and leave home their marriages will become more like their parents' marriages, which they feel are so much more segregated than their own. However, many other factors affect the type of relationship which a couple want, or are able, to have. For example, an ideal of complete equality between the sexes may contribute to a very close, joint type of relationship between a courting or newly married couple. However, if the demands of the man's work become greater, while the woman is increasingly tied to her domestic role by the arrival of children, their relationship will inevitably become more segregated; the ideal of equality, which previously led to a closer relationship, may now lead to frustration; if the wife seeks employment outside the home in order to redress the balance of equality, the result may be an even greater degree of role segregation as the couple's domestic work load is increasingly divided between them or delegated to servants.

Mr and Mrs Dover discussed their marriage, and compared it with that of their parents, in this way:

[Mr Dover] I'm very satisfied indeed with my marriage; no matter what differences we have, the thought of not having my wife around makes me sick inside.

[Mrs Dover] It's quite successful really. We have struggled through fifteen years and the next fifteen won't be so hard financially. It's also been a very interesting marriage because we've moved around. On the whole I would say it's a happy marriage.

[Mr Dover] I like my wife's company. I can sit without talking, yet if she isn't there I would be very lonely.

[Mrs Dover] I think ours is based on a better understanding than my parents' was, even though they have been married for forty-seven years. They are happy in their own way but I think we are much happier. We have a much better man and wife relationship than my parents.

[Mr Dover] Yes, *they are not so much man and wife, as man and woman*, and they go their own ways and are completely different. She always knows to a penny what my salary is and we have a joint account. Whereas her mother never knew what her father had and vice versa. They didn't know each other's business; they had no trust. We have this sort of trust. Whatever I've got my wife's welcome to it.

Mr and Mrs Dover's use of words, in contrasting man and wife with man and woman, illustrates well a point which we shall come to later in this discussion, in which we attempt to compare the relative importance of the married relationship to each of the partners: in this context it would be significant that they did not talk of *husband* and wife, but rather of *man* and wife.

Man and wife

Several couples felt that though they are closer than their parents were, yet they are not necessarily happier, since their standards of what makes for happiness in a marriage are different.

[Mrs Chilham] I think ours is a very happy marriage. We have our ups and downs, but doesn't everybody?

[Mr Chilham] The longer it goes on the better it gets. When I hear of other people's marriages I'm very happy. I consider ours to be very normal.

[Mrs Chilham] It's certainly much better than the sort of thing my parents had.

[Mr Chilham] It's certainly much better than my parents inasmuch as it's a different type of marriage. But I think you tend to see the pitfalls that your parents fell into and you don't fall into the same ones. We're not separate as a couple. It's what I would call a proper marriage.

[Mrs Chilham] It's difficult to know from the outside. I guess that my mother would say that she had a happy marriage.

[Mr Chilham] Yes, I think my father would say that his marriage was ideal. He never even cleaned his boots all the time he was married. He thought it was his right to get drunk once a week. He did think a lot of his children and I think it was a typical marriage of that time. I don't think they would call it unhappy.

[Mrs Chilham] I mean if you compare it to my parents' they always had terrible rows which we don't. Yours didn't, did they?'

[Mr Chilham] My mother didn't row with my father. She just gave in. Oh, I think our marriage is better than most of our friends have. My wife understands me better than a lot of other wives understand their husbands. I'm mainly thinking now of my business colleagues. In business it's very important too, and I think there's a tremendous part of the wife in one's success. If one's wife plays hell, and objects to your work, this plays hell with the job, but if she lets you get on with it and understands you then everything's O.K.

We shall return to the significance for the marriage of the wife's attitude to her husband's work and of the demands which his career makes on her; a high degree of commitment by a husband to his work can cause his wife to feel dissatisfied with their marriage.

On the whole, then, the couples whom we studied felt that their marital relationship was a close one and valued this closeness. However, this did not seem to imply that the partners shared equally in all the household tasks and in decision-making. Rather it seemed that the household tasks were divided between those which were the responsibility of the husband and those which were customarily done by the wife. And though all the sixteen couples said that any important decision would be discussed by both of them together, nine out of the sixteen agreed that the final decision was made by the husband.

Mr and Mrs Newington talked at length, and perceptively, about their marriage and their comments illustrate many of the generalizations which we have made. Mr Newington earns £2,000 a year and is in his early thirties; his wife is a few years younger and they have two young children. Mrs Newington saw their children as the long-term focus of their life together.

Our most important decisions are those concerning the children and their future. There are so many things. To bring them up in a certain way, and having to have the right job and the right home, etc., but the most important thing is their education, and even with that it's important to go at it *en famille* as it's all connected with family life. It's so easy to be busy all weekend, and then it's Monday, and by the time you think about it they're all grown up anyway.

Mr Newington stressed the importance of communication in their relationship,

Most of our problems get discussed so much that it turns out there's only one decision we can make. I think everything is fully discussed to its logical conclusion.

[Mrs Newington] I think with most smaller issues my husband makes the decisions. However, before we married even, we discussed how we would educate our children, and we are in agreement about most big issues.

[Mr Newington] We probably have a frank relationship and *talk* to each other about ourselves and our marriage as much and a lot more than other people.

Man and wife

Mr Newington described how the day-to-day activities of the home are divided between them,

I do the garden and the car, but very little in the house. I don't cook; I do dry up most weekends and evenings, under protest, but I don't do any housework unless the place is particularly untidy, when I might take out the Hoover. I kept very clear of the kids when they were young. I told my wife they were hers till they were a year old. I didn't feed them, or amuse them or anything. I did things like putting up shelves, and so forth. I feel it's a natural and normal sort of division; I don't do anything that's really a woman's province, though I do light the fires which my mother always does in my own home.

The question 'From what do you get your chief sense of security?' was asked of husband and wife at their individual interviews, an interview from which the other partner was usually absent; therefore there is rarely a question of the presence of the partner affecting a respondent's reply. The replies, shown in Table 8.3, illustrate the different attitudes of

TABLE 8.3. Bases for Sense of Security among Sixteen Couples

Sense of security is based on	No. of husbands	No. of wives
Husband/wife/marriage	2	15
also mentioned:		
other personal relationships	0	3
religious beliefs	1	1
financial security	0	2
Job/career/skills	7	0
Money/insurances/savings	5	0
Own personality/'within self'	1	1
Do not know	1	0
Total	16	16

husbands and wives to their marriages and the great importance which work has for many husbands; thus, while all but one wife replied that her husband was the source of her sense of security, only two of the husbands felt that their wives were

similarly important for them.* Twelve of the sixteen husbands
derived their sense of security from some aspect of their work;
most answered the question briefly, in such terms as 'simply
being an established civil servant', 'being able to pay the bills',
'having confidence in my own ability to earn a reasonable
salary in a number of jobs from finance to general management'.

Mr Graveney spoke at greater length and we shall use his
case when considering some implications of the different
values which husband and wife may place on their marriage.
He is a general manager, who has worked his way up from a
working-class background and a first job as a junior clerk;
from a starting wage of 25s. a week, he now earns nearly
£5,000 a year. Mr Graveney said,

> I get my chief sense of security from the fact that I'm adequately,
> or should I say more than adequately, insured myself and my wife
> and daughter are provided for. I'd like a bit of capital, but there's
> lots I still want to spend money on first, and I'm not too bothered
> about that. All the insurance policies I have are endowment policies
> and when I retire I should be able to put my hands on £20,000 to
> £25,000 cash. I think it's from this sort of thing that I get my feeling
> of security.

(Interviewer: 'What do you feel is your greatest achievement?')

> I suppose just the fact that I qualified and started with nothing,
> or very little and that I now occupy the position that I do and have
> a nice home and standard of living and so forth. For the future, I
> would just like to see the company make half a million pounds
> profit and to develop well.

(Interviewer: 'What would you say are the most important
things in your life?')

> My home, family life and my business, although I'm sure my

* When asking this question the interviewer first waited for a spontaneous reply from the respondent; then she attempted to find out if any
other factors contributed to the respondent's sense of security. In spite
of such extended questioning most of the wives persisted in asserting that
their husband was their sole source of security.

wife wouldn't agree with the order in which I've put them. I think probably I wouldn't put either before the other, and this is difficult for my wife to understand, but it's in my wife's interest for me to do the job well otherwise I'd get the sack, and it's also in my own personal interest. If I didn't do it well I should end up with ulcers. It's inevitable that the higher up you move in business, the more incursion it makes into one's private life and I think wives find this hard to accept. I don't think that I've neglected the family. I don't think it is neglect to the family. It's just that the more senior you are the more responsibility there is to be filled. This is something that women must recognize: that they have a fuller and more comfortable life as a result of this work. You can't have both, position, earnings, and a nine-to-five job.

Mrs Graveney's replies at her interview may highlight the different attitudes which can exist between husband and wife towards the husband's work. She too comes from a humble background and indeed feels that it is their social mobility which has provided the foundation stone of their marriage: thus she said,

Sex is definitely not the foundation for us. I would say it was our need for each other. I think you can need each other without sex. For example, after my husband studied and qualified, he went into bigger and better jobs and after the sort of background we had both had, we needed each other to face the consequences of this.

The Graveneys live stylishly, in a comfortable modern house with a large garden, giving frequent dinner parties and taking their holidays abroad. Mrs Graveney, however, seemed to be one of the least happy of our respondents.

I've been married for twenty-three years, now, during which time my husband's wishes, the house and Marianne, my daughter, have always come first and I feel now that I want a life of my own. I don't know whether this is as a result of moving, or whether it's a change of relationship between my husband and myself. I suppose this is just a little rebellion inside of me. His work has always come first, and we're pushed very much into the background. I feel we've lost communication and can't converse together any more. When he comes home at night I have to listen to all the problems of the firm's activities, and when that's over, out come the books and papers and he works all night. I'm a bit sick of his industry, or any other, for that matter. He lives for his work. I suppose it's just him. But after all these years I've had enough of it.

(Later, the interviewer asked: 'From where do you get your chief sense of security?')

From my husband. Knowing that no matter what happens, that he will be here. Not just providing for me, that means nothing, but *just being here with me* [our italics]. He is more important than the provision he makes. I'd rather live and be poor and happy, than have position and wealth and have an empty life.

(Interviewer: 'What did you expect of marriage before you got married?')

I don't think I had any expectations. I don't know if this is a good thing. I suppose in a way I expected it to be all lovey-dovey and thought it would be a merging of two people, merging their personalities and getting the best out of the relationship. Oh, hell! I thought marriage would give me more happiness than it has, and it's not really given me any happiness, not the marriage itself. I have a nice house, and I can afford things, and I have a nice daughter, and my husband has a nice position, but deep down I have not had the happiness I expected. I suppose this was because we were not compatible from the beginning. It always goes back to this thing of my husband seeing me as one of his other possessions.

Perhaps it would be valuable to emphasize some aspects of Mr and Mrs Graveney's interviews. First, there is the dominant part his work plays in both their lives (during her description of a typical weekend Mrs Graveney mentioned Saturday afternoon, Saturday evening, Sunday morning and Sunday afternoon as times when her husband might be likely to do office work). Secondly, there is the fact that, though each values their relationship with the other, Mr Graveney feels that he makes his contribution to the relationship through his work and his financial provision, while his wife expressly says that 'he is more important than the provision he makes'. Thirdly, it may not be coincidence that this crisis in their relationship occurred within eighteen months of moving away from their home area, an area where both had lived since childhood: thus just when her husband moved his place of work and was absorbed in a taxing and responsible new job, Mrs Graveney found herself thrown back on her marriage as a crucial source of support in the absence of her kin and before she had built up new friendship patterns.

It might be useful to consider the marital relationships of our managers, and in particular that of Mr and Mrs Graveney, in terms of theoretical work on conjugal role-relationships and social network.

In Elizabeth Bott's terms very few – perhaps only one – of our couples lived solely in one close-knit social network; most have one or more loose-knit networks of friends and colleagues from earlier stages in their life cycle. This was illustrated by the answers to the question asking whether the couple's friends and relations lived mainly locally or were scattered at a distance from their own home. Only one couple out of the 86 said that most of their friends and kin lived locally. Sixteen said that some of their kin lived locally while some were scattered further afield, and the majority, 62 of the couples, said that their kin were scattered. A confirmation of this pattern is provided by the fact that, of the 73 husbands who still had one or both of their parents living, 52 lived more than twenty miles away from them; and of the 76 wives who still had one or both of their parents living, 52 lived more than twenty miles away from them. As we showed in Chapter 6, a majority of our couples had a comparatively loose-knit network of friends, 48 having some of their friends living locally while some lived at a distance, and 21 replying that most of their friends lived at a distance. Of course, the fact that kin and friends live at some distance from the anchorage point of a network does not necessarily imply that the network will be a loose-knit one, though it would seem to make it more likely. However, most of the women who were personally interviewed said that their best friends did not have similarly friendly relations with each other and, indeed, that many of their best friends had not even met each other.

In addition one must remember that most of the husbands, and some of the wives, had day-to-day contact with people who, though they were not defined as friends, yet must be counted as part of their social network. For a wife, these people might be neighbours or the mothers of her children's friends. For the husband they would be the people with whom he worked. Such a work group can form an intensely strong and demanding network, particularly if its members are highly committed to the work on which they are engaged. If the demands made by one part of an individual's network – for instance the demands of his office colleagues – conflict with the demands of members of another part of his network – for instance, of his wife and family – then tension and conflict will result.

In general it appeared that the wives in our sample had more loose-knit, but more durable and intense networks than did their husbands – a possibility which Elizabeth Bott's classification does not seem to allow for, since she treated her couples as one, rather than two, anchorage points. Many wives mentioned that it was considered to be their responsibility to keep up the couples' links with kin, both on the husband and the wife's side of the family; and many kept up relationships by means of letters, phone calls and occasional visits with friends who lived at a great distance. If Bott's hypothesis is applied to these couples, it would follow that the wives would have an ideal of a more joint conjugal relationship; but their husbands, living from day to day in the comparatively tight-knit network of the work situation, might prefer a more segregated relationship. In making this distinction between husband and wife it should be remembered that almost all our couples lived in comparatively loose-knit social networks and had a more egalitarian and joint type of conjugal relationship than did any of the families whom Bott described as having a 'segregated' conjugal relationship.

The example of Mr and Mrs Graveney may illustrate some of the differences between husbands and wives in our sample. Mr Graveney valued his wife and daughter, but felt that it was through his work that he made his chief contribution to their welfare. He gives his wife a personal allowance equal to his own and expects her to lead a life of her own, though he would disapprove of her taking a job. They never go out together, except when they are invited to friends' houses, and his only domestic responsibility is their garden. When asked about their marriage Mr Graveney said 'It's much the same as anybody else's'; but Mrs Graveney spoke bitterly, 'On the whole I think we can call it a complete failure.' Mrs Graveney had expected marriage to be 'all lovey-dovey . . . a merging of two people'. The early years of their marriage were years of struggle: 'I used to get up at six o'clock on Sunday and work till ten o'clock at night,' he said. Mrs Graveney, too, was busy at this time, caring for her home, husband and young child, carrying on a wide variety of local community work, and seeing a lot of their many local friends and relations. In effect they were an example of a tight-knit network segregated conjugal relationship type of couple. Then they moved house. Mrs Graveney lost the props of her tight-knit network, but Mr Graveney, absorbed in his new job, continued to behave as though theirs was a segregated conjugal relationship. Mrs Graveney yearned for a more joint conjugal relationship; she said 'I'd love to go to the theatre, even only one in two months. I'd love to go regularly, or to a good concert. But my husband won't take us as he's not interested: he says he'd like to go but never has the time. And over the weekend I feel it should be a family time, so I don't go on my own. I do make an effort to keep us together.'

How general is the problem which we see in the case of Mr and Mrs Graveney? Do other couples disagree, implicitly or explicitly, about the nature of their relationship? The sample may perhaps be taken as representative of a section of the middle class; they are predominantly employed in industry, they tend to be strongly work-oriented, and they are, on the whole, comparatively recent recruits to the middle class, their parents or grandparents being manual workers. We hope, therefore, that any generalizations which we make may be true, not only of our sample, but also of the sub-group of the middle class to which the majority of them belong.

We have seen that most of our couples agreed that their relationship is 'closer' than that of their parents. We have seen that to a large extent this closeness expresses itself in the couple's relationship with their children in the weekend activities of the family group. We found that a couple's description of a characteristic weekend tallied well with the impression which we had gained of their marriage. Those couples who had a relatively segregated relationship tended to spend their weekend on separate activities, while those with closer relationships spent more time together, shopping, gardening, watching television, taking the children out, visiting friends or being visited. Yet this aspect of the marriage may be closely related with the couple's life-cycle stage: it may be that as the children grow up and leave home the closeness of the relationship decreases. Certainly our study revealed considerable differences between husbands and wives in their attitudes to their marriage, differences which seemed likely to increase rather than decrease in the future.

Husbands and wives had different ideas, as we have shown, about the source of their sense of security, and Table 8.3 illustrates well these different attitudes. For many wives their marriage provides them with their strongest and most valued identity; it is a protection against the insecurity which comes from frequent moves, giving them a substitute for the relationships which less mobile wives might have with kin or long-established friends. In this sense a wife is much more dependent on her marriage than is her husband. Yet in marriages such as those of our managers the husband is the partner with the greater power. He brings to the family a comfortable income and a good social status; he is the decision-maker and the link with the outside world; it is he, through his work, who decides where the family shall live and how long they shall live there. But with his considerable involvement in his work life, the husband is much less dependent than his wife on the married relationship for the security and personal esteem which everyone needs.

As the couple go through the characteristic life cycle – as the children leave home, the role of housewife becomes a very part-time job, the husband becomes more and more involved in his work – the differences between the partners' lives may lead to marital stress. In all this the husband's work is a critical factor. His commitment to work tends to decrease his commitment to the marriage; his promotion involves uprooting his wife and family from other sources of support and security; the demands of his work make it difficult for her to follow a career of her own and so find alternative sources of identity and esteem in her own work world. It may be that spending time and energy on developing and sustaining a close relationship with his wife is the price which the manager has to pay for the success of his career.

MARRIAGE AND CAREER

We have seen that a husband's attitude to his work affects, and may be affected by, the couple's marital relationship. Indeed his attitude to the balancing of his home and work roles may be crucial in determining their marital happiness,* though his wife's attitude to his work may also be important. In the long-term sense, of course, most wives value their husband's work effort for the security and financial reward it brings to them and their family. Day-to-day attitudes, however, may be different, more ambivalent and antagonistic. Just as a husband can claim 'I do all my work for my wife' and then work so hard that he hardly ever sees her; so a wife may value her husband's contribution to the family budget while yet grudging the time he spends earning it.

In an attempt to clarify the patterns of relationships involved we have constructed two typologies to illustrate various dimensions of the couple's attitude to the husband's work. Of course, the construction of a typology produces stereotypes of individuals who are unlike any individuals found in reality: in

* Lotte Bailyn (1970) discussed some effects of husbands' attitudes. She concludes 'A husband's mode of integrating family and work in his own life is crucial for the success – at least in terms of marital satisfaction – of any attempt of his wife to include a career in her life. There is evidence, as a matter of fact, that identifying the conditions under which men find it possible to give primary emphasis to their families while at the same time functioning satisfactorily in their own careers may be even more relevant to the problem of careers for married women than the continued emphasis on the difficulties women face in integrating family and work' (p. 108).

this sense a typology blurs reality. The first typology is based on attitudes to work, that is, on whether work is seen as an end in itself or whether it is seen as a means to an end. A wife who held the first attitude would agree with the statement in our questionnaire: 'A man ought to get the main meaning in his life from his work.' A wife who held the second attitude would be more likely to agree with the statement: 'A man's a fool to drive himself only in order to achieve a moderately greater income and vastly greater responsibility' (see Appendix 1). Similarly, a husband in the first group would work because of the challenges work presented to him and the satisfaction and status he obtained from meeting the challenges. A husband with the second attitude would work in order to earn money so as to be able to do something else. We have called the first attitude 'work-oriented' and the second attitude 'non-work oriented'. The great majority of our managers are work-oriented and so their wives fall into categories 1 and 2.

Wife's attitude to husband's work	Husband's attitude to work	
	Work-oriented	*Non-work-oriented*
Work-oriented	1. Supportive wife – as housekeeper, hostess, etc.	3. Pushing wife – marital discord
Non-work-oriented	2. Wife feels neglected – resents his involvement with his work	4. Home-, child-, leisure-centred couple

The second typology is an attempt to elucidate these two categories of the first. In considering these typologies it is important to bear in mind a point which was well put by Blood and Wolfe (1960, p. 96):

In general, answers to the question, 'What have you tried to do to help your husband along in his work?' disclose more about the

Man and wife

wife's relationship to the husband than they do of tangible assistance in the husband's mobility. The reason a woman stands behind a successful man is not so much in order to make him succeed as because that's the kind of man a woman likes to stand behind. This is not to dismiss the wife's role as meaningless but to describe it as negligible in comparison to the personal-achievement motive and occupational skills of the husband. . . . To the marriage, however, what the wife does to help her husband in his work role is a sensitive indicator of how they feel about each other, what they mean to each other, what they do for each other.

We based our typology on the wives' answers to the question

In your relationship with your husband, how do you see yourself? Please tick one place on the scale following each statement. Do you see yourself as:

1. someone to share your husband's relaxation,
2. someone with whom he can talk over his problems,
3. caring for the house and children,
4. someone who enjoys entertaining his work colleagues,
5. a help to him with his work in practical ways e.g. reading through reports,
6. a social asset to him in his career.

Respondents were asked to place each possible role on a scale which ran thus: 'essentially so, very much so, to a large extent, to a certain extent, not really'. Table 8.4 shows the relative importance of the roles to the wives as a whole, with the five-point scale simplified by combining the first three positions together and the last two together. It shows that the majority of the wives saw their role in relation to their husband's work as being essentially a supportive and domestic one and only a minority took a more positive part in his work life. The typical wife saw herself as someone who cares for the house and children while her husband is at work and who helps him to sort out his worries and relax when he comes home to the nest in the evening.

When we looked more closely at the answers which individual wives gave to this series of questions, it became clear that there were characteristic patterns of answers and it was

TABLE 8.4. The Importance Attached by the Wives to Different Roles in Relation to Their Husbands

	Sharing husband's relaxation	Talking over his problems	Caring for house and children	Entertaining colleagues	Helping with his work	Being a social asset
Wife sees role as being						
Important*	72	70	77	39	15	32
Not really important†	14	16	9	45	71	52
Does not apply or she does not know				2		2
	86	86	86	86	86	86

* This includes those who saw themselves in these roles 'essentially', 'very much so' or 'to a large extent', i.e, positions 1 to 3 on a 5-point scale.

† This includes those who saw themselves in these roles 'to a certain extent' or 'not really', i.e, positions 4 and 5 on a 5-point scale.

upon these patterns that the typology was based. The answers
of 29 of the wives could not be put into any category; the
other 57 could be placed in one of three categories which we
have called domestic, supportive and independent. *Domestic
wives* characteristically rate the first three roles only as
important to them; that is, they see themselves as doing all
that they can in the domestic and personal sphere to help their
husbands, but do not see themselves as becoming involved in
the work life itself, either as hostess, social asset, spare typist
or whatever; 26 wives fell into this category. *Supportive wives*
characteristically rate all five roles as being important to them;
that is, they are willing to become involved, not only with the
husband's life at home, but also with his work life; 16 wives
fell into this category. *Independent wives* may rate themselves
high on role 3 in a bitter spirit of 'I'm just his housekeeper';
or they may not rate any of the roles as being of great importance to them. This may be done reluctantly, in that their
husbands do not allow them to be more closely involved, or it
may mean that they have separate interests of their own; 15
wives fell into this category.*

Mrs Petham is an example of a wife who falls into the

* Our categories differ slightly but significantly from those put forward
by Blood and Wolfe (1960) and Bott (1957) both of which might be thought
comparable. Blood and Wolfe divided the wives in their sample into col-
laborative, employment, supportive and peripheral. The last two of these
types are the most similar to the wives in our sample. Perhaps it is a
measure of the more ambitious and aggressive nature of American society
that the domestic wives in our sample (which in the American study are
called 'peripheral') consider, rightly, that they are a positive support
to their husbands in their work.

Bott puts forward a typology of family organization. She says 'In
complementary organisation the activities of husband and wife are different
and separate but fitted together to form a whole.' (As in our 'domestic'
category). 'In *independent organisation* activities are carried out separately
without reference to each other, in so far as this is possible.' (In terms of
our independent category, the independence may be reluctant as far as
the wife is concerned.) 'In *joint organisation* activities are carried out by
husband and wife together, or the same activity is carried out by either
partner at different times.' (In the terms of our question this means an
involvement of the wife in her husband's work life as we have described
for the 'supportive' category.)

supportive category; she and two other supportive-type wives, Mrs Ickham and Mrs Chilham, are discussed on page 59 in the section on 'Conjugal relationships at times of career crisis'. It might be valuable at this point to refer back to the earlier section. Mr Petham is a regional sales manager and his wife was a secretary until the arrival of their children. They are both in their early forties and have had a mobile married life, having lived in five different parts of the country. Mrs Petham's conjugal role profile, representing her attitudes to the six roles the questionnaire presented is shown on Table 8.5 section (b). Mr and Mrs Petham talk about his work every day and she enjoys her involvement with clients and colleagues; she says 'at the moment my husband is fifteen minutes from his work and I have been in to visit it a lot. I call whenever I'm in town and take the children in. He talks about his work a lot and I feel I know a lot about it and the people who work there.' She is involved in a certain amount of entertaining of customers and says,

This involves having a certain amount of social graces so you can cope with anything – having an ability to listen and to be sympathetic. It is important to make a good impression on boss and colleagues. It's important to appear to be capable and to be able to help your husband if he needed you to talk things over to and listen to him. As my husband has to entertain customers, his boss likes to know that wives are O.K. on this level.

Mrs Petham doesn't like the mobility which her husband's career involves but is willing to put up with it for the sake of the benefits which promotion brings. She said,

When we move I always go back into my shell and become very much a housewife. I'm miserable and suffer greatly from the fact that I haven't spoken to a soul all day. However, this doesn't last long with children, because I meet their friends' mums and then we're off. Anyway, normally a move involves promotion and higher salary – and so a bigger or nicer house or a better neighbourhood.

Mrs Petham gets her sense of security from her husband: 'I tend to leave things to him as he has the strive and energy that I lack. I am pleased in a way to let him be Mr Fix-it.

TABLE 8.5. Conjugal Role Profiles of Three Types of Wife

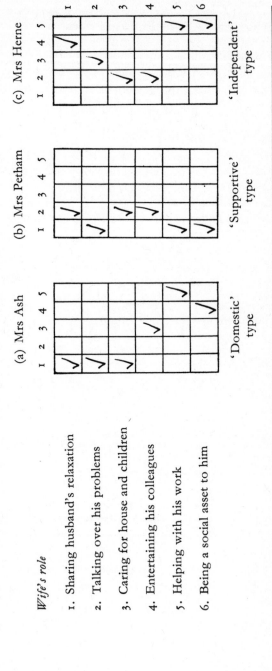

	(a) Mrs Ash 'Domestic' type	(b) Mrs Petham 'Supportive' type	(c) Mrs Herne 'Independent' type

Wife's role

1. Sharing husband's relaxation
2. Talking over his problems
3. Caring for house and children
4. Entertaining his colleagues
5. Helping with his work
6. Being a social asset to him

But when I'm called upon to do anything I can rise to the occasion, and, for example, when he was away on the course at Cambridge, nothing went wrong without him.'

Mr Petham values his wife for the encouragement and support she has given him: 'I'm lucky to be able to have an intelligent wife who can discuss things at any level I want to discuss them at.' They have a joint bank account and many of their interests, though not their political convictions, are mutual. Mrs Petham said 'I would like all my children to go to university. If I had a daughter I would like her to be intelligent; I should like her to marry someone with whom she could have an equal partnership, someone who was successful, and had money.'

Mrs Herne is an example of a wife who falls into the *independent* category, though in hers, as in many cases, it is a rather reluctant independence. Her husband is a financial manager in a nationalized industry, with a responsible, demanding and well-paid job; she is a graduate who took her first job as a teacher at the age of twenty-two. They are both in their thirties and live on a sociable housing estate of high-quality houses. Mrs Herne's conjugal role profile, representing her attitudes to the six roles the questionnaire presented, is shown on Table 8.5 (c). On average they talk together about his job once a week. Mrs Herne said,

I expected more 'togetherness' from marriage than has actually turned out, with cosy evenings, and homemaking, and doing such things as making lampshades and so forth. However, my husband left home at seventeen and has got to be very independent. I feel I'd like us to spend more time together and do more creative home-building, but in fact I do it all myself.

When a woman with these sorts of expectations finds herself married to a man with a high degree of commitment to his work, conflict between them seems to be almost inevitable. The focus of this conflict often seems to be the amount of time and interest which the husband invests in his work, as compared with the amount of both which he invests in his family. Mr and Mrs Herne are a couple who feel this conflict of interests. Mr Herne earns around £5,000 a year; he said 'I have no desire to be a millionaire; I would be quite happy if I could earn £15,000', and later 'Getting ahead in the world to me is concerned with getting ahead of other people, to be better than somebody at something, to be above the people you are with. The satisfaction of doing the job and the enjoyment of the job and the challenge of it are all important to me'.

Mr Herne then enjoys his work and is strongly work-oriented. His home life is relatively unimportant to him it seems: he says, for example,

My home and locality do not make much difference to me, but I know it does to my wife and so it does to me. I feel I could live almost anywhere without being unhappy. I plan my home life in no way at all: my wife does all that. My long-term plans are generally dictated by my job. For example if the work requires that I should go abroad, I will go abroad.

Mr Herne spends several hours yachting on both Saturday and Sunday, leaving Mrs Herne at home with their children in the South London suburb where they live. Mrs Herne said,

All marriages have problems and I moan about him not being at home enough. It took me a long time to accept this and I was very resentful of it at first. I feel that to a certain extent we are growing apart. . . . I feel I am not the sort of woman who is going to be able to help my husband and my influence is not important in terms of his job. Ideally I would have liked a husband who was more of a father – the only time over the weekends he spends with us is Sunday morning.

When they were interviewed together Mr Herne explained,

A lot of the day is spent apart doing very different things and there is little time in the evening to adjust to each other. I find it difficult to get interested in the domestic scene with minute family details and she can't possibly be aware of all that goes on in finance. I find it difficult to switch off from my day life to a common evening interest.

But when he was alone he was more brutal: 'There's absolutely no platform of communication between myself and my wife,' he said; 'I would like to be able to go home and talk about my work and get an intelligent response instead of the non-committal nod I usually get.' Interviewed on her own, Mrs Herne explained how she saw it.

I tend not to listen when my husband talks about his work as it is hard to maintain an interest if the person being talked about is just a name, as people from work do not come and visit us and there is little contact. For example, I can't give the name of my husband's boss or staff, though I do know his secretary as she is the one that I talk to if I phone him. Once my husband caught me out as he spent one whole evening talking about a project and asked me about it the next day and I couldn't remember anything that he had said.

There is something of a vicious circle here, since the more absorbed Mr Herne becomes in his work, the less time he has for communicating with his wife, by sharing in their family responsibilities and talking with her about his work; on the other hand, the less there is of this sort of communication between them, the harder it is for Mrs Herne to take an intelligent interest in her husband's work and for him to feel part of their day-to-day family life.

Mrs Ash is our example of the third, and most typical category of managers' wives. We have called her role *domestic* in that it is chiefly played in a domestic setting. This is not to say, however, that she is simply a housekeeper for her husband; she feels that helping her husband to talk over and work out his problems, and sharing in his relaxation are just as important as caring for the house and children. Her conjugal role profile is shown on Table 8.5 (a). Mr Ash is a national distribution manager earning £4,500. His wife left school at sixteen, after passing the school certificate, and married young. They are now in their forties and with only one child left at home are able to have an attractive and carefully furnished house.

Mr and Mrs Ash both used the word 'close' in describing their marriage.

[Mrs Ash] It's odd really because we're not a bit alike, but we do get on. Compatible is a horrid word, but rather appropriate.

[Mr Ash] My marriage relationship is like living and breathing and it's no less intense than the day we married. I can't conceive of going on holiday separately. I get far less pleasure out of a party if Mary is not there.

[Mrs Ash] Our marriage is much more complete than our parents'. They just jog along. It wouldn't do for me.

(Interviewer: 'What do you mean by close?')

[Mr Ash] It means a complete acceptance almost like another limb – no sensation of being apart – and everything between two people being completely free.

Mrs Ash's life since her marriage has been fully occupied with caring for her husband, children and home; she also gets pleasure from her artistic interests. She said

My husband has always discussed his work with me and I always feel I know the people he is talking about and indeed I have met a lot of them. I have never really felt that my husband and I were growing apart, though this might be true of the last few years as my husband has become more successful and I have felt it fleetingly. If anything went wrong we would talk it over with each other; I think we could. My husband changed his job last year and as it was a new job it was time- and thought-consuming. I appreciated that for a few months he would be preoccupied and that he would have to go away quite a bit. I made a particular effort to understand this. I have never resented the time my husband has to spend on his career; I take it for granted.

Mrs Ash was able to talk knowledgeably about the reasons for the many moves her husband had made (nine since their marriage) but nevertheless felt that her role was largely a passive one. 'I feel it is important to act as a sort of "safety valve". But I feel a bit inadequate because there's nothing I can do anyway and I can't even offer concrete advice. I just have to be there and listening.'

Mr Ash's career has been both hectic and successful. 'I work like hell,' he said; 'I'm always looking for the next thing to do. For example, I oil paint as a hobby and I can't do it fast enough. This is my personal view of myself, and also what my employers say of me.' Like many of the managers (see Chapter 4) his career has been largely a matter of accepting the promotions which were offered to him, rather than a matter of his planning his career and applying for the jobs he wanted. Accepting such promotional challenges he took the family up to the North of England and back down to the South again in the space of three years, with the result that the two elder children chose to leave home prematurely and the youngest child became extremely unsettled. Mr Ash realizes that his career has meant sacrifices for his wife: 'She has never questioned my ability. She has accepted that I would take anything that came my way and has put up with a good deal of personal misery in the process. I can't overstate its importance to me.'

Mr Ash probably realizes that his attitudes to work and success are highly ambiguous. On the one hand he says, 'Everything I do is concerned with the fact that I am married. I seldom do anything without thinking it is all connected. I have no desire for success – I do it all for my wife. If she wasn't there, there are many occasions when I would walk out. Marriage is my motivating force.' But on the other hand he can say 'Success means no more to me than my personal job satisfaction and more money.'

Yet both agree on the closeness of their marriage, that their interests are mutual. Domestic chores such as cooking and washing up are shared and both look forward to Mr Ash's retirement as a time when they will have more time to enjoy their leisure together. In the meantime perhaps the *three-day weekend* would be a good idea for couples such as Mr and Mrs Ash, particularly at that stage in the life cycle when children dominate the weekend and work the week. If Monday were 'marriage day' it might be easier for the ideal of a close conjugal relationship to co-exist with a high degree of commitment to work on the part of the husband.

CONCLUSIONS

In drawing up and describing our typology we have so far avoided the problem of explaining *why* a wife should fall into one category rather than another. We are reluctant to do so, since the variables are so many, the patterns so complex, and

our material so slight by comparison with reality. Nevertheless we feel that we must attempt to make some generalizations, however tentative. For the great majority of the wives
in our sample their marriage is the most important thing in
their lives, providing them with emotional as well as financial
security. Their attitudes to the role of wife, however, are
varied, according to their upbringing and education, their
experience of the world of work, their relationship with their
husband, and so on. The wife who falls into the *domestic*
category comes typically, we hypothesize, from a working-
class background or has had limited work experience; she does
not expect or want a role outside the home and feels more at
ease in her home environment. The wife who falls into the
supportive category comes typically from a lower-middle-class
home, or from a job as secretary; she too does not want a role
outside the home, at least while her children are young, but
she is familiar enough with the office world to feel that she
has a role to play in relation to her husband's work life. The
wife who falls into the *independent* category may be forced
there by her husband's desire to keep work and home
separate; more typically her middle-class home background

TABLE 8.6. Bases of Sense of Achievement among
Sixteen Managers

	Greatest achievement felt to be	*Most important thing in life*
Good job – holding responsibility	10	6
Sporting achievements	1	—
Educational attainments	3	—
Wife and children	4	13
Own integrity	—	1
Good salary/high standard of living	1	1
Friends	—	1
Good health	—	2

Note: Totals add up to more than sixteen since more than one item
in each category was mentioned by several respondents.

and her higher education have led her to want identities apart from her identity as wife and mother.

We have looked in greater detail at Mr and Mrs Ash, and placed them last in our discussion of the typology, because we feel that their example shows most clearly some of the ambiguities and stresses of such marriages. As Table 8.6 shows, while the managers characteristically felt that their wife and children were of greatest *importance* in their lives, they felt that their greatest *achievements* were made at work. For many, as for Mr Ash, the challenges presented at work were irresistible, whatever sacrifices might have to be made at home. So long as wives accept a passive role or a supportive, work-oriented one, all may be well. But the spread of the ideal of a close, companionate type of marriage, coupled with the rising level of education of women, may mean that the sacrifices will become increasingly unacceptable.

To both the men and the women in our sample their marriages were very important. But there were subtle differences in the degree of importance, as our tables crudely indicate. Thus, for example, the typical manager felt that his wife and children were the most important thing in his life, but that his work supplied him with his sense of security and his sense of achievement. His wife, however, seemed to have a greater stake in the marriage, finding in it her chief source of identity formation. Thus Mrs Dover said, 'We have a much better man and wife relationship than my parents.' And Mr Dover replied, 'They are not so much man and wife as man and woman, and they go their own ways and are completely different.' The implication seems to be that in their married relationship he 'is' primarily a *man* (significantly, the word which is also used to mean a human being), perhaps secondly a sales manager, and only third a husband and father. By contrast, she 'is' primarily a *wife*, with the implication that for her the married relationship is of the greatest importance.

In their attempt to live a close, companionate marriage, the woman has to adapt more than her husband. This may be one reason for the confusion which we found among the women about 'who I really am'. Our fieldwork was completed before the ideas of the Women's Liberation Movement attracted popular attention in this country. We found little evidence among the women in our sample of dislike of the nuclear family, resentment against the marriage tie, or very great frustration in their chief roles of wife, mother and housewife. But we did find a sense of uncertainty about identity among the women. Looking objectively at the managers and their wives, the dependent position of many wives is clear, even if they are unaware of, or at least unresentful of, their position. If these wives were to define being liberated as following a career of their own, that is, as getting their salient identities from occupational roles, they might handicap their husbands in the mobile and competitive world of industrial management.

Thus we see another area of *tension* in the lives of the managers and their wives. Many wives are in an ambiguous position, in that the relationship which is most salient to them is one in which they are the less powerful partner, and one in which their roles as wives are dependent on and determined by their husbands. Yet the husbands, too, are in the position of having their most salient role under the control of others; the competitive nature of their work situation means that they, and so, indirectly, their wives, must accept such constraints as frequent mobility and a commitment to work of most of their time and energy. We would expect the tension to become greater as the drive for greater efficiency in British industry meets our increased concern about the quality of personal relationships, and of marriage in particular.

CHAPTER 9

Ambition and Ambiguity in the Middle Class

In the previous three chapters we may have overdrawn the cosy domesticity of the wives and the homes of our managers. Generally content with their lot as housewives, and conscious of the advantages of a modest affluence, these wives do not give the immediate impression of being tense and anxious strivers. Indeed, as we showed in the last chapter, the wives could be seen as resentful – not of their lack of rewards – but of the way their husbands' work life took them away from the close conjugal relationships they needed or demanded. We saw the paradox of the man who involved himself intensively in his work 'all for his wife' whereas, we suggested, his wife would have preferred him to devote more time to what she defined as 'family life'. Thus we might conclude that, at least for their section of the middle class, 'ambition' and 'success' are not such overwhelmingly dominant values as the literature suggests.

Sociologists have shown an increasing interest in the study of values in recent years. Kohn (1959) showed that in America there were clear clusters of values associated with the middle and the working class and Gross and Gursslin (1963) produced a useful model of beliefs and values for the two classes. They see the central middle-class value as the attempt to achieve upper-status positions. From this they claim that there is competition for these positions which, in turn, requires the use of individual initiative and its acceptance as a value with the necessary rejection of group mobility as a value. Middle-class children, they say, are trained earlier and more rigorously than are lower-class children. They are taught the general characteristics that will help them to compete successfully in the middle-class world. These include, self-discipline, responsibility, initiative, adequacy in school performance, and restraint of physical aggression and sexual exploration

237

(ibid., p. 171). We have an illustration of this in Wyllie's account of *The Self-Made Man in America* (1964, p. 63):

> The ambition to succeed may be and always ought to be a laudable one. It is the ambition of every parent for his child. It is emphatically an American ambition: at once the national vice and the national virtue. It is the mainspring of activity; the driving wheel of industry; the spur to intellectual and moral progress. It gives the individual energy; the nation push. It makes the difference between a people that are a stream and a people that are a pool; between America and China. It makes us at once active and restless; industrious and overworked; generous and greedy. When it is great it is a virtue; when it is petty it is a vice.

We are not entirely happy with the American literature since it deals with very crude categories, thus deflecting attention from interesting variations within each category. Also we are not convinced that the American and British middle class can be necessarily assumed to have congruent values. We would consider the fear of downward social mobility to be a different kind of motivating force from the positive motivation for upward mobility. We suspect that the solid middle class in Britain puts more stress on stability, style and 'gentlemanly' values, leaving the striving to the *parvenu*.* Certainly the elucidation of the values of sub-groups within the middle class still remains a fascinating research task. John Raynor's admirable text on *The Middle Class* provides a useful starting point. He sees a distinction between the personal goal of independence for the higher managerial and higher professional groups, the goal of career for the lower-managerial and newer professional groups, and the goal of respectability for white-collar workers. Presumably our managers fall into his middle-middle class whose main goal is career.

Success, in occupational terms, becomes an almost compulsive drive. It is here that we find the spiralists for whom there is a steady fusion of career and family life, which means being both socially as well as geographically mobile, the family being assistants

* Pahl, R. E. in 'Middle Class Values' (unpublished paper) explores the worlds of Rat and Badger and Winnie the Pooh for evidence of this stable, family-centred, middle-class style.

in the process of 'getting on' and making a success in their careers. There is, in this group, a certain restlessness deriving from the need to be more productive and more successful. Every step upwards occupationally opens up the possibilities of conquering further horizons, and, therefore, they continuously and insistently demand of themselves effort in reaching these goals.*

Even this attempt to provide different value systems for three sub-categories of the middle class still leaves us dissatisfied. If we take our own sample we find some men from manual-working backgrounds and some from higher professional backgrounds, while their wives show a similar diversity in social origins. Are we to expect such a heterogeneous category to share the same values? To what level of generality do we have to go before meaningful statements can be made about the category as a whole? Raynor states categorically,

The over-arching value which dominates child-rearing in all groups in the middle class and which is directly related to the social structure is the value of achievement. . . . The emphasis laid by middle-class parents on independence, training, autonomy and standards of excellence stems from a belief they hold that the world is there to be manipulated to their advantage and that this will be more likely if satisfaction in their careers is obtained. (p. 90–91)

We are not convinced, even for a sub-category of the middle class, that values and beliefs are held so unambiguously. We suspect that there is a greater degree of ambivalence within the middle class than many sociologists and other observers have hitherto assumed. It has certainly been noted by Josephine Klein (1965) that 'The middle classes do not form static categories.' She is particularly shrewd and perceptive about what is *not* known about the subject under discussion. She goes on to say:

In each social category, in each occupation, will be some who have entered because it was their father's or their uncle's. Others are on the way up, others on their way down from fathers in the higher professional or business world. Geographical differences, with a related difference in the local definition of social strata,

* Raynor, 1969, pp. 88–9.

239

further complicate the picture. Any of these people may move to another town. Each generation increases the possibilities for change. (Vol. 1, p. 319)

In our discussion of the career we have already expressed our doubts about its adequacy as an all-embracing concept to provide a central focus for middle-class life. We are now going to consider ambition and success as basic driving forces for the middle class. Before leaving the general issue of middle-class values we would simply like to pose some questions which may perhaps stimulate other researchers. First, is the desire for upward social mobility widely shared throughout the middle class and is it equally strong at all levels? Does the upper-middle class, for example, strive to move into the upper class as strongly as the lower-middle class may want to move into the middle-middle class? Secondly, is the desire for their children's high achievement maintained consistently or is it a latent value which emerges only at certain times during their education and early career? At what point does a parent's striving on behalf of his offspring cool off? Thirdly, are middle-class girls exempt from this parental pressure and, if they are not, how do they manifest their internalized striving values when they are married women? Is it simply handed on to male offspring? This is an issue on which we throw a certain light below. Fourthly, if personal mobility and achievement are core values, this must create a certain conflict and stress *within* the middle class. It is not clear how the political solidarity of the middle class is maintained when, presumably, a large proportion must be competing with each other. One answer, we suggest, is that there is a collective interest in maintaining dominance over the working class and this leads to alliance with the elite and not with the masses. Finally, what are the implications of the middle class seeing education as a means to material success rather than as an end in itself? What tension does this create between those in the middle class who have absorbed different values with regard to education – in particular, of course, the teachers – and the rest? These are only some of the questions which could be considered. The social situation of our managers is complex and poses many questions. Our only comfort is that there appear to be no better answers elsewhere.

We could argue that the emerging style of the 'new middle class', in Britain anyway, is not the self-conscious, status-seeking typical of the American literature, but rather a contented domesticity, centred round shopping trips on Saturday and annual camping holidays with the children. Mr Frith, one of the most dynamic men in our sample, whom we considered in Chapter 4, provides a striking example of this lack of a strong materialistic outlook in life. 'We live the same as we did when I had £800 a year, and our personal acquisitions don't change much, except that we have a car, a home and we can send our children to the schools we want to.' He went on to say that for him material possessions were not very important and he wouldn't strive particularly to get them.

There was a time when they were important and that was when we had no money. When I was an undergraduate, and when I started work, I was impressed by the acquisitions of others and this made me dissatisfied. I thought I would not have great earning power in the job I had undertaken. But my environment has changed, and I've found that this feeling died out when I found I could get happiness out of simple things. Material things mean little now. . . . For example, cars waste money and two cars is ridiculous. We can get along with one having the car every other day. Two is very much of a luxury.

Thus, if we combine the domestic contentment of some of the wives with their husbands' relatively modest materialistic aspirations, we could paint a picture that would appear to be very different from that conventionally held for the middle class. Certainly this discrepancy is sharp if the comparison is made with the American middle class or the more aggressive Continental manager. However, before leaping to generalizations about the causes of Britain's slow rate of economic growth, the implications of this study for joining the European Economic Community or to detecting parallels with studies of affluent manual workers, it is necessary to pause. We need to consider whether the middle-class managers and their wives whom we are describing are not, to some extent, deceiving themselves. We need to be a little cautious about accepting at face value some of the articulate accounts of their life style and aspirations which they gave at an interview. The British managers may be slightly more modest or self-effacing than their American or Continental counterparts; their wives may be less brash – or less honest. Ambition and success are not such acceptable words in our culture as they may be in America. Perhaps in Britain the ambitious man forces the pace and disturbs our innate conservatism. In America it may be that the ambitious man is admired and encouraged, since change and high rates of individual social mobility are part of the national ideology. Here, although the rates of social mobility are much the same as in the United States, we perhaps do not acknowledge the qualities of those who are individually mobile so readily. We do not admire the *nouveau riche* or the *parvenu*; we emphasize style, manners, vocabulary and distinctive ways of speech and so forth. Manners, not money, maketh the man to a greater degree perhaps than we are happy to acknowledge, even in Britain in the seventies.

THE WIFE: PUSHER OR DROP-OUT?

We were particularly interested in the *beliefs* and *attitudes* held by our managers' wives. We wanted to know how much they supported the general competitive values of our society and how much they supported, encouraged and even pushed their husbands to be strivers. Similarly we wanted to know how much they were 'the drop-out behind the throne', concerned to foster home-centred, familial values, which would serve as a source of moderation to the more aggressive values of ambition and success in the husbands' work world. We later turn to discuss some of their husbands' attitudes and, in particular, consider whether success in any role other than their work roles can serve as a basis for 'success'.

Our research technique for the wives was to present them with six statements about a man's career, and respondents were asked to tick the appropriate box, depending on how true they believed these statements to be. The full questionnaire and the detailed instructions are reproduced on pages 277–8. In each set of statements there are three 'pushing statements' – these were concerned with the content of the man's job, the opportunity to exercise power and the social relations at the workplace. The three non-pushing statements were concerned with family, marriage and personal identity. Table 9.1 reproduces the statements in the order that they were given in the questionnaire and the totals of those who recorded pushing beliefs are bracketed. This indicates that a pushing belief would involve either believing the statement was true, or false, depending on its content. We have grouped the five-point scale in the way indicated by the footnotes to the table. It is unlikely that respondents would work out what we were trying to find out before completing the schedule and thus we hope that replies reflect a relatively unselfconscious series of responses.

It will be seen from Table 9.1 that those holding pushing beliefs outnumber those holding non-pushing beliefs by two to one. Of course, when asking whether respondents thought these various statements were true, we were not concerned with whether they individually approved of the statements. In general, it can be seen from the table that the statement that elicited the least ambiguous response was that which stated 'Men are more satisfied if they are fully stretched at work' – 61 wives believed that that was true. A further 49 wives believed that it was also true that 'A man's career is like a race and naturally he must compete to do well.' These are high proportions of our total: no non-pushing belief rates such high scores. Indeed the highest total for a non-pushing position was of 39 women who agreed that 'Men who are "Married to their work" make less good husbands', and this is somewhat ambiguous, since it is quite possible that women holding both pushing and non-pushing beliefs could agree with that. It could be argued that the statements which are more accurate reflections of pushing beliefs are those (i.e. 3 and 4) which get the highest totals. Thus the deficiencies of our research design may mask an even greater degree

TABLE 9.1.

Beliefs

No.	True*	False†	Not sure‡
1. Men that rise to the top quickly often lose touch with their family and old friends	19	[9]	56
2. Men who are 'married to their work' are less good husbands	39	[12]	33
3. Men are more satisfied if they are fully stretched at work	[61]	2	21
4. A man's career is like a race and naturally he must compete to do well	[49]	7	28
5. The worries of a senior position are compensated for by a more exciting and interesting life	[35]	11	38
6. The happiest men are those who don't take their work too seriously	22	[35]	25
			201

* Those who indicated that the statements were 'always true' or 'generally true'.

† Those who believe the statements are untrue.

‡ Those who believe them to be true sometimes or who are not sure.

Totals of pushing beliefs are bracketed.

Pushing beliefs		*Non-pushing beliefs*	
	9		19
	12		39
	61		2
	49		7
	35		11
	35		22
	201		100

(Total answers 502 which together with 14 'do-not-know' answers equals 516, i.e. 6 × 86.)

of agreement that work is basically tough and competitive and that men are most satisfied in situations when they are fully stretched.

In Table 9.2 we set out in greater detail the actual pattern of responses and it will be seen that many of those holding 'pushing' beliefs also, at the same time, hold non-pushing ones.

TABLE 9.2.

	Beliefs		Attitudes
Respondents with			
4 or more pushing positions		10	5
3 pushing positions			
with no non-pushing positions	6		3
with 1 ,, ,, ,,	11		4
with 2 ,, ,, ,,	9		4
with 3 ,, ,, ,,	4		1
		30	12
2 pushing positions			
with no non-pushing positions	5		1
with 1 ,, ,, ,,	8		7
with 2 ,, ,, ,,	11		15
with 3 ,, ,, ,,	1		7
		25	30
1 pushing position			
with no non-pushing positions	4		1
with 1 ,, ,, ,,	5		4
with 2 ,, ,, ,,	8		12
with 3 ,, ,, ,,	2		11
with 4 ,, ,, ,,	0		1
		19	29
0 pushing positions but			
1 non-pushing position(s)			2
2 ,, ,, ,,			2
3 ,, ,, ,,	1		4
4 ,, ,, ,,			2
		1	10
Those showing no pushing positions and			
no non-pushing positions at all		1	0
		86	86

This may, however, imply less ambiguity than appears at first sight. A comparison of Table 9.1 with Table 9.2 gives some indication of the apparently conflicting or inconsistent beliefs that are most likely to be held. The 'pushing' beliefs were connected with the competitive nature of the career, the need for men to be fully stretched at work, the compensations that the quality of the work life provides for the greater 'worries' of a senior position, and that men should take their work seriously. The non-pushing beliefs that were likely to be held *at the same time* as two or three of the pushing beliefs were that men 'married to their work' make less good husbands or a belief that men should not take their work too seriously. The inconsistency appears therefore primarily between the nature of their husbands' worlds of work and their husbands' situation within it and the imputed effect of this work life on their life outside. The statement which produced the greatest ambiguity was the one which made a direct link between work and non-work relationships, 'Men that rise to the top quickly often lose touch with their family and old friends'; 56 of our wives were unsure about the truth of this. Few of their own husbands had yet reached anything that might be described as the 'top' and few would know other men in that situation; in addition the word 'often' may have confused them. The statement which produced the sharpest division was about taking work 'seriously'. Although 35 women believed it was untrue that the happiest men do not take their work seriously, 22 believed the reverse to be true.

Thus there are more women who believe that their husbands live in a basically competitive world, where work is demanding and must be taken seriously. Now it is quite possible to believe that the world is hard and thrusting without necessarily liking it. We therefore devised another six statements against which our respondents could record their personal *attitudes*. Our procedures are similar and we again had three statements which were more pushing in tone and three that were more relaxed. We set out the details in Table 9.3 and the striving responses are again bracketed. The first point which comes out clearly is that, unlike the situation with

The wife: pusher or drop-out?

TABLE 9.3.

No.	Attitudes	Agree*	Disagree†	Not sure‡
1.	Once a man has got a reasonable salary and a respected position he should spend more time on his family and other interests	26	[17]	41
2.	A man ought to get the main meaning in his life from his work	[10]	35	39
3.	A man should not be too friendly with colleagues in case he is their boss one day	[9]	51	24
4.	A man's a fool to drive himself only in order to achieve a moderately greater income and vastly greater responsibility	31	[18]	35
5.	If a man has ideas it is only natural he should want the power to put them into practice	[59]	3	22
6.	Men should not get too involved with their work as this would interfere with a happy married life	14	[36]	34
				195

* Those who indicated that they agreed or agreed completely with the statements.

† Those who disagreed with the statements.

‡ Those who were not sure about or agreed to a certain extent with the statements.

Totals of pushing attitudes are bracketed.

Pushing attitudes	17	Non-pushing attitudes	26
	10		35
	9		51
	18		31
	59		3
	36		14
	149		160

(Total answers 504 which together with 12 'do-not-know' answers equals 516, i.e. 6 × 86.)

regard to beliefs, where the pushing responses outnumbered the non-pushing by two to one, here the *non*-pushing attitudes gain most responses – 160 to 149. This balance in firmly held attitudes reflects an even greater ambivalence and ambiguity than was the case with regard to beliefs. The greatest degree of consistency was shown by agreement with the statement 'If a man has ideas it is only natural he should want the power to put them into practice', 59 out of 84 women holding this attitude. Thirty-six women disagreed with the notion that involvement with work necessarily interferes with a happy married life. The non-pushing attitude most likely to be held was disagreement with the statement that 'A man should not be too friendly with colleagues in case he is their boss one day' (51 cases) and disagreement with the statement that 'A man ought to get the main meaning in his life from his work' (35 cases). The statement which produced the greatest uncertainty and ambivalence was 'Once a man has got a reasonable salary and a respected position he should spend more time on his family and other interests'; 41 women were unsure what they felt about this. This may be partly, as one woman wryly noted, because a 'reasonable' salary implied responsibility and responsibility demanded time and without time you cannot have other interests.

It was striking that not only did fewer women hold pushing attitudes than held pushing beliefs, they are also more likely to hold both pushing and non-pushing attitudes. Thus there is not only a tension between what is believed to be true and the wives' attitudes to it but wives also hold attitudes which are inconsistent with each other. The former point is clearly illustrated in the following table. This is based on a 'pushing scale' on which inconsistent beliefs or attitudes cancel each other out. For example, those with, say, two pushing attitudes and two non-pushing attitudes end up in the 'ambivalent' category (Table 9.4).

So while it seems fairly clear that most women *believe* that the world of work is competitive and that it is true that men are, or need to be, stretched, their own *attitudes* to this are less clear and about half our sample indicate non-pushing views. This

TABLE 9.4.

	Beliefs (%)	Attitudes (%)
Pushers	62	29
Ambivalent	23	23
Non-pushers	15	48
	100	100

is one of a number of basic ambiguities at the centre of middle-class life which we are concerned to explore in this chapter. Certainly many wives were aware of this ambiguity and were ready to comment on their questionnaires or enlarge on the point to our interviewer. Many saw the advantages of having a 'successful' husband and simply hoped that this would not be too much at the expense of his health, their marriage and family life. An implicit acceptance of the centrality of work is shown in those replies which view the home as a place where the husband relaxes and is soothed before another foray into the tough world. As the wife of a chartered mechanical engineer put it 'I feel that a man should be completely engrossed while at work but should try to leave office work at the office. I feel he will work better for a complete break when he gets home to his family. My husband takes great interest in our garden. This I'm pleased about because I feel it gives the maximum relaxation that I'm sure any man working, particularly in business today, needs.' Similarly the wife of a product manager felt that holidays should be taken 'with the planned result of better application after the vacation'. The thirty-three year old wife of a man who carried the sales responsibility of a turnover of £4 million wrote 'My husband has a hobby – bird watching – thus the main meaning in his life is not his work, although he is equally striving in both respects. Without his birds he would not get the relaxation and be revitalized to face the rigours of workaday life.' Ideally, of course, wives wanted their husbands to be successful without too much effort: they wanted to have their cake and to eat it too.

I feel a man should have a job he likes and enjoys doing. This I feel is the most important consideration. He will then have the incentive to get to the top – not just because of the money and power that goes with the top positions, but because he has an interest and therefore can't help but get on. There should be no question of him spending 'so many hours' with his family. It's a question of give and take, between work and home.

There was also a feeling expressed by some that certain men had innate abilities which must not be wasted or under-used. 'Some men are satisfied to secure a balance between home and business life. Others must drive themselves. I think this drive should not be thwarted if it is seriously to fulfil a need within himself but that he is a fool to do it purely for financial gain.' Another wife argued that 'many men do not have to "drive" themselves to get a better position because it would be more harmful for these men not to have greater responsibilities'. For wives married to such men it seems that chance has provided them with a social position they simply have to make the best of. 'I feel very strongly that a man in a senior position needs to be able to talk to his wife – thinking, dreaming, planning; unfortunately I know many a wife who forgets that at this time she is in the same position as his doctor or confessor – chat or listen and then forget it ever took place. She must be a safety valve with the emphasis on the *safety*' (her emphasis).

Unfortunately for many wives it was quite clear that their husbands were not going to get to the top effortlessly as a result of their overflowing talents: 'In many cases he is striving to earn a greater income so his wife and family can enjoy a reasonable standard of living in this highly competitive world.' Many wives said that of course this should not be at the expense of his health and happiness: 'Much as I like to see my husband getting ahead and enjoy the advantages that go with it, I would be quite prepared at any time for him to take a drop in salary if it meant him doing the work he really wanted to do.' A number of wives had specific reasons for wanting their husband to spend more time at home – one had a spastic and epileptic daughter and she felt that her husband's position and over-conscientious approach to his responsibilities did not leave him the time to give her the extra care and attention his wife felt she needed. Another wife, daughter of divorced parents, resented the work her husband did at home, instead of playing with the children or just being 'father'. Other women simply reacted against what they felt was a crude materialism:

I feel that it isn't worth killing oneself for the thought of more money or promotion. My husband already works very hard and although he says he enjoys it I don't think it does anybody any good to live and work at top speed all the time. All I wish is for him to be happy at work and remain healthy, and if promotion means hours of work, worry and entertaining most nights people neither of us particularly like, well our happiness and pleasure means more to me at any rate than wealth and ambitions. (Forty-one-year-old wife of a commercial director.)

It is difficult to be honest, because as a selfish woman one would want a husband at home and without worries as much as possible. The children benefit too from seeing more of father. However, if a man is dissatisfied with his work you can't hold him back. . . . Personally as long as my husband is happy, we are fed, clothed and housed and the children educated satisfactorily, I don't mind what he does provided it isn't illegal (and preferably not in a slaughter-house or a glue factory). Probably the happiest wives are those of teachers and the unhappiest are those of tycoons and export managers. . . . A man with a fairly easy job (i.e. well within his capacities) and two or three outside interests (i.e. a sport, a club – say Rotary – and, say, painting, gardening or church) would probably be a very contented man and husband, and his wife would be happy too. (Thirty-two-year-old wife of a district sales manager.)

It is very hard to give an objective picture of what the majority of our wives felt on this issue. They were torn in their own attitudes and doubtless their replies would vary from day to day or from week to week as they had different experiences in the family or as the work load of their husbands varied. Probably, if one had to come to a firm conclusion, most would agree with the woman who wrote 'Some fortunate people are able to get satisfaction and a good salary without becoming too involved – this, of course, is the ideal position.'

'SUCCESS' FOR THE MANAGERS

We were able to explore the husbands' attitudes to ambition and success in the personal interviews. We asked our sixteen managers what they thought 'getting ahead in the world' meant for them, what their main achievements were, in their opinion, and also what were the most important things in their lives. Inevitably such general questions did not provide precise answers and it is not possible to give a general summary of typical attitudes to be found among our sixteen managers. Indeed the contrasts were striking: in the same way that many wives felt a tension between the values of family and the values of work, some husbands felt a similar tension. This came out very clearly in answer to our questions about their aspirations for their sons. It was often felt by those who saw a tension between the demands of work and the demands of the family that these could more easily be combined in a profession. They saw the difficulty of combining the ruthless and competitive qualities needed to further their 'careers' and the gentler qualities, associated with their 'real' selves.

Mr Bourne is a civil servant who saw getting ahead in the world as simply 'career success – an increasing responsibility and the rewards for it. I think one just does get ahead in the world and I don't think it's a thing one questions. You just do as best you can without being obsessive about it.' This is what we shall take to be the 'solid' middle-class approach to career and success: without too much questioning one simply accepts the increasing responsibility and rewards. But these rewards are not the most important thing in Mr Bourne's life: various things combined to create a particular style. 'It all hangs together. It's difficult to place things in order. I can't quantify. For example, my family, my job, friendly relations with other people, social contacts – these are all important but it's hard to put them on any priority scale. I suppose if it came to the crunch and I had to give up some of them then I would have to order them, but for me personally they all hang very much together.' Mr Bourne is the son of a civil servant and now gets his chief sense of security from 'simply being an established civil servant'. His father 'was a man who, to a fault, accepted responsibilities to his family and to his job to the extent that he killed himself doing it. He died relatively young, I think to a certain extent he died of overwork, or at least this helped.'

Clearly Mr Bourne's father had rather too much zeal and this perhaps leads his son to be more detached about his work. However, his father was fond of classical music and his mother read a great deal. 'Looking back,' he remarked, 'I remember reading more than doing anything else. We had a house full of books, and I worked through them indiscriminately.' For Mr Bourne there has been little change in life style over the generations. 'I think life is fixed in the London suburbs, except in terms of technology (for example the television), the style of life now is remarkably similar to what it was thirty years ago. And as far as suburban areas like this are concerned, I simply see the 1960s as the 1930s writ large.'

The tradition and style is continuing: Mr Bourne wants his son (aged twelve) to be happy,

Much as he is now. . . . I was flattered when I was talking to his housemaster at school, when he remarked that my son is a very civilized boy. I feel I have achieved something, though I don't know to what extent I am responsible for it. He has got a sense of humour, and the same funny stories amuse us both. He is considerate. I wouldn't say he is a repository of all the virtues, but I think he is an engaging personality and would be a pleasant sort of young man. I think he will ultimately make a good citizen. That sounds really corny and square, doesn't it? As far as the job is concerned, one would hope that he would finish up in some professional capacity. I have no strong feelings one way or the other about this: it's a case of seeing which way he is going to develop.

He was then asked from what he would hope his son would get his chief sense of happiness and he replied:

This is something that struck me the other day looking back, when I was talking to my wife, remembering the times when I was happy, and they were almost inevitably when I had established a good relationship with someone else, either my wife, my children, friends or simply anyone, and I would hope my son would find happiness in the same way. In fact I don't think there is any other way, though I suppose some people think of it in terms of making money.

Mr Bourne wants to provide his children with an education that will open up the maximum number of options. He thinks 'a public-school education is more directed towards making a whole man' and he wants them to go to university 'not for the sake of achieving a degree', although, of course, he would like them to get one 'though in no particular subject'. More important is 'making them into more complete people'. Universities, in his view, provide a setting in which they can develop their personalities and come to terms with themselves.

Mr Bourne has little cause to strive, to be anxious or to be worried about the effects of competition on his character. From a solid-middle-class home, with an Oxbridge degree and the means to establish his children 'in a profession', he can afford to say his main achievement is his home and family. Furthermore he is not even obliged to pretend to be ambitious, on the contrary: 'In the Civil Service as compared with industry I think it's part of the game to pretend that you're not really trying. If you are open about wanting to succeed you are regarded as an outsider and it won't get you anywhere.' The young Bourne boy is being brought up to provide the perfect husband for the daughters of our managers in industry. We asked the wives about the kind of man they would like their daughter to marry. Characteristically none said they would like them to marry someone in a job similar to that of their own husband: men who were kind, considerate and in 'a profession' were the ideal. Clearly it is considered that this 'effortless' success or security is more likely to be found in the professions than in industry.

This concern with the right mix or balance of various life interests was also expressed by the Newingtons. We have considered Mr Newington's attitude to his career (page 96), and his attitude towards his son reflected a similar non-striving style.

I'd like him to have a full appreciation of life and that covers everything. People, the way things are done, music, old things,

architecture, furniture and an understanding of new things. It's
a whole outlook. I'd like him to be sensitive. . . . I'd like him to get
his happiness from his relationships with other people. . . . I'd
like my children to receive the education necessary for them to be
the full people I'd like them to be, and I think this is more likely
to come from a fee-paying school, because of the environment,
attitude of the staff, numbers and attention, tradition and discipline.
These things are all better and are more conducive to a rounded
personality. As far as qualifications are concerned, I'd certainly
like them to have pretty good basic academic achievements behind
them. I think this is necessary for this full personality I've talked
about, and it would give them a chance to go on with other things.
This is something I lack myself, and it limits one's field.

Mr Newington, the son of an engineer, left his public school
before taking his 'A' levels.

We will return to discuss some of the implications of this
secure-middle-class view of the full personality later in this
chapter. Now it is perhaps worth remembering that other
managers see things rather differently, even if they too come
from a middle-class background. Mr Ickham, to return to
another of the case studies we presented in Chapter 4, had a
clear idea of what he wanted his son to be like – 'like me'.
He then went on to say:

I would also like him, unless he's a complete idiot, to have a
better education than I have. I'd like him to go to university. I
don't really mind what he does as long as it's what he wants to
do, but I'd like to give him the opportunity to do anything.
Perhaps a lawyer would be nice, although I wouldn't encourage
him to be an accountant, or even if he went into industry that would
be O.K. I hope he'll be a good mixer, and get on with people and
be able to drink his pint and play a good game of golf. I wouldn't
like him to be an effeminate little guy. I'll probably beat him over
the head to play golf. If he's girly I'll accept it, but I won't be happy
about it. I don't intend to push my kids though. I think this is a
great mistake. I wouldn't want to push them into a career but I'd
like to make them try things. I think one of my father's faults was
that he was too easy going if I wouldn't do something and he was
too soft. I shall be different with my kids and push the little blighter
a bit and tell him if he says he can't do something that of course
he can do it.

When Mr Ickham was asked about education for his children, he said:

> I'd like my son to have one such as I've had, as far as school was concerned, but with further education. . . . If I can afford it I'll send him to a public school, but I'm quite happy with a good state school, if he's getting a good education. If he's thick though, he won't get far in the state system, so therefore I will have to fork out to buy him a better one than he necessarily deserves.

Mr Ickham is unashamedly materialistic. He would like a yacht, two cars, a nice home, plenty of money to spend and so forth. 'At this stage the income is more important. When we have bought a lot of things that we need and the family is set up, then income, I think, will be less important to me, but I'm prepared to struggle quite hard for a lot longer.' A similar point of view was held by Mr Kingston who said that material things are important: both he and his wife like to have them and he feels this is a natural desire. He claimed to be extravagant and doesn't care – he would like to get £15,000 a year (not allowing for inflation) together with a proportion of the company's profits, which could run into thousands. His wife writes,

> I find that my husband is so one hundred per cent involved in his work, seven days a week and evenings, that he literally does not have any relaxation. I should be very grateful for some knowledge-able advice as to whether it is my duty to encourage this way of life if he is happy, despite the effect on his health, or whether I should fight for some of his time.

By the time of the interview she had become more reconciled: 'His work is not only his hobby, but his life, and he has no spare time . . . he will never alter. . . . In the past this caused considerable upheavals.' Mr Kingston claims that the most important things in his life are his wife and home . . .

The demand for money also motivates Mr Olantigh, who is driven on by a determination not to live in the circumstances in which he was brought up, since his father had squandered the family money. 'We were poor and that is why I am keen on saving money. It's become a hobby with me and it gives me a lot of confidence.' However, he is unlike Mr Ickham and Mr Kingston in that he values money more 'for the sense of independence and security that it brings' rather than for the accumulation of material things. 'We can afford not to keep up with the Joneses.' He has saved money over the years ('in my best year I managed to save over £800') and hopes that, unlike his father, he will be able to set up his son in business if that would help him. His son must first get qualified: 'One of the finest exams in the world is to take your degree or qualifications working at night.' Somewhat inconsistently he would like his son to be a professional – 'such as a lawyer' – rather than an entrepreneurial businessman, where presumably some initial capital would be more useful. For Mr Olantigh getting ahead 'means success in business judged by financial rewards'. Like Mr Kingston he works very hard: he leaves home at 7.15 a.m. and gets home late; generally he hasn't finished clearing up from dinner until 9.30 p.m. and then he works at his desk until 11 p.m. Mr Olantigh says he 'wastes' a lot of time at weekends. For example he 'has' to go and visit his mother at weekends when he could be working the Stock Exchange (from which he has successfully added to his income) or saving money by doing his own decorating. Indirectly, then, Mrs Olantigh senior is 'a financial burden' to her son. Mrs Olantigh wishes that her husband would spend some of his money (he kept his previous car for twelve years), but nevertheless felt her marriage was 'wizard and is better than anyone else's I know'.

There is little doubt that our managers worked hard. Either by bringing work home or because of a lengthy journey to work, most had long working days. Even Mr Bourne, the civil servant, did extra work (on another job) at the weekend. Why do they work so hard? What are they working for? Is it that they are simply less able and have to work long hours to do what a man of greater ability could finish by 5 p.m.? Are they working in order to achieve promotion and thus more money? How can they say (as most of them do) that they are working hard for their wives and families when the very fact of working prevents them from being with the people for whom they are said to be working? None of the managers complained about the burden of work – although of course their wives did – are we then to assume that they enjoy it?

These, and similar questions, are not easy to answer: they perhaps provide pointers to future lines of research. In this final section we become more speculative and try to make some generalizations which arise from the evidence provided by our 86 managers and their wives.*

We have shown that the managers work very hard but it is not clear why or what for. We spent a considerable amount of time getting detailed information on how they spent their weekends. There was, in general, little to distinguish the way they spent their 'free' time from the way skilled manual workers spent theirs. Saturday mornings might be spent in going shopping in a near-by town. The family might have coffee out and the husband might have his hair cut. In the afternoon, typically, sport dominated the men's lives. Some still played; others watched on television or at the stadium or local playing fields. Fathers sometimes took young children out, but not always. Evenings were spent watching television or with friends. Few had lavish holidays or had clear aspirations for bigger houses or cars. Most of the help which they received from their parents was in kind, for example baby-sitting rather than in cash. Maybe they would inherit a little capital on the death of one or other of their parents but only in a minority of cases would even this be likely. By and large they were more interested in income than capital. The men appeared to have few interests apart from their work, although we took considerable pains to probe this in the extended interviews.

WILLING SLAVES TO THE SYSTEM?

These middle managers in British industry appear to be willing slaves to the system; only their wives complain and even they

* We also draw on other research which one of us has done over the past decade; some of this is reported or referred to in the section on 'Newcomers in Town and Country' in *Whose City?* by R. E. Pahl (1970).

are not sure whether they ought to. Certainly the wives accept that the system offers their husbands little choice. Of course, it may be that there is nothing more satisfying than work and that time with one's wife and children or simply reading a book is 'wasted'. However, it is worth considering why these men see work as a central life-interest when other employees quite clearly do not.* It could be argued that managers are more effectively exploited than the men they manage. They have internalized an ideology of self-coercion. They suffer the full force of the competitive society they support. The area sales manager must work on his books over the weekend because his opposite number in a rival firm is doing the same. They must work hard to produce more, for if they did not somebody else would, markets would decline and even managers can become redundant. They have no security. Their only reassurance is movement forward and upward. For them life is a hierarchy and success means moving up in it. Marking time and staying in the same position is interpreted as dropping out. Typically they have a longitudinal view, of developing and of becoming. They expect different things to happen over a period. There is a logic of change that pervades middle-class life. This commitment to change in the class of conservatism is simply one of the paradoxes with which we are faced. Very often it is the fear of falling rather than the positive aspiration to climb which pushes these men on. Those who had an experience of downward social mobility in their family history were among the most determined to have a successful career. They work, then, because they are trapped in a competitive society: above all they do not want to fall. The men were not, however, usually prepared to admit that they were driven on for selfish, materialistic reasons. They would talk of 'challenge' and 'responsibility' as well as family commitments. Their wives would believe it to be true that men are more satisfied if they are fully stretched at work, but

* Dubin, 'Industrial workers' worlds: a study of the "central life interests of industrial workers"', and Orzack, 'Work as a "central life interest" of professionals'. Both articles are reprinted in *Work and Leisure* edited by Smigel (1963).

disagreed with the idea that a man should get his main meaning from his work. Thus a man is expected to view his wife and children as the most important thing in his life and yet get most of his satisfaction away from them working at his job. Few of our managers had worked through these ambiguities and paradoxes. That is why some of our material is apparently contradictory or ambivalent. It is a commonplace of any sociological textbook to contrast the affective ties of the family with the achievement-oriented and affectively neutral values of the wider industrial society. What we are trying to describe is the way this tension works out among British managers and their wives.

Undoubtedly, the more highly educated and more confident wives provide a threat to those whose interest it is to keep managers as willing slaves. As long as wives feel that it is their duty and privilege to act as decorative housekeepers then few problems arise. In one of the pilot studies for this research we interviewed an accountant as one of half a dozen interviews on a Hertfordshire estate. He was a man in his thirties in his third appointment and during busy periods he did not get home until 10.30 p.m. As he put it 'I've just got to earn money. One of my joys in life is to sit down and read the newspaper from cover to cover and I get fed up when I can't do this.' When asked how he saw his home he replied, 'A haven of peace to return to. Somewhere where I can get a bit of sympathy when I need it.' This particular man epitomized, more dramatically than any of our sixteen managers, the exploitative approach to his wife (who was incidentally an extremely attractive blonde and by no means dumb). When asked about his wife he replied as follows,

I haven't gone far wrong with what I've got: she's always here when I come home and always willing to hear my moans. She makes me feel wanted. I get a pleasant sensation from her at times. She helps me to recharge after hectic days. Basically what I look for – home to me is somewhere where I can do what I please rather than what someone else pleases and my wife tolerates it; where one gets mollycoddled to some extent – if one can put it that way.

He was then asked what qualities his colleagues looked for in their wives. 'By and large they look for the same things I look for: reasonable level of comfort; decent standard of food. . . . I've always been thankful I've got a good housekeeper.' He went on to say that one of the factors that influenced him to 'take the final plunge' was that his wife had been brought up in a 'careful household' and would therefore be a 'competent manager' of his money. He thus has a joint account with his wife, 'giving her a freer hand money-wise than some of my colleagues do'. Apparently they 'wouldn't dream' of a joint account. A further factor he took into account before marrying his wife was whether she was prepared to move about the country.

You've got to get it sorted out early whether she's prepared to move: if the girl says no, then black mark. It seems to be one of the factors people take into account. I had a friend – a Cambridge graduate – who married a local girl who refuses to move. He's stuck: he can't realize his full potential.

This mobile housekeeper who cooks well, is careful with his money and provides a 'pleasant sensation' at times may be the pattern of the past. Future managers' wives may be less likely to accept such a role. Even if the men do not question their work-dominated lives, their wives are likely to demand more *time*. Money is not necessarily an adequate compensation for time. Already the indications from our study suggest that wives are more sensitive to the basic ambiguities in the situation. Those who have been contemporaries with their husband at school, college or university or who have shared a similar pattern of life before marriage in some other way are unlikely to be so ready to lose their husbands to the demands of 'the system'. It is significant that both in our pilot studies and in the extended interviews with our managers there is an emphasis on ensuring that offspring should either marry or train to be a *professional*. It was rare for anyone to have ambitions for themselves to have, or for their children to have, their own business or organization. The entrepreneurial role appeared to carry few attractions.

However, the professional was perhaps seen as someone who could hold his own against the system. His skill would be his capital and this could not be devalued. He would not be obliged to move about. It is similarly assumed that he would not be obliged to work long hours but would have the ideal 'balance': a high status and respected position, 'enough' money and more autonomy in making his important life-plan decisions. This myth of the non-striving, relaxed 'professional' is one of the most interesting and elusive themes that has appeared in our work on the middle class. Managers in industry, and very often their wives to an even greater extent, have a curious vision of this professional life style. It is probably based on an inflated notion of the importance of education. When couples stress the importance of university education so that their pre-school-age sons will be able 'to enter a profession of their own choice' we suspect that this is an aspiration for 'the plateau'. They have discovered that the competitiveness of industry within and between firms makes it impossible to level off. Someone else is always pressing for the same job. Hopefully 'the profession' allows one to level off. The highly trained lawyer, for example, is above competition: he simply applies his mind to complex problems for a limited time each day and grateful clients provide sufficient reward for him to live (inevitably) in a Georgian house, to entertain and to live a cultured life, knowing about music, painting and literature. In this myth, time is free for wife and children and there is no fear of demotion, redundancy or shortage of money to drive one to work in the evenings.*

Basically we consider that what we may be detecting is the beginning of a middle-class reaction against competition. While

* Of course those who read this passage and work in the legal profession or, to change the example, are university teachers may find all this incredible. Life in some industrial concerns is positively sheltered compared with the cut-throat competition of many university departments. However, it is true that academics have security of tenure and, like civil servants, in this respect are in a stronger position than other professionals. However, we are not so much concerned with the falseness of the myth so many managers and their wives hold but rather with the implications of such a belief.

fundamentally believing that we live in a competitive society, a minority, particularly of the wives, are questioning the effects of such competition. Thus the concern for university education for their offspring, for more 'choice' and for the profession as the ideal occupation, all reflect a desire to get into a situation where competition and its consequences may be minimized.

We hasten to emphasize that our suggestions are very tentative. Our analysis of the material on our managers and their wives has revealed three areas of ambiguity. First, there is the ambiguity between the discrepant beliefs and attitudes of the wives; secondly there is the discrepancy between satisfaction and meaning in a man's life, and thirdly there is the ambiguity connected with wanting to be professional or uncompetitive in a competitive world.

Perhaps we should consider these men and women in a broader perspective. We may see them as examples of the new middle class created by the expansion of managerial capitalism in the first half of the twentieth century. The nineteenth-century entrepreneur, with his emphasis on the accumulation of capital and the development and continuity of dynastic financial empires, has clearly gone. In his place have come huge management empires. As organizations have got larger managerial functions appear to have increased. Similarly the new, technically-complicated growth industries have a high ratio of managers to workers. Particularly during the past twenty-five years there have been more opportunities in this section of the labour force than any other. Thus from 1951 to 1961, for example, the average annual compound rate of increase for male workers in higher administrative, professional and managerial occupations was 3·8 per cent, far higher than any other major cluster of socio-economic groups.* The average compound rate of increase for managers in the same period was 4·9 per cent a year. This rate of change was, of course, far higher than the expansion, say, of places in institutions of higher education. It is a striking reflection on the rigidity of

* Rose Knight, 1967, Tables 3 and 8. See also Harold Rose *et al.* (1970, pp. 14–17).

our society that this increase did not appear to lead to any dramatic increase in rates of social mobility from the working class, as Clements's study (1958) clearly illustrates. However, it did mean that many men were able to acquire extra qualifications by studying in the evenings and by moving into managerial positions. Many men were carried forward by the expansion of industry to jobs which perhaps stretched them to the limits of their capacity. The birthrate in the middle class was low in the late 1920s and 1930s and hence the cohorts which entered the labour force after the ex-servicemen's bulge of the late 1940s had a relatively easy run. Thus, to return to our sample, Mr Herne, who was born in 1934, started as an apprentice in 1952 and was a systems-engineering manager before he was thirty.

The chaotic expansion of British management brought forth many reactions. First came the ideology of the 'career' and the attempt to hold some men in certain organizations with a spurious logic of progression and career planning. Secondly came the expansion of graduate entry and training schemes (of which Mr Eastwell is a very good example from our sample), and finally there has been the development of the business schools and the production of M.B.A. whizz-kids. The Madingley course which, significantly, developed in the early 1950s was concerned with general education, particularly in economic problems.

We are suggesting, then, that we are describing the 'battery managers' of the mid-twentieth century. They have not had time to acquire the relaxed and 'cultured' style they so much admire and would like for their children. They simply have not stopped to think and consider the implications of what has happened to them. The opportunities were there and it seemed logical to take them or to struggle to get them. Their wives have more time to think and have acquired more doubts. Free from the all-embracing ideology of 'management thinking' in the world of work, wives can ask whether all the long hours of effort are worth it. If a family really does not see the need for a second car why work hard to get more money? Once the fear that things may get worse has been overcome, the search for the plateau, the levelling off, may be on. We are arguing that, as indications of this, the wives' attitudes are more significant than their husbands'.

Looking ahead it might be of interest to consider the 'professional' style of life, and the ideal of companionate marriage, which combined may well have an impact on future generations of British managers. We are reluctant to build much more from a few straws in the wind. One thing is, however, very clear. Our managers will nearly all have twenty to thirty more years' active work life ahead of them. Their wives, many of whom are content to be at home with the children now, may get more resentful of the demands made by their husbands' work when the children have left home. However, we are not at all sure about this. It is equally plausible that those who now express some resentment will become more resigned. It is very unlikely that their husbands will change. They are what their work lets them be. Few show any clear indications that they would turn down a promotion. Only Mr Bridge, among our sixteen personally interviewed managers, had a clear personal strategy for marking time (see page 100).

This, then, is a work-dominated generation without capital or 'culture', using that word in a restricted and elitist sense. These are men who rarely question their own values – they are too much involved in the next work problem or hurdle. They trust in their own expertise or ability to take on responsibility and their wives trust in them, often obliged to do so by the mobility which has taken them from friends and kin. Typically first-generation managers, with a conception of career that is retrospective, they show their ambition most clearly in their aspirations for their children. Perhaps they will have prospective careers, such as it is imagined those in 'professions' may have. The wives may sometimes be defended from stress by their lack of education: if all they miss is a chance to spend longer looking round the shops on a Saturday they are more likely to be satisfied. Certainly there are absolutely no signs of a collective discontent.

If our managers were deeply concerned about wider social,

political or economic issues we found little evidence of it. Of course few had the time to be activists in any political sense. Their political skills were entirely devoted to manoeuvring at work. Political activity appeared to them to be individual activity and problems were seen as problems of individuals. Husbands who worked hard were diagnosed as individuals of that 'type'. It did not seem to occur to the men that other managers doing very similar work with similar responsibilities might earn much larger salaries: presumably such men would simply be considered to be 'lucky'. Men like our managers must be extraordinarily easy to manipulate. Someone more senior in the hierarchy has simply to say 'we think you're the man for the job' and off he goes like a lamb. He may discuss the implications, as far as he can see them, with his wife but of course she knows next to nothing about what the consequences of acceptance might be and her husband has little else to go on than the opinion of his superior. The more managers insist on this individualistic conception of themselves and their position, the less power they have and the more easily can they be bought off with £500, a car or a new title for an old job. Managers feel absolutely no affinity with the skilled manual workers with whom they do productivity deals. Despite being in a relatively vulnerable position, often having to respond to intuitive decisions or even whims of 'the board', they obey without a murmur, happily taking more work home to the dismay of their wives. Few appear to be concerned about wider issues such as economic development in third-world countries or even the slums of our own cities. Collective action and collective concern were not their style. Few even concerned themselves with local pressure-group activity.

We are suggesting that the main force for change is their wives. Increasing possibilities for higher education for girls and changing conceptions about the position of women in our society are, as we suggested in the last chapter, leading to different expectations about the nature of marriage and family life. When our managers are on the board they may not be able to manipulate their middle managers so easily. However, we admit that we are by no means sure which way things will change. We must stress the ambiguity and ambivalence in the attitudes we have probed. It is possible that this category of people in our society will become more materialistic. Most of our couples have achieved only a modest degree of affluence: the incentives of a larger house, a second car, more lavish and longer holidays may keep middle managers in Britain hard at the grind until the end of the century at least. Their wives may continue to have doubts, particularly those with more education, but they appreciate their comforts and may begin to find that Cornwall is much less nice than Greece for holidays. They may not therefore feel inclined to undermine the ideology which the industrial system has imposed on their husbands. Already the industrial system is using sensitivity training to keep its systems of manipulation operating smoothly.

However, many young people today, particularly those at university, appear to be obsessed about the quality and style of personal relationships. The subtleties and nuances of behaviour are understood with probably greater perceptiveness than their parents ever had. The 'feminization' of young men, which has been one of the unintended consequences of the expansion of coeducational higher education, may have helped to make many more young men sensitive to the feelings of the young women they know or live with. Marriage is probably entered into far more seriously and on a basis of greater equality than it has been at any time in the past. It seems less likely that young men who have been to university since the mid 1960s will ever imagine that they are marrying a docile housekeeper. If middle managers of the late 1970s and 1980s have been socialized at university, where personal relationships are so highly valued and acutely understood and, crucially, if they have married young women with similar backgrounds, they are less likely to be such willing slaves. This might imply an acceptance in Britain of a less affluent and less materialist style of life. How a demand to work less hard will square with Britain's entry into the Common Market is difficult to see. However, there seems little doubt that increasing education and an increased awareness of the nuances and subtleties of personal relationships will lead to different demands for, and expectations of, family life. A combination of more confident, educated and self-conscious wives and sensitivity training for their husbands may lead to a demand for more time in which to develop the marital relationship. It remains to be seen whether time or money will be most valued.

The Questionnaire which Was Sent to the Wives

UNIVERSITY OF KENT AT CANTERBURY

FACULTY OF SOCIAL SCIENCES
Project on the Career Pattern of Managers
Survey of Wife's Attitudes

1 September 1967

Dear Madam,

Please forgive me addressing you so formally but I am very much hoping that you will help me by answering some questions and I think it right that the information you give me should be treated as strictly confidential. For this reason your name will not appear on this form.

Perhaps I should briefly explain the nature of my inquiry. I am particularly interested in the interaction between a man's home and work life. When I have discussed this with managers on courses, such as the one your husband went on at Cambridge, I have been struck by the necessity of knowing more of the wife's attitudes – for example when a man moves his job his wife very often has to deal with moving the house. I am afraid that husbands aren't always the best people to describe their wife's attitudes and so I have decided to ask you directly. Maybe you have discussed these matters with your husband before, however on this occasion I would like to have *your own* replies without the benefit or otherwise of his advice!

I know that you will have to give up some of your time in order to complete this questionnaire and naturally you may well ask – what good will it do? I must give you an honest answer: I don't know. At the moment I am doing this work as a sociologist because I consider it to be an interesting and important topic. I hope it will be possible to publish something on the results of this study and I will be satisfied if this does no more than illuminate a small aspect of our complex society. Of course these results should be of interest to those who advise companies on personnel matters: some companies might well wish to reconsider their policies in the light of this and similar studies. I must emphasize here that it will be quite impossible for any information you give me to be identified as relating to you. No names will be used and the results will be presented in statistical tables. If you would like to see a copy of the report when it is published please let me know and I will ensure that you do.

I very much hope that you enjoy answering the questions. I have provided as much space as possible for comment but if you require still more space do please carry on on a separate sheet of paper. If you find any part of the questionnaire particularly interesting and would like to write to me personally I would be very glad to correspond with you. Naturally I would prefer to be able to discuss the questions with you at an interview – but I am just hoping that they will all appear clear to you.

It is very important for me to have all the forms back by *September 11th* at the latest. If you happen to be away on holiday during this period *please* do let me have the form as soon as you possibly can after you come back. Of course I need hardly add that you are not obliged to answer any question if you do not want to. However, in order to make the investigation a success I must rely on your cooperation. *Even if you think you are most untypical please do your best to answer all the questions.* It is only by getting the full range of responses that this study can carry weight.

With very many thanks for your help,

Yours sincerely,

Dr R. E. Pahl, Lecturer in Sociology.

Rutherford College,
University of Kent at Canterbury

The questionnaire which was sent to the wives

1. YOUR EDUCATION

(a) At what age did you leave school? ....

(b) What sort of school was it?

Technical ☐	Direct Grant ☐	Comprehensive ☐
Secondary ☐	Grammar/ ☐	Elementary ☐
Modern	High	Fee-paying/ ☐
		Convent

(c) Please list below all the qualifications which you gained either at school or after leaving, as a result of either full- or part-time study, e.g. secretarial diploma, degree, 'O' level in 3 subjects, S.R.N.

Dates From To	Institution in which you studied	Qualification gained

2. YOUR JOB HISTORY

(a) What was your first full-time job? ....

(b) How old were you then? ....

(c) Please list below all the jobs – full-time, and part-time if for more than about 10 hours a week – which you have had since then. Please give details – more than just 'secretary'. Please indicate if any of these jobs was in the same organization as your husband by placing a tick in Col. 4.

Dates From To	Full- or part-time	Type of Job – Both name and nature of work	Col. 4

(d) Do you have plans for work outside the home in the future?

Appendix 1

3. YOUR MARRIAGE

(a) How did you meet your husband?

(b) What was the date of your marriage? ....
    How old were you then? ....
(c) How many children have you? ....
(d) And what are their ages? ....
(e) And how many more children do you *expect* to have? ......
(f) Ideally, how many children would you *like* to have? ....

Comment

(g) How do you see yourself now? Please tick one place on the
    following scale opposite each statement.

       1 = Essentially so
       2 = Very much so
       3 = To a large extent
       4 = To a certain extent
       5 = Not really

	Scale					
Someone who is:	1	2	3	4	5	
1. Providing interesting activity for your children.						1
2. Creating a comfortable and well-run home.						2
3. A companion to your husband.						3
4. Concerned with interests of your own, e.g. pottery.						4
5. Keen to do a paid job now and again.						5
6. Keen to follow a career of your own.						6
7. Active in local clubs, church or other organizations.						7
8. A friendly person in your neighbourhood.						8

(h) In your relationship with your husband, how do you see yourself? Please tick one place on the following scale opposite each statement.

Scale

1 2 3 4 5

1. Someone to share your husband's relaxation.

2. Someone with whom he can talk over his problems.

3. Caring for the house and children.

4. Someone who enjoys entertaining his work colleagues at your home.

5. As a help to him with his work in practical ways, e.g. reading through reports.

6. As a social asset to him in his career.

1 2 3 4 5	
	1
	2
	3
	4
	5
	6

Comment

4. SOCIAL ACTIVITY

(a) Everybody has a circle of friends, some of whom may live in the immediate town or neighbourhood, while other friends, acquired during a lifetime of different jobs and different homes, may be scattered over a wide area and be kept up with through visits and letters. If you think of your own circle of friends would you say they are:

Tick once only

1. Mainly local (say up to ½-hour's journey) ☐
2. Mainly scattered about ☐
3. Equally divided between 1 and 2 ☐

This is rather a difficult point to get clear so any comments would be welcome.

Comment

(b) What about your relatives? Would you say they are

Tick once only

1. Mainly local ☐
2. Mainly scattered about ☐
3. Equally divided between 1 and 2 ☐

Comment

(c) Could you think about the local clubs to which you belong, and bodies to which you may have been elected, the church which you attend, e.g. Music Club, Young Wives Group, W.I., Parish Council, W.V.S., Social Club, Parent Teacher Association, etc. *Counting only those which you attend fairly regularly*, please list them below. Please say also whether you are an office holder in any of these clubs or organizations.

Name of club, organization or church	Office held	No. of attendances per year

5. YOUR RELATIONSHIP WITH YOUR HUSBAND'S WORK

(a) Does your husband talk to you about what went on at his work:

Tick once only

1. Every day ☐
2. Most days ☐
3. Perhaps once a week ☐
4. Less often than once a week ☐
5. Never ☐

(b) And do you feel?

Tick once only

1. You would like to know more about what goes on at his work. ☐
2. He should talk and worry less about his work when he is at home. ☐
3. You talk together about his work about the right amount. ☐
4. You can help him actively in his work. ☐

(c) If he talks about his work, does he talk:

Tick once only

1. Mainly about the people he meets and works with. ☐
2. Mainly about the work itself and its problems. ☐
3. About both people and work. ☐

Have you any other feelings on this subject which you feel the questions do not cover?

(d) Does his firm arrange occasions when colleagues and their wives can meet each other socially? Yes/No If so, are these occasions:

Tick once only

1. More than once a year ☐
2. About once a year ☐
3. Less than once a year ☐

(e) What sort of occasions are these? ....
(e.g. office party, formal dinner, etc.)

(f) What are your feelings about these occasions? ....

(g) It would be helpful to know if and how well you know your husband's colleagues' wives.
Have you, for example, been to any of their houses for a meal? ....
Or invited them to your house by themselves during the day? ....
And could you call any of them real friends? ....
How many of your husband's colleagues' wives do you know? ....
How well do you know them? ....
And how did you meet them? ....

Any other comment (Please enlarge on and explain your answers above)

6. YOUR FEELINGS ABOUT YOUR HUSBAND'S CAREER

(a) If there is a question of your husband taking up a new job, how much weight would you yourself give to the following aspects. Please tick one place on the following scale opposite each statement. 1 = Essential; 2 = very important; 3 = important; 4 = do not mind; 5 = not important:

275

Appendix 1

Scale

I 2 3 4 5

1. Educational facilities of the area.

2. The region where the job is.

3. Separation from your family or friends.

4. The actual day-to-day work which your husband would be doing.

5. The pay, prospects and general character of his job.

6. Fringe benefits and other special advantages.

7. Your own work or career.

Tick in the
appropriate box

Comment

	Yes	No
(b) Do you sometimes think your husband should change his job now?	☐	☐
Does he sometimes think he should change his job now?	☐	☐
Do you sometimes think you should move house now?	☐	☐
Does he sometimes think you should move house now?	☐	☐

Comment (please explain if 'yes' above)

(c) Most people have had times when they thought they might move to a new job, but when for one reason or another the move did not come off. Could you think of times when you and your husband have seriously considered possible moves, and fill in details about these occasions below.

The questionnaire which was sent to the wives

Date	Type of job which was under discussion	Region you would have had to live in	Reason why you did not move
1.			
2.			
3.			
4.			

(Perhaps this is a moment to stress again that all the information given here is completely confidential.)

(d) What are your feelings about moving from the place where you live? What have you found to be the chief advantages and disadvantages *for you* of recent moves? (Continue overleaf if necessary)

(e) Here are some statements about a man's career. How accurately do they reflect what you yourself *believe*? Please tick one place on the following scale opposite each statement: 1 = Always true; 2 = generally true; 3 = sometimes true; 4 = you are not sure; and 5 = you believe it is untrue:

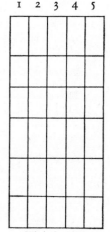

Scale

1 2 3 4 5

1. Men that rise to the top quickly often lose touch with their family and old friends.
2. Men who are 'married to their work' are less good husbands.
3. Men are more satisfied if they are fully stretched at work.
4. A man's career is like a race and naturally he must compete to do well.
5. The worries of a senior position are compensated for by a more exciting and interesting life.
6. The happiest men are those who do not take their work too seriously.

Tick in the appropriate box

(f) Here are some more statements. How much do you yourself *agree* with them? Please tick one place on the following scale opposite each statement. 1 = Agree completely; 2 = agree; 3 = agree to a certain extent; 4 = not sure; and 5 = disagree:

Scale

1   2   3   4   5

1. Once a man has got a reasonable salary and a respected position he should spend more time on his family and other interests.

2. A man ought to get the main meaning in his life from his work.

3. A man should not be too friendly with colleagues in case he is their boss one day.

4. A man's a fool to drive himself only in order to achieve a moderately greater income and vastly greater responsibility.

5. If a man has ideas it is only natural he should want the power to put them into practice.

6. Men should not get too involved with their work as this would interfere with a happy married life.

Tick in the appropriate box

I have included an extra sheet of paper to give you space to add your comments on the last question and on the questionnaire as a whole. Please enlarge on any of your answers if you feel it would be helpful for me, and add any point which you think has not been covered.

Interviewer's Check List of Topics, Themes and Questions for the Personal Interviews

LIFE STYLE

1. *What sort of a house is it?*
   Number of bedrooms, reception rooms; state of care and type of garden; situation (country, estate, suburb); garage and type of car(s)?
2. What do you like most, and like least, about *the situation* in which your house is? e.g. type of neighbourhood, access to facilities, nearness to friends or relatives, etc.?
3. What aspect of your house gives you the greatest pride?
4. What *magazines and newspapers* do you take?

Also add observations on

how much care is lavished on the house? What are the furnishings like, e.g. prewar, postwar, contemporary, antique?
are there pictures, records or books about? What sorts of books?
how much is home child-centred? Are there toys scattered about?
Is the garden obviously used for playing in?
What is the balance in the arrangement of the house between things considered 'beautiful' and those of a more 'sentimental' type – photos and so on? What interests and leisure activities are suggested by the things in the house? How self-conscious is the 'taste'?

WIFE'S INTERVIEW

1. *What sort of person do you see yourself as?*
   How do you think these other people see you? Husband; parents; siblings; best friend (specify); neighbours; other members of clubs to which you belong (specify); work colleagues (if applicable); boss; tradespeople (check alternative reference groups). (Try to explain any discrepancies in above role identities. Try to get some *hierarchy of role identities* as she sees them.)

Appendix 2

2. *Do you think you have been, or will be, a different person at different times in your life?*

What were you like, or would you like to be like, if it is in the future, before marriage, after marriage but before having children, when you had young children, with older children, when the children have left home, when your husband retires? (Try and get her self-conception at appropriate stages in her life cycle.)

3. *From what do you get your chief sense of security?*

Husband, parents, children, home, social standing, education, jobs, looks, money, beliefs, friends? (An alternative approach to her conception of her self and her central life interests.)

4. *Socialization*

What sort of person was your mother/your father? With which did you get on better? How did you get on with siblings? Who really was the strongest influence on you when you were a child?

What sort of a home was it, e.g. cultural and social atmosphere? What sort of situation was it in, e.g. country, suburb, etc.?

What time before you left home was the happiest, and what the unhappiest?

In what ways do you feel yourself to be most like, or most unlike your parents? And in what ways does life in your home resemble or differ from life in your childhood home? (Biography affecting self-conception: relationship between family of origin and family of procreation.)

5. *Aspirations* (Actual or Hypothetical)

What would you like *your daughter* to be like? What sort of job do you expect her to do? What sort of person would you like her to marry? What would you expect to be her chief source of happiness? (How much mental mobility? Is she fixed in her cultural patterns and expectations over three generations? How much awareness and acceptance of *change*? Aim at *daughter* as means of self-identification. If no children ask *if* she had a daughter.)

What sort of *education* do you want for your children? What sort of qualifications would you like them to end up with? Do you think you have different ideas about education from your own parents?

Check list of topics, themes and questions

6. *Expectation of married relationship*

   What sort of *married relationship did you expect* to have before you married? Has it turned out as you expected? Why is it different, if it is? (Her definition both of 'relationship' and how it may have changed.)

7. *Source of support*

   Many married couples find that they have a feeling of growing apart, because husband and wife live in such separate worlds. If this were to happen to you . . . to whom would you turn to talk it over? *Prompt:* Parents, friends, doctor, priest?

8. *Sex*

   (FIRST: Ask if she minds talking about sex: if doubtful don't continue.)

   How important is sex, to you, to your husband, in your marriage? Have your feelings about sex changed? What is, or has in the past been, your chief worry about sex? Whose job is it to tell the children about sex? (Is this the foundation now or was it in the past? If *not* very important then what were main 'important' factors in marriage? Duty?)

9. *Personal plans*

   What are your weekends like? What do you all like to do? Do you feel there is a conflict between the demands of your husband and your children? Whose home is it predominantly at the weekend – your husband's for rest, your children's for amusement, yours? (Emphasizing *choice:* what *she* would like, viewing it on her own.)

10. *Employment*

    (Check whether she has a job, or has plans for one: see first questionnaire.)

    If yes – what is, or will be, your chief reason for working? If no – what do you feel about people like you working, when their domestic commitments make it possible for them to work? (Home–work role tension: is this *defined* as a 'problem'?)

11. *Personal autonomy and husband's attitudes*

    What does your husband feel about *your weekday life,* when he's not at home? About your job, if you have one or are thinking of having one? About the clubs to which you belong? Your pattern of life when he is not at home? Do you feel you have a life of your own? (How much is her life 'her own' and how much does she feel constrained or moulded by spouse?)

12. *Friends and neighbours*
    (a) *Neighbours:*   How well known? What is *definition* of a "good" neighbour?
    (b) *Three Best Friends:*   Do they know each other? How well does husband know them? How met? where live? what contact?

      Explore networks.

13. *Social skills and other – direction*
    e.g. 'When you move to a new area how do you – or how would you – set about *making friends* for yourself and finding friends for your children?'
    e.g. Friends in for coffee or tea? How often? How do you feel about having people in?

14. *Voluntary associations*
    (see first questionnaire for details)
    (a) Assessment of *importance* of these activities. Are they missed?
    (b) Reasons for such activity – 'ought' you take part? duty or whim?
    (c) General view of role in 'community'. (What does she think she is?)
    (d) Religion?

15. *Constraints*
    (a) Mobility. Drive? Car? How much use? How get about?
    (b) Human slave – cleaning, with children, in garden, other?
    (c) Mechanical slaves – washing, dishes, gadgets, etc.

16. *Attitude to husband's work pattern*
    (a) Is he *away from home* much? How do you feel, what adaptation?
    (b) Distance/time from work – far separated? Does it seem remote – have you been to his work place?
    (c) Fringe benefits. What do you get? How important are they?

17. *Moves* (last one or two in detail)
    What things talked about when a move is planned? How do you set about choosing a house? Do you find a house and then a school or vice versa? (if move a lot). How feel about sending children to boarding school? If you had to move next month what would you miss most?

Check list of topics, themes and questions

1. *What sort of person do you see yourself as?*
   (Hierarchy of role identities, as for wife)

2. *Do you think you have been, or will be, a different person?*
   (As for wife's interview, but also ask whether he feels he might have been different with a different wife, a different job, or living in a different locality)

3. *From what do you get your chief sense of security?*
   (As for wife's interview)

4. *Socialization*
   (As for wife's interview)

5. *Aspirations*
   (As for wife, but emphasize son instead of daughter)

6. *First job*
   How chosen? Any plan?

7. *Subsequent jobs*
   Explain how got into each (full detail). How did you hear about them (ads., privately)? Pros and cons of each – discussed with wife?

8. *Overview of career*
   How *orderly*? Logical progression or sharp jumps? Does he think he's come a long way? Does he feel frustrated by *lack* of progression?

9. *Self-assessment of career*
   How has he done in comparison with father/brothers/best friends at school/other significant others? If you think of your career as 0–100 how far up it are you now? What job represents 100?

10. *Important determining factors* (other than own abilities)
    Social background – dress, accent, etc. Friends/graft. Support of own family/wife (specify)? Or merit (amplify)?

11. *Future prospects*
    Whom would you talk it over with? Colleagues at work, friends, wife, boss, or whom (and how influential is each?)? Do you have a *plan* for the next few years, for the long term? What is it? How realistic? If no plan, why not?

12. *Income*
    Run through each stage if possible. What income do you have now? Is this adequate recompense for responsibility you have? What do you expect? Highest realistic income?

13. '*Getting ahead in the world*' – meaning for him.
    What is important for you in life? What *really* matters – work, non-work, home, friends?

14. *Voluntary activities*
    What organizations/clubs/church, etc. does he belong to? Expressive or instrumental? Voluntary work – treasurer, fund raiser, etc. What out-of-home, non-work activities – sport (golf, sailing, squash) or hobbies (car rally, bird watching). (Try to assess what the home locality means – if anything – to him. Does the *place* have significance for his style of life?)

15. What are his greatest *achievements* in life so far? And what does he expect in the future? Are such achievements all work centred? How much have his aspirations been modified through experience? How much does he want *material* things – dishwasher, two cars (and sports car?), etc., and how hard would he want to struggle to get these material awards?

16. People all have *plans*, for the day, for the week, for the month, for the year and for a longer period. How much is he conscious of this *planning* process? How far ahead is he planning? Are they all *work* plans or do his wife, family and other non-work activities also figure? Probe his notion of *balance* or *mix* in his plans. How much *choice* does he think he has now? What times in the past did he have more/less choice? Try to go over important plan-deciding periods.

17. Does he feel he is likely to get what he wants by his own efforts alone or by collective action? What class and how vote?

HUSBAND AND WIFE TOGETHER

1. *Decision-making*
   (a) Ask them to name what they consider to be *important* decisions and *order* these in importance.
       Prompt: Children's education; sort of house or car; wife taking a job; holidays, use of leisure time, who and how they entertain.
   (b) Were decisions taken primarily by one or other? Probe which?
   (c) *Recreate* decision-making process particularly for last move of house/job and decisions about schooling (where relevant). (Interviewer to choose the most relevant thing to explore.)

Check list of topics, themes and questions

2. *Conjugal relationship expressed*

(a) *Home activities:*	sharing (?) Children and household tasks at weekend. *Probe* Saturday p.m., Sunday a.m. What ordering of priorities?
(b) *Free time:*	What is this? Segregated/joint activities, e.g. joint activities – going out together: frequency, where, when – holidays – ideally and actually (last). Are there separate styles or joint styles – and what is essence of this style?
(c) *Entertaining:*	Burden or pleasure for one or both? Specify recent examples. Who, when, topics of conversation, purpose, attitudes, etc.

Whose needs and demands come first when? And how much does their conjugal relationship affect *his* work life (summarize feelings)?

3. *Kin links*
   (a) Mostly wife's, husband's or both? Probe balance between two.
   (b) Strength of links. How is contact maintained?
   (c) Which are closest? Why?
   (d) What sort of obligation and responsibilities do husband and wife feel they ought to have towards relations? Difference between two?

4. *Self-assessment of relationship* (both)
   How would each describe it? How does it compare with relationship their respective parents had? Or your friends now? (*Check:* reference groups)

Problems and Procedures of Interviewing
by Marie Corbin

ANYBODY who has ever stood on the doorstep of an unknown house, mustering a smile and a greeting for its unknown occupants, will appreciate at least some of the feelings of an interviewer arriving at such a house to talk to her respondents. People who have not been the subjects of a sociological interview may not find it so easy to imagine what the person opening the door feels about the imminent encounter with an inquisitive stranger. An enormous literature exists in the social sciences on interviewing techniques and methodology in general, but this appendix does not seem to be the appropriate place to discuss it. Rather I would focus attention on the more direct problem of how a small number of ordinary people reacted to the intrusion into their lives for one day of an equally ordinary interviewer, who was frequently cold, wet, tired and crumpled from a train journey half way across England, and who was often as nervous of meeting them as they seemed to be of meeting her.

Sociological reports seldom reflect the more mundane personal experiences involved in gathering sociological data, and sometimes when perusing elegant theories and complicated tables it is difficult even to remember that what these reflect are the results of just such experiences. The connection between the reality of people's lives and the sociological models used to analyse them often seems to be a very tenuous one, because, somewhere along the line, these experiences must finally reduce to numbers, holes in computer cards, tables and chapters of books, if any attempt is to be made at generalization and comparison. However, the image of efficient, 'scientific' investigators systematically collecting coherent facts and neatly formulated opinions to be fed unproblematically into an even more efficient computer falls far short of what characterizes much sociological investigation.

Any kind of interviewing involves at least two people at any one time in what is basically a highly artificial situation with its concomitant discomforts, embarrassments and prejudices. Two people, hitherto unknown to each other, and often of different age, sex, background and disposition, come together fleetingly for the sole purpose of one of them finding out as much as possible about what the other thinks on a defined range of topics. While two people are involved, it is essentially a one-way process, and one that is subject for its effectiveness to the willingness of the people being interviewed to invite a complete stranger into their homes, and to answer questions with patience and honesty. Interviewers may phrase questions carefully so that they are not leading, devise means of checking the consistency of answers by approaching one topic in a variety of ways, order questions in a particular way to minimize the effect of one answer upon another, and ask the same questions of different respondents so that answers are comparable, but they cannot control effectively how a person will react when facing them across a room over a sheaf of papers. From the interviewer's standpoint a single interview is one step in a series of meetings whose ends are well defined, whose purposes are clear, and all of which can be viewed as part of a larger whole. For the interviewees, the interview is an experience in most ways unrelated to the rest of their lives, and the point of which is not always entirely clear. It is interesting, I think, to consider how people do act in such circumstances.

ARRANGING THE INTERVIEW

Most sociological or anthropological studies take as their field of interest either the whole of, or a random sample of, the population of a community, a work place, an institution, or a limited geographical area. This study, however, has been concerned with a small collection of people who can be called managers because of the positions they hold, although their jobs differ greatly in responsibility and salary. No two of the personally interviewed managers work for the same company. While all can be called 'middle class' because they are managers, they come from varying family backgrounds, educational levels, and regions of Britain. No two were born in the same town. Perhaps, though, for the practical problem of interviewing some of the managers, the most significant factor was that no two of them live in the same town.

In fact, the eighty-six managers and their wives who completed the mailed questionnaires (Appendix 1) lived as far apart as Edinburgh and Cornwall. Place of residence was one of the main criteria used in the selection of a smaller number of managers to be asked if they were willing to be interviewed in their own homes, in the hope that it would be possible to gather a detailed case history on at least one manager from each region of Britain. The other criteria used for the selection of this smaller group were the types of jobs they held, the extent to which they had moved jobs and residence, and the sorts of family backgrounds from which they and their wives came, as well as R. E. Pahl's personal knowledge of the men from being a tutor on the Madingley course (page 6). As so much travelling was involved and money was limited, only twenty-nine of the eighty-six couples were asked if they would be interviewed, on the assumption that about twenty would agree.

A letter was sent to the wives of the twenty-nine managers explaining that we would like to follow up the mailed questionnaire with a personal interview and asking if they and their husbands would be prepared to help. Of the twenty-nine, five refused outright, their reasons varying from 'not sufficiently extrovert' or 'not enough free time' to expressions of general disapproval of personal interviews. No replies were received to six of the letters. Of the remaining eighteen couples who did agree to be interviewed only sixteen actually were. One interview was abandoned because of ill health in the family, and in the other case the husband withdrew his acceptance at the last moment. At this stage there was insufficient time and money to bring the total number of couples interviewed up to twenty by seeking the help of the remaining managers and their wives.

The fact that the couples did live so far apart, and that the interviews were carried out during a period when many couples were away on holiday (June to October 1968), made it difficult to arrange interviews. Most appointments had to be made well in advance in order that both husband and wife should be free to see me on the same day, and that couples living in approximately the same area should be interviewed during the same week. The final arrangements were made through the wives, by letter or telephone, and often included an invitation for me to have dinner with the couple on the day of the interview. I was also sent lists of hotels, detailed road instructions and even maps by many of the couples who lived in fairly distant suburbs or country areas.

The couples were asked if it would be possible for me to talk to the wife in the afternoon and the husband in the early evening, as well as to both of them together later in the evening. Most of the interviews were conducted in this way, but for a number I met the husband first in the evening, then talked to him and his wife later in the evening, returning the following morning to interview the wife. On average I needed to talk with both husband and wife separately for three hours each, and with both of them together for a minimum of an hour and a half. The actual schedule depended largely on the arrangements the couples themselves had made and often on the peculiarities of the local public transport. For most of the interviews I arrived at the house between 1 and 2 p.m., and on many visits I was still there at 11.30 p.m. or midnight.

THE INTERVIEWS

The personal interviews with the couples were intended to provide case histories to illustrate points brought out in the more general study. As such they had two basic aims. The first was to clarify or amplify some of the answers on the original questionnaires, and the second was to construct as complete and detailed a picture as possible of most aspects of the lives of the couples, with particular reference to the relationship between their family life and the husband's career.

So that different questions could be pursued to differing degrees with each couple and could be directly related to the information they had already given, the interviews had to be fairly unstructured. Consequently a formal questionnaire with set questions in a predefined sequence was not used. Instead a list of topics to be covered during the course of the interviews was drawn up, and this was used primarily as a guide for the interviews. The list is reproduced as Appendix 2 above. The actual questions asked did not necessarily correspond to those appearing on the list, and where one topic led more naturally into another this sequence was followed rather than the more arbitrary ordering on the list. The same starting questions on a particular topic were used in nearly all cases, though the whole of the interview was kept at a 'conversational' rather than a 'question and answer' level, unless a respondent was particularly reticent in which case many more direct questions had to be asked.

The direction of these questions and the interpretations of the answers are fully discussed in the main body of the book. In this section I wish simply to mention some of the difficulties encountered in asking the sorts of questions needed to give the required information. The list of topics and questions taken as a reference sheet for the interviews indicates the sorts of answers at which it was hoped to arrive, but unhappily for social scientists, if perhaps fortunately for the rest of the world, most people do not go around thinking of themselves, their lives and the way they lead them in the same terms that social scientists use to describe them.

THE WIFE'S INTERVIEW

The interview with the wife was primarily concerned with finding out the sort of life she led, and to what extent this, and the way she viewed it, was determined by the fact of being a manager's wife. The interview had two main sections, the first attempting to form some general picture of her ideas about herself and how these had changed over a considerable period of her life; the second asking mainly for detailed, factual accounts of some aspects of her day-to-day life.

However, to arrive at a 'hierarchy of role identities' or 'self-conceptions at appropriate stages of the life cycle' by asking people a series of questions about how they saw themselves, was a process that not only took a great deal of time, but was also frequently unproductive. During the course of the interviews the questions were approached in a number of different ways, all of which tried to avoid introducing the concept of role. Many of these questions were not successful, particularly with the women. Often the questions, however phrased, produced in response a series of adjectives which the women would use to describe themselves, such as 'ordinary' or 'patient'. These adjectives were seldom in combination with any noun other than 'woman', and generally did not refer to any particular situation. Answers tended to be along the lines 'I'm fairly ordinary' or 'I've more confidence now than I used to have'. Attempts to follow up these answers by getting the women to tie them into particular circumstances or changes in their lives also had little success, and it was difficult to enlarge on the questions without predetermining the answers. Their ideas about themselves as mothers, wives, career women and so forth, and the conflicts engendered by the differing demands of these roles were much more adequately expressed in the second half of the interview when they talked about the organization of their home life, their attitudes to their husbands' work, and their own involvements outside the home.

There was a noticeable difference in the ease with which the men and women replied to these particular questions, and it did seem that the men were much more immediately aware of conflict between their home lives and their work lives. On the other hand, the men in general were much more articulate in expressing their ideas about themselves, and appeared to be more accustomed to this type of self-analysis. For many of the women, the whole of the first section of the interview seemed too abstract, and they were frequently disconcerted by the questions, commenting that they found them difficult to answer and that they did not spend much time thinking about themselves. Some apologized for their answers, either because they did find difficulty in expressing adequately what they wanted to say, or because they thought that what they did think was so 'uninspired' as to be of no interest. Yet others were worried that the whole procedure was too introspective to be a good thing, or that an honest self-appraisal would tend to sound immodest.

Many fairly specific questions were needed to build up a picture of the 'social and cultural atmosphere' of the homes from which the wives came. As initial responses to more general questions about the sorts of things they used to do at home were often of the 'what most families do, I suppose' type, a considerable amount of time was spent on this part of the interview, even though very detailed information was not required. In most cases a whole series of questions were asked on the father's income and occupation, and the leisure activities of the family – how much entertaining they did, whether or not they themselves had friends in, how much they went out together as a family and what sorts of outings they were, how they spent their evenings, and whether or not they read, listened to music, played cards, and so forth.

Most wives were more comfortable with the second section of the interview which was concerned with their own activities. As the questions were straightforward there were few problems, although the exploration of the wife's contacts with her neighbours and friends, and the accounts of the moves the family had made were fairly time-consuming.

All the women asked said they were willing to talk about sex, though more often than not their replies were brief and they showed some signs of embarrassment. If anyone else was present during this section of the interview the questions on sex were omitted entirely, and if the wives were at all uncomfortable the subject was not pursued. Where possible these questions were linked with comments the wives had made on their written questionnaires about family size, and in these cases the subject developed more naturally.

The extent to which the wives were prepared to discuss their problems and difficulties varied. With some the interview was the opening of a floodgate, and questions designed to procure a glimpse of their personal lives brought forth highly detailed accounts of grievances, dissatisfactions and frustrations. Most were more cautious in their replies and seemed deliberately concerned to try to view their own situation objectively.

THE HUSBAND'S INTERVIEW

For the husband the main focus of the interview was on his own career, what he thought it was, and what it meant to him. The interview was in three parts, the first of which was identical to that for the wife and suffered from similar, though less acute, problems. The second section asked for a complete and detailed account of the husband's occupational history, his attitudes towards his work and the income he received, while the third was more concerned with his interests outside work and their effects on him, his future plans, past achievements, and the everyday organization of his life.

As the section on careers mainly called for descriptions of events, the questions were easy to answer, if rather involved and complicated in detail. Most of the men, especially those who were conscious of having come from humbler origins, were pleased to be asked to describe the various stages leading to their present positions. While they were all quite willing to discuss their financial situations, they were more reluctant to talk about the reasons for their various promotions. Their diffidence in this respect seemed again to be related to the fact that to talk of their successes on such specific occasions involved them, directly or indirectly, in citing their own abilities. Often they prefaced their remarks on this subject with an apology for 'blowing their own trumpets'. In fact, their careers and achievements were generally only viewed in retrospect as having any logical basis, and they frequently gave the impression that their present positions had been arrived at as the result of a number of purely fortuitous steps.

The questions in these two sections to a certain extent presupposed a much more structured overview of their careers and work life than most of the men appeared to have. In this sense they had difficulty in talking about planning in general, and about planning in relation to their careers in particular. When they did talk of plans they referred to the immediate future in terms of days or weeks, and then these plans were concerned with the day-to-day organization of their lives both at home and at work. The idea of 'balance and mix' in their plans was consequently difficult to pursue.

Attempts to find out how conscious any manager was of how different he as a person might have been with a different wife, a different job, and living in a different place, met with little response. Most managers thought that all these factors had affected them in some undefined way, and that they were at least partially products of their personal experiences in these areas, but to ask them to divorce the man from the experiences was perhaps a futile enterprise. Similarly the reactions of the men, when asked to choose from interrelated parts of their lives the thing that mattered most, suggested that this was an abstraction that had little meaning for them. Some men chose health and happiness, but most asserted that their wives and families were their primary concerns. They were often aware of the seeming contradiction between the stated importance of their families and the amount of time and attention they devoted to their work. Some claimed that their wives thought they put work before all else, and many wives confirmed this. In turn, the men believed that what they did was for their families. As the man who considered the most important factor in his life to be his belief in a god might be unable to demonstrate this to others by the amount of time he was seen in prayer, so the managers often found it difficult to reconcile, even for themselves, the apparent discrepancy between their beliefs and their performances.

In fact, throughout their interviews the men were often concerned with analysing their own answers and what these answers said about them as men. They would also frequently see the general direction of the questions and proceed to discuss the topic in depth with little or no prompting from me. As many men also queried the relevance of particular questions (and they showed no hesitation in remarking that they thought certain questions were silly), it was not easy on occasions to keep the interview confined to the subject in hand. The discursive nature of many of the interviews was added to by the insistence of many of the men on trying to distinguish between parts of their answers that should be recorded and others that were supposed to be 'off the record'. They were, in general, more articulate in expressing their views both on the topics under discussion and the interview itself than were the women. On the other hand, they were much more reluctant to comment on problems relating to their families or their wives.

Appendix 3

THE JOINT INTERVIEW

The interview with both the husband and wife together was the shortest of the interviews, covering only four major topics, but was the most difficult to conduct. The first topic, 'decision-making', had similar problems to that on 'planning' in the husband's interview. Most couples knew what they considered to be important steps taken, or to be taken, in their lives, but they did not tend to think of these as being decisions or processes involving a series of steps taken by one or other or both. Most decisions were arrived at after vague talk around the subject for a considerable period of time, and the final outcome was seen as being something that 'happened'. Couples were frequently unable even to remember what their considerations had been at the time, except in the most general way. Some of the men said there were few actual decisions involved in their careers, as they would not consider the acceptance of an offered promotion to be a decision on their part. On several occasions I was asked what I meant by a decision, which I normally countered by asking them to talk about what they meant by a decision. Under such circumstances, the 're-creation of a decision-making process' turned out to be a fairly elusive pursuit.

Like most general topics in the interviews, the questions on how the couples spent their leisure time and their attitudes to entertaining and so forth needed a considerable amount of probing on specific instances and examples. The same was true of the information on kin links, although the questions were confined primarily to their respective parents and siblings with a few more general questions on the extent to which the couples maintained contact with more distant members of their families.

The briefest answers given to any questions from all the interviews were usually those to direct questions about their marriages. Even people who had commented independently on their dissatisfactions with their marriage in other parts of the interview almost invariably concluded, perhaps unsurprisingly, that their marriages were far better than those of other couples.

The problems faced in the joint interview were not so much inherent in the questions as in the interview situation. Inevitably the fact that a third party was included affected individual responses on more personal questions. I was often aware of the hesitancy with which both husbands and wives responded in the joint interview. In particular, wives who had been fairly loquacious when on their own remained relatively quiet. Attempts to involve both parties equally in the interview by referring remarks specifically to the husband or the wife did not always succeed. Where they did succeed, it sometimes proved to be such a viable means of bringing out both sides of the picture that on occasions a tactful retreat or change of subject was called for to prevent differences of opinion developing into the continuation of long-standing arguments.

GENERAL PROBLEMS

The main problem with the interviews was the attempt to glean a large amount of detailed information from each couple in a very short period of time. Most couples gave their time and energy willingly enough, but at the end of the day many of them were showing signs of restlessness. As an interviewer I found it extremely difficult to maintain throughout, in most cases, eight hours of interviewing the degree of concentration necessary to ensure that all questions were followed up completely. In many interviews I had to choose between pursuing one question to a satisfactory answer and leaving out many of the other questions. Had sufficient money been available it would have been preferable in some ways to have made several visits to each couple to try to cover exhaustively and systematically the wide range of topics on the list. As it was, because of the pressure of time, many of the ambiguities of answers went unnoticed or were the result of insufficient time. On the few occasions where we did have a break overnight the answers were more complete.

However, an attempt to split interviews into various stages over a longer period does involve asking those who have said they are willing to be interviewed to give up an even greater amount of time to the study. It is not only possible that such a suggestion would discourage many couples from participating in the first place, but might also run the risk of them changing their minds when only part of the data has been collected. It is hard to assess to what extent this would have been true of these sixteen couples, as many of them told me not only to get in touch with them again if I needed more information, but to drop in to see them should I ever be in their area.

On the other hand, even arranging one visit caused organizational problems. Many women had had to make special arrangements for collecting children from school, and husbands had made special efforts to come home early from work (a fact which many wives commented on favourably). A few interviews, or at least parts of them, had to be carried out in places other than the couples' homes to fit in with the family schedules. I accompanied one manager and his young son to the local swimming pool, where he alternated between cheering his son in the races and answering my questions. I drove with wives to pick up children from school, scribbling frantically as we went. I went to the office of one manager and spent a couple of hours in competition with his work colleagues and his telephone, and I interviewed yet another in the bar of my hotel.

The need to adjust to family timetables meant that frequently I was unable to talk to both husband and wife privately. Mostly the wives were on their own during the afternoons, with the exception of children and, in one case, a teenage niece. For most of the husbands' interviews the wives were present. Even though I knew the wife's presence was probably influencing her husband's answers, as an interviewer and a guest it was not possible for me to suggest that she should leave us alone. Sometimes the couples themselves anticipated the difficulty. On several occasions the wife remarked that if the interview with her husband was anything like her own, it was only fair that he should also have the opportunity to talk with me in private. Other times the husband suggested to his wife that she should 'go and do something in the kitchen'.

The problem of having the wives present was not that they answered for their husbands or actively interfered with what they were saying (with one exception), but was simply that many of the questions bore directly or indirectly on the relationship between the two of them. If part of the interview was done in private and the other part with a third party present there was usually a change in the type of answers I received, and one manager did confess to me afterwards that he had found his wife's presence inhibiting and had not been as frank during the time she was with us.

As the interviews did touch on some fairly personal aspects of the lives of the couples I had decided not to use a tape recorder for these interviews. This decision was reinforced by my own self-consciousness when using a recorder and a personal conviction that many other people feel the same way. The length of the interview and the constant interruptions and changes of locations would also, I think, have made the use of a tape recorder more obtrusive than in many other interview situations. I did ask a number of the couples if they would have minded the interview being taped, and most said it would have put them off in one way or another.

Problems and procedures of interviewing

As I write very quickly I was able to take down almost complete answers, recording factual information in note form but keeping verbatim records of opinions and ideas. Immediately on returning from the interviews the reports were dictated and typed. This rather cumbersome method of recording the data allowed us to keep very detailed accounts of the interviews and did not cause a great analytical problem afterwards as there were only sixteen of them.

THE COUPLES' EXPECTATIONS

The couples had agreed to participate in a situation in which they were largely unsure of what to expect and, as most of the interviews had been arranged well in advance, they had had some time in which to anticipate them. It seemed that many of the couples had spent some time pondering what form the interviews would take. Apart from guessing games as to whether the interviewer herself would be young or old, easy going or 'terrifyingly academic', both husbands and wives had wondered exactly what sorts of questions they would be asked. The men found it hard to imagine what more they could be asked about their careers than was already known. The women were particularly worried that they would not be able to give 'correct' answers, or that questions would show them up as not being well read, well informed, or well educated. They were frequently relieved to find that the questions were primarily concerned with their personal opinions and activities relating to home and family and their own life histories.

Several wives told me that they had looked out and read on the previous night the copy of the Pahls' article from *The Graduate Appointments Register*, April 1968 (which had been sent several months previously as a matter of course to all who completed the mailed questionnaire), so that they would know more about what was going on and would be able to discuss it more intelligently. One couple told me they had discussed my forthcoming visit at some length and decided that it would not be worth my while coming such a great distance unless they were prepared to answer fully anything I cared to ask. One man confided to me, in the absence of his rather shy wife, that she had been so nervous about the whole thing that she had tried for several days to persuade him to telephone me to cancel the appointment. As he had apparently been responsible for accepting in the first place, he had refused to do so. He said he was glad he had refused as he felt she had enjoyed it and that it had been good for her. It was, in fact, a very successful interview.

The expectations of actual questions were well demonstrated by one wife who had been convinced that the one thing I was sure to ask her was whether or not she knew how much her husband earned. In preparation she had asked him the night before, 'not', she claimed, 'that I didn't know; I just wanted to make sure I'd got the exact figure right'.

The couples who did not tell me that they had had some apprehensions about my visit were in the minority, and the points about which they had worried varied tremendously, from some of those mentioned above to the wife whose major preoccupation had been whether I would like all the dishes included in a fairly elaborate dinner prepared in my honour. The most general expectation, however, seemed to have been that the interview would be much more structured and that the questions would have been more narrowly defined.

RECEPTION

To describe the diversity in the houses and life styles of the managers would be almost as difficult as to describe the differences in the couples themselves. The couples were a mixture of the middle-aged and the young, the tidy and the untidy, the elegant and the casual, and so were their homes. As their incomes varied so did their surroundings, though it did not necessarily follow that those with the highest salaries lived in the most luxurious style. All lived in suburban areas, though the houses ranged from the small semi-detached, through the 'box' on the new estate, to the recently built 'Georgian' detached.

Some couples, usually among the older and better-paid managers without very young children, lived in large, expensive houses with elegant and 'tasteful' furnishings that gave the general impression of affluence. Such houses were inevitably neat, tidy and well polished. Most of the remaining managers had young children, and the houses reflected this, the emphasis being on family use rather than on uncluttered appearance. It was, of course, difficult to judge such things as 'the extent to which the home was child-centred' and 'how much care was lavished on the house' as I had the distinct impression that many wives had cleared up before I arrived. If not, they are indeed greatly to be admired for their abilities as housewives. I was in general impressed by the extent to which preparations had been made for my visit, and often when I arrived afternoon tea had been laid out, tables set for dinner and a meal already prepared. The women were dressed and poised for the encounter, and one felt it necessary to apologize for her appearance in slacks when I inadvertently arrived a little earlier than anticipated.

While most couples were polite and distant and in some cases obviously nervous at the beginning of the interview, the length of time I was in the house, my participation in the activities of the family, and the nature of the questions themselves overcame this reserve. Only two interviews never reached an informal stage, and proceeded very much on the basis of brief answers to a series of direct questions. In only one of these two cases was I made to feel I was really being a nuisance. This was also the only case in which the couple did not say they had enjoyed the interview and indeed did not appear to have done so. The two more formal interviews took much less time, and when I left the houses I knew much less about the way the couples actually lived than I did after the other interviews, where frequently a chance remark or conversation over dinner gave a greater insight into their lives than any direct question. In some of the other cases I was incorporated into the home to the extent of being given, among other things, babies to bottle feed, children to read to, dogs to play with, dishes to dry, tables to set, and recipes to copy during my visit.

The reception I met with from the majority of the couples would have been envied by any interviewer who has ever had a door slammed in his face. Obviously the extent to which the wives and I had been in touch beforehand, the couples' previous knowledge of the study, and the fact that in most cases I had come a long way to talk to them, set the interviews on a different footing from most. However, the amount of personal kindness and hospitality I met with was overwhelming and could in no way have been taken for granted. I was invited to lunch or dinner or both by all but four of the couples, and one of these four apologized for not being able to do so because of prior commitments. Some of these invitations were issued in advance of my visit, on other occasions I was asked to stay and take 'pot luck'. The meals I ate with the families ranged from a lunch of baked beans on toast to a candle-light dinner of considerable expertise served amid an impressive array of linen, cut glass and silver. Whether I was treated lavishly or whether I had what was going, I was made to feel welcome. I was plied with cups of tea, coffee and sandwiches, and drinks. Concern was expressed for my comfort and safety, and I was driven to my hotel, seen onto my train, and offered accommodation for the night. One couple living not too far away insisted on driving me all the way home, and I caught one wife slipping a packet of biscuits into my briefcase for my return journey. It would be interesting to know if this kind of hospitality would have been typical of the majority of couples who were not interviewed, or if indeed it was the more 'extrovert' and hospitable couples who had agreed to be interviewed in the first place.

When the interviews were over, most couples volunteered some kind of comment on their feelings about them. Happily nobody thought it had been too gruelling an experience, though many heaved a visible sigh of relief when the stream of questions finally ended. The most frequent comments referred to the 'therapeutic' value of the interviews and many people said it had been rather like spending an afternoon or evening on the psychiatrist's couch. Other remarks ranged from the very frequent 'What on earth can you do with all that stuff?' through 'I don't see what it's got to do with my career' and 'It's the first time I've stopped to think of some of these things – it was very interesting', to 'It's been lovely to have someone listen to me for all these hours without once contradicting me.' On the other hand, I was asked if I ever felt I would like to argue with them about what they did think, and one man attempted to turn the tables on me by asking me 'potted' versions of many of my own questions. With considerable delight he informed me that it was only fair I should take my turn as I was leaving with so much information about him and his wife. He, along with other husbands, jokingly said he hoped I never decided to change my job and go in for blackmail.

The extent to which the couples were interested in my work and home life varied, but most did have some questions once the interviews were over. They were particularly interested in my own relationship with my husband and how this was affected by my work in general and my particular task of chasing round the country interviewing managers. Most were also curious about how the other couples who had been interviewed had received me in their homes. Many asked who else besides themselves was being interviewed, as most knew of each other from their participation in the Madingley course. I avoided giving names on such occasions to prevent identification from the published results on such small numbers. In one case this was not possible as two of the couples were fairly close friends and they had already exchanged the information that they were being interviewed. The inquiries about the

participation of other managers named by them were often surrounded by a certain amount of innuendo about the approachability
of the person and the likelihood of my 'getting any information out
of him'. Almost all the couples expressed an interest in seeing the
published results of the study and how the information they had
given would be used.

COMMENTS

Even though before my visit I knew much more about the couples
than they knew about me, I was unable to approach the interviews
without some qualms. I was asking for a great deal of their time,
and many of the questions were personal. I also knew that interviewing can be an uncomfortable experience if respondents are
suspicious, hostile, fidgety, nervous, pressed for time, or think
that the interviewer is a nuisance. It therefore came as a very pleasant
relief to be shown not only the hospitality I have already mentioned,
but also a great deal of patience and frankness with my delving into
their personal lives.

My own preconceptions about the middle class, based on reading other studies of the middle class and, to a certain extent, my
own experience of being middle class, had led me to suppose that
the couples would be more reluctant to discuss many of the topics
with a complete stranger. Had most couples known specifically
what questions were to be asked, I think they might well have
refused to be interviewed at all. (One couple told me this was true
of themselves, but added that they had enjoyed doing it and to have
missed it would have been a pity.) As the couples had agreed to the
interviews without having much idea of what was entailed, I
stressed at the beginning of each interview that they should
stop me if there were topics or questions which they did not wish
to discuss. Though in some instances I was clearly given the briefest
possible response, nobody ever refused to answer a question. This
in itself is not surprising, since an evasion is more socially comfortable than a direct refusal. What did surprise me was that I was given
much more detailed information on some topics than was demanded
by the questions. As most questions were completely open it was
entirely up to the couples to answer in the length and detail they
saw fit. A great deal of the very personal detail was given spon-
taneously, as such topics were seldom pushed in any way.

On the whole it was about their personal relationships that the
couples were most surprisingly frank, although the women were

more inclined than the men to be talkative about their marital problems than were the men. The extent to which past and present grievances, disharmonies or unfortunate experiences were recounted varied, but many of the remarks made were not consistent with the image of the reticent, 'putting a good face on it', middle-class Briton.

Not all couples were as open in their replies as others, and many probably had no problems or unfortunate experiences to reveal. Also, as the remarks were usually made in the absence of the spouse, some husbands and wives had more opportunities than others to talk about their difficulties. I had not expected that, after such a short acquaintance, I would be given information such as that one wife did not think she liked her husband any more, that one husband thought that his wife hated the sight of him, that one couple thought their marriage was a complete failure.

Even if one disregards the extremely revealing comments of the few couples who did appear to be facing very immediate problems, the responses to the questions throughout were much fuller than I had anticipated. Some of the couples obviously enjoyed talking about themselves, and most seemed to feel they were doing a service in giving information and so contributing to a scientific investigation and an existing body of knowledge. Having previously worked in a society where attitudes to personal information are very different, and where such information is treated as private property to which other people have as little right as to another man's wife or house, I found the tacit acceptance that I should be given the fullest possible answers to be striking. However, in such a society, where most relationships are confined to the local community, to have information about another person is to hold power over him. In contrast, in our own society people are accustomed to giving information to various representatives of the State, and often have experience of being asked for their opinions on various issues from the merits of different soap powders to the adequacy of the present government. In such circumstances the social scientist is, I suppose, just one more stranger asking questions.

I did wonder, though, if the couples who talked so freely to me were, for example, so frank about their marital problems to members of their own social circles. The lives of these particular couples seemed to centre around the husband's career to the exclusion of almost everything else. To the extent that members of their social circles were people who could influence the husband's career they may well have been in a similar situation to that faced by members of a face-to-face community. It is easy to understand why a wife might be reluctant to tell the wives of her husband's colleagues, subordinates or bosses that she had never been sexually satisfied in her marriage. For these few couples, the presence of an impartial interviewer who was completely removed from their work and social life, may simply have provided an outlet for many things which otherwise would have been left unsaid.

The frequent references to the psychiatrist's couch also seemed indicative of how many couples saw the interview situation, and I often felt that my position was regarded as being similar to that of a lawyer, a doctor, a psychiatrist or a priest. The acceptance of this peculiar, impersonal, professional role was implicit in many of the attitudes I met with. One manager who, without any prompting from me, talked about the worries he had had about his sexual life also commented 'I'm not embarrassing you am I? After all, you are a sociologist.' I am convinced that this same man under other circumstances would have hesitated to raise the subject with a young woman he had just met.

Obviously the exact type of relationship that is formed between an interviewer and the people being interviewed is something that the interviewer cannot control entirely, even though the nature of this relationship and how the interviewees classify the interviewer will affect the kinds of information given. For example, the very facts that I am young, married, working, university educated and dress in a particular way possibly all affected the answers I was given by the couples. It is impossible either to demonstrate these effects or to eliminate them – the most one can do is to be aware of them. It would probably have been difficult for a man to have talked to the women in the same way I was able to. Simply because I am a woman and a wife I shared interests with the other wives, and this helped to make the relationship a relaxed one. I could listen to their problems and enjoy doing so. This is not to say that the responses a male interviewer would have received would have been any less valid or interesting, but in all probability they would have been different. Similarly the information a male interviewer could have elicited from the men would probably have varied from the answers I received. On the whole, I shared much less common ground with the men, and it did seem on occasions that because I am female they were less prepared to take me seriously. The interviews in which I met the husband first, or met him when his wife was not present, were often characterized by a fair amount of reserve on the husband's part.

Appendix 3

However, the effect on the interview of a person's reaction to the interviewer was best exemplified by one manager who was extremely antagonistic to me at the beginning of the interview. As a husband he disapproved of his wife's job on the grounds that she allegedly neglected both himself and the home as a result of it. He definitely seemed to feel that the place for any reasonable wife was in the home and nowhere else. From several of the remarks he made during the early part of the interview, it was obvious that at least part of his unhelpfulness was a direct response to the fact that I was yet another married woman who was treating her husband in an unwifely way by leaving him in order to run round the country interviewing managers. Fortunately his interest in the point we were discussing about his own career overcame his initial hostility so that the latter part of the interview was more satisfactory.

I found the recording of detailed case histories by means of one very long and loosely structured interview to be almost a cross between the methods of participant observation and the more structured methods of the social survey. Participant observation requires that the anthropologist should establish an informal and often fairly close relationship of trust with his informants if there is to be any guarantee that the information gained is reliable. Interviewing for social surveys depends far less on the relationship between interviewer and respondents, and interviewers are expected not to talk too much about themselves or become too friendly with respondents in order that biases are not introduced by the very fact of the relationship. The control in the survey situation is in many ways the distance between the people; for participant observation it is the prolonged interaction over several months.

In these particular interviews I was conscious of the need to establish some kind of confidence with the couples if the sorts of information required were to be forthcoming. On the other hand, I knew I was only making one visit and that it would be possible for me to detract from the validity of the information by becoming too involved with the couples, however pleasant such an involvement might be. In theory it should be possible to establish confidence simply by courtesy towards and interest in the interviewees. In practice it can be difficult to spend eight hours in a person's home, share their meals and listen to their problems, and at the same time remain polite, detached, and largely uncommunicative. I found the balance between prejudicing the answers to questions which covered almost every aspect of the couples' lives, establishing a relationship that would allow the interviews to be successful, and holding a civilized conversation over dinner to be a very precarious one.

The collection of material on the complicated interrelationships of self-images, opinions, ideas and behaviour in a very short period is an arduous task. Few people have sets of ideas and beliefs that are consistent or even well thought out. When talking at length in a flexible interview situation, or in answering related but differently slanted questions, people will often come out with statements that are inconsistent or ambiguous. Obviously it is possible for a person to hold two conflicting but equally valid beliefs at the same time, or to have self-images that vary with circumstances. To assess the relative importance or 'truth' of conflicting statements purely on the basis of the statements themselves requires a much greater understanding of individual motivation than most interviewers have. In many situations a person may hesitate to respond directly to one type of question for a variety of reasons, but if the subject is approached in another way may be quite happy to give the information. Often the problem is simply one of communication, giving the correct cue for the desired response. Such approaches are very much part of any social study, but in the final analysis people will only give the information they want to give, no matter how circumspect the interviewer's approach. In this sense it is easier to check the consistency of opinions than it is to elicit factual information that a respondent is unwilling to give.

Even if an interviewer is filling in a questionnaire by ticking relevant boxes, the results are to some extent dependent on his judgement of an answer. If the interview involves recording long and complex answers the problem of selective recording places even more emphasis on this judgement. Any interviewer will have some preconceived ideas about the answers expected – not to have them would be almost inhuman. However, the temptation to leave out the bits that do not fit or to record selectively on the basis of these preconceptions is balanced by the desire to be objective and to evaluate each piece of information independently of them. Even so, it is not always possible to record every single word that is said, and somewhere along the line interviewers will judge the weight they can give to various types of statements, based on their experience with the respondent and taking note of his reactions either consciously or subconsciously. To the extent that this is true, the answers recorded are not objective, but dependent on the subjective interpretations of the interviewer.

If the person doing the interviewing is also solely responsible for

305

the analysis of the recorded data, the weight he attaches to statements or his evaluation of them, are part of the analysis taking place at the time of the interview. However, I felt that in these interviews my function was primarily to gather the information, and that the final analysis of it did not rest with me. For this reason I attempted to keep complete records of what was said, and to make notes of the couples' reactions, the interview situation and my own feelings about particular interviews, to try to eliminate as much as possible the filtering or prejudging of information. On the other hand, it is never possible to record on paper statements that represent completely accurately eight hours of social interaction, or to hope that the records of statements will represent the full reality of the lives of the people interviewed.

Social scientists use case histories in much the same way as novelists may draw upon the behaviour of their friends for the characters in their latest works. The social scientist with such material on people who are not only literate but are also likely to read the report of his findings, faces a similar problem to the novelist who casts his friend as the arch villain in his latest best seller. Frequently he must choose between leaving out valuable information or comments, and causing embarrassment or resentment among the people studied. Either way, he may suffer qualms about his right to report in print on the personal experiences of others, even if names are changed and circumstances varied.

Many of the experiences I shared with the managers and their wives were not part and parcel of the specific questions I went to ask. Yet the experiences are valuable information in their own right, and add to the picture we can draw of the 'middle-class manager'. The anonymous, typewritten reports on the conversations I had with, and the observations I made on, the sixteen couples were not only the product of a detached and disinterested interview, but also the result of, for me, a personal and frequently enjoyable experience. However, once these experiences had become reports they were simply data to be drawn upon and manipulated in much the same way as statistical tables – they became depersonalized. Every effort has been made to disguise the couples who were interviewed, and given the fact that they were dispersed throughout England, it is highly unlikely that anyone else will recognize them. However, I think that most of them will recognize themselves. I hope they will appreciate that it is only the data that have been manipulated and not they themselves.

List of References

ABRAHAMSON, M., 'Cosmopolitanism, dependence–identification and geographical mobility', *Administrative Science Quarterly*, pp. 98–106, 1965.

ACTON SOCIETY TRUST, *Management Succession*, 1956.

ADAMS, B. N., and BUTLER, J. E., 'Occupational status and husband–wife social participation', *Social Forces*, pp. 501–7, 1967.

AXELROD, M., *A Study of Formal and Informal Group Participation in a Large Urban Community*, Unpublished Ph.D. dissertation, University of Michigan, 1954.

BAILYN, L., 'Career and family orientations of husbands and wives in relation to marital happiness', *Human Relations*, pp. 97–113, 1970.

BARNES, J. A., 'Class and committees in a Norwegian island parish', *Human Relations*, pp. 39–58, 1954.

BECKER, H. S., and STRAUSS, A. L., 'Careers, personality and adult socialization', *American Journal of Sociology*, pp. 253–63, 1956.

BECKER, H. S., and CARPER, J., 'The elements of identification with an occupation', *American Sociological Review*, pp. 341–8, 1956.

BECKER, H. S., 'Notes on the concept of commitment', *American Journal of Sociology*, pp. 32–40, 1960.

BELL, C. R., *Middle Class Families*, Routledge & Kegan Paul, 1969.

BERGER, P., and KELLNER, H., 'Marriage and the construction of reality', *Diogenes*, pp. 1–24, 1964.

BERGER, P., and LUCKMANN, T., *The Social Construction of Reality*, Allen Lane The Penguin Press, 1967.

BERLEW, D. E., and HALL, D. T., 'The socialization of managers: effects of expectations on performance', *Administrative Science Quarterly*, pp. 205–23, 1966.

BEYFUS, D., *The English Marriage*, Weidenfeld & Nicholson, 1968 and Penguin Books, 1971.

BLAU, P. M., *Exchange and Power in Social Life*, John Wiley, Chichester, 1964.

BLOOD, R. O., *Marriage*, The Free Press of Glencoe, Illinois, 1962.

BLOOD, R. O., and WOLFE, D. M., *Husbands and Wives*, The Free Press of Glencoe, Illinois, 1960.

List of references

BOTT, E., *Family and Social Network*, Tavistock Publications, 1957.

BOX, S., and COTGROVE, S., 'Scientific identity, occupational selection and role strain', *British Journal of Sociology*, pp. 20–28, 1966.

BOX, S., and FORD, J., 'Commitment to science: a solution to student marginality?', *Sociology*, pp. 225–38, 1967.

BRACEY, H., *Neighbours*, Routledge & Kegan Paul, 1964.

BRIM, O. G., and WHEELER, S., *Socialization after Childhood: Two Essays*, John Wiley, Chichester, 1966.

BURNS, T., 'The reference of conduct in small groups: cliques and cabals in occupational milieux', *Human Relations*, pp. 467–86, 1956.

BURNS, T., *Ambiguity and Identity*, Unpublished MS., University of Edinburgh, 1966.

CARPER, J. W., and BECKER, H. S., 'Adjustments to conflicting expectations in the development of identification with an occupation'. *Social Forces*, pp. 51–6, 1957.

CHRISTENSEN, H. T., *The Handbook of Marriage and the Family*, Rand McNally, Chicago, 1964.

CICOUREL, A. V., *Method and Measurement in Sociology*, Free Press of Glencoe, Illinois, 1964.

CLARK, D. G., *The Industrial Manager: His Background and Career Pattern*, Business Publications, 1966.

CLARKE, A. C., 'Leisure and occupational prestige', *American Sociological Review*, pp. 301–7, 1956.

CLEMENTS, R. V., *Managers: A Study of Their Careers in Industry*, Allen & Unwin, 1958.

CLEMENTS, R. V., *Local Notables and the City Council*, Macmillan, 1969.

CRICHTON-MILLER, N., 'The mobility of graduates', *The Graduate Appointments Register*, pp. 6–20, 1966.

DAHLSTROM, E., *The Changing Roles of Men and Women*, Gerald Duckworth, 1967.

DAHRENDORF, R., *Class and Class Conflict in Industrial Society*, Routledge & Kegan Paul, 1959.

DALTON, M., *Men Who Manage*, John Wiley, Chichester, 1959.

DONNISON, D. V., 'The movement of households in England', *Journal of the Royal Statistical Society* (series A), pp. 60–80, 1961.

DOWNS, A., *Inside Bureaucracy*, Little Brown, Boston, 1967.

DUBIN, R., 'Industrial workers' worlds: a study of the "central life interests" of industrial workers', in Smigel (1963).

ETZIONI, A. (Editor), *Complex Organizations: A Sociological Reader*, Holt, Rhinehart & Winston, New York, 1961.

FELLIN, P., and LITWAK, E., 'Neighbourhood cohesion under conditions of mobility', *American Sociological Review*, pp. 364–76, 1963.

FIRTH, R., HUBERT, J., and FORGE, A., *Families and Their Relatives: Kinship in a Middle-Class Sector of London*, Routledge & Kegan Paul, 1970.

FLETCHER, R., *The Family and Marriage*, Penguin Books, 1962.

FOGARTY, M., RAPOPORT, R. and, R. N., *Sex, Career and Family*, Allen & Unwin, 1970.

FORM, W. H., and MILLER, D. C., 'Occupational career pattern as a sociological instrument', *American Journal of Sociology*, pp. 317–29, 1949.

GANS, H. J., *The Levittowners*, Allen Lane The Penguin Press, 1967.

GAVRON, H., *The Captive Wife*, Routledge & Kegan Paul, 1966 and Penguin Books, 1968.

GERSTL, J. E., 'Determinants of occupational community in high status occupations', *Sociological Quarterly*, pp. 37–48, 1961.

GLASER, B. G., *Organizational Scientists: Their Professional Careers*, Bobbs-Merrill, Indianapolis, 1964.

GLASER, B. G., and STRAUSS, A. L., *The Discovery of Grounded Theory*, Weidenfeld & Nicholson, 1967.

GLASER, B. G. (Editor), *Organizational Careers: A Source Book for Theory*, Aldine Publishing Co., Chicago, 1968.

GLASS, D. V. (Editor), *Social Mobility in Britain*, Routledge & Kegan Paul, 1954.

GLUCKMAN, M. and DEVONS, E. (Editors), *Closed Systems and Open Minds*, Oliver & Boyd, Edinburgh, 1964.

GOFFMAN, E., 'On cooling the mark out: some aspects of adaptation to failure', first published in *Psychiatry*, 1952, and reprinted in Rose (1962).

GOLDBERG, L. C., *et al.*, 'Local – cosmopolitan: unidimensional or multidimensional', *American Journal of Sociology*, pp. 704–17, 1965.

GOLDNER, F. H., 'Demotion in industrial management', *American Sociological Review*, pp. 714–24, 1965.

GOULDNER, A. W., 'Cosmopolitans and locals: towards an analysis of latent social roles', *Administrative Science Quarterly*, pp. 281–306, 1957 and pp. 444–80, 1958.

GOULDNER, A. W., and H. P., *Modern Sociology*, Rupert Hart-Davis, pp. 168–77, 1963.

GROSS, G., and GURSSLIN, O., 'Middle class and lower class beliefs and values', in Gouldner and Gouldner (1963).

List of references

GRUSKY, O., 'Corporate size, bureaucratization, and managerial succession', *American Journal of Sociology*, pp. 261–9, 1961.

GRUSKY, O., 'Career mobility and managerial political behaviour', *Pacific Sociological Review*, pp. 82–98, 1965.

GRUSKY, O., 'Career mobility and organizational commitment', *Administrative Science Quarterly*, pp. 488–503, 1966.

HAGEN, E. E., *On the Theory of Social Change*, The Dorsey Press, Homewood, Illinois, 1962.

HARRINGTON, M., 'Co-operation and collusion in a group of young housewives', *Sociological Review*, pp. 255–82, 1964.

HARRINGTON, M., 'Resettlement and self image', *Human Relations*, pp. 115–37, 1965.

HARRIS, A. I., and CLAUSEN, R., *Labour Mobility in Great Britain 1953–63*, Government Social Survey, 1966.

HARRIS, C. C., *The Family*, Allen & Unwin, 1969.

HAUSER, P. M., 'Observations on the urban-folk and urban-rural dichotomies as forms of western ethnocentrism', in Hauser and Schnore (1965).

HAUSER, P. M., and SCHNORE, L. F. (Editors), *The Study of Urbanization*, John Wiley, Chichester, 1965.

HAUSKNECHT, M., *The Joiners*, The Bedminster Press, New York, 1962.

HAVIGHURST, R. J., and FEIGENBAUM, K., 'Leisure and life style', *American Journal of Sociology*, pp. 396–404, 1959.

HELFRICH, M. L., *The Social Role of the Executive's Wife*, Bureau of Business Research, Ohio State University, 1965.

HOCHSCHILD, A., 'The role of the ambassador's wife: an exploratory study', *Journal of Marriage and the Family*, pp. 73–87, 1969.

HOMANS, G., *Social Behaviour – Its Elementary Forms*, Routledge & Kegan Paul, 1961.

HOUSE, J. W., *et al.*, *Mobility and the Northern Business Manager*, Report to the Ministry of Labour, Papers on Migration and Mobility in Northern England No. 8, University of Newcastle upon Tyne, 1968.

HUBERT, J., 'Kinship and geographical mobility in a sample from a London middle-class area', *International Journal of Comparative Sociology*, pp. 61–80, 1965.

HUGHES, E. C., 'Institutional office and the person', *American Journal of Sociology*, pp. 404–13, 1937.

KATELMAN, D. K., and BARNETT, L. D., 'Work orientations of urban, middle-class, married women', *Journal of Marriage and the Family*, p. 43, pp. 80–88, 1968.

KEMPER, T. D., 'Reference groups, socialization and achievement', *American Sociological Review*, pp. 31–45, 1968.

KLEIN, J., *Samples from English Cultures*, Vols. I and II, Routledge & Kegan Paul, 1965.

KLEIN, V., *Britain's Married Women Workers*, Routledge & Kegan Paul, 1965.

KNIGHT, R., 'Changes in the occupational structure of the working population', *Journal of the Royal Statistical Society*, pp. 408–22, 1967.

KOHN, M. L., 'Social class and parental values', *American Journal of Sociology*, pp. 337–51, 1959.

KOMAROVSKY, M., *Blue-Collar Marriage*, Random House, New York, 1962.

KORNHAUSER, W., *The Politics of Mass Society*, The Free Press of Glencoe, Illinois, 1959.

KRIESBERG, L., 'Careers, organization size, and succession', *American Journal of Sociology*, pp. 355–9, 1968.

LADINSKY, J., 'Occupational determinants of geographic mobility among professional workers', *American Sociological Review*, pp. 253–64, 1967.

LEHMAN, E. W., 'Opportunity, mobility and satisfaction within an industrial organization', *Social Forces*, pp. 492–501, 1968.

LESLIE, G. R., and RICHARDSON, A. H., 'Life cycle, career pattern and decision to move', *American Sociological Review*, pp. 894–902, 1961.

LEVENSON, B., 'Bureaucratic succession', in Etzioni (1961).

LITWAK, E., 'Geographic mobility and extended family cohesion', *American Sociological Review*, pp. 385–94, 1960.

LITWAK, E., 'Occupational mobility and extended family cohesion', *American Sociological Review*, pp. 9–21, 1960.

LITWAK, E., 'Reference group theory, bureaucratic career, and neighbourhood primary group cohesion', *Sociometry*, pp. 72–84, 1960.

LITWAK, E., and SZELENYI, I., 'Primary group structures and their functions: kin, neighbours and friends', *American Sociological Review*, pp. 456–81, 1969.

LUCKMANN, T., and BERGER, P., 'Social mobility and personal identity', *European Journal of Sociology*, pp. 331–43, 1964.

LUCKMANN, T., *The Invisible Religion*, Collier-Macmillan, 1967.

MCCALL, G. J., and SIMMONS, J. L., *Identities and Interactions*, Collier-Macmillan, 1966.

List of references

MCCLELLAND, D. C., *The Achieving Society*, Van Nostrand, New York, 1961.

MCCLELLAND, W. G., 'Career Patterns and Organizational Needs', *Journal of Management Studies*, pp. 56–70, 1967.

MCGIVERING, I. C., MATTHEWS, D. G. J., and SCOTT, W. H., *Management in Britain*, Liverpool University Press, 1960.

MCKINLEY, D. G., *Social Class and Family Life*, The Free Press of Glencoe, Illinois, 1964.

MANT, A., *The Experienced Manager – A Major Resource*, The British Institute of Management, 1969.

MARTIN, N. H., and STRAUSS, A. L., 'Patterns of Mobility within Industrial Organizations', *Journal of Business*, pp. 101–10, 1956. Reprinted in Glaser (1958, p. 205).

MERTON, R. K., *Social Theory and Social Structure*, The Free Press of Glencoe, Illinois, 1957.

MILIBAND, R., *The State in Capitalist Society*, Weidenfeld & Nicholson, 1969.

MILLS, C. W., *White Collar*, Oxford University Press, 1951.

MITCHELL, J. Clyde (Editor), *Social Networks in Urban Situations*, Manchester University Press, 1969.

MIZRUCHI, E. H., *Success and Opportunity*, The Free Press of Glencoe, Illinois, 1964.

MOORE, W. E., *The Conduct of the Corporation*, Random House, New York, 1962.

MORSE, Nancy C., and WEISS, R. S., 'The function and meaning of work and the job', *American Sociological Review*, pp. 191–8, 1955.

MOTZ, A. B., 'Conception of the marital role by status groups', *Marriage and Family Living*, pp. 136 and 162, 1950.

MUSGROVE, F., *The Migratory Elite*, Heinemann, 1963.

MYRDAL, A., and KLEIN, V., *Women's Two Roles: Home and Work*, Routledge & Kegan Paul, 1968.

ORZACK, L. H., 'Work as a "central life interest" of professionals', in Smigel (1963).

PAHL, R. E., *Urbs in rure*, L.S.E. and Weidenfeld & Nicholson, 1965.

PAHL, R. E., *Whose City?*, Longman, 1970.

PLATT, Jennifer, 'Some problems in measuring the jointness of conjugal role-relationships', *Sociology*, pp. 287–97, 1969.

PRESTHUS, R., *The Organizational Society*, Random House, New York, 1962.

RAPOPORT, R. N., 'The male's occupation in relation to his decision to marry', *Acta Sociologica*, pp. 68–83, 1964.

List of references

RAPOPORT, R., and R. N., 'Work and family in contemporary society', *American Sociological Review*, pp. 381–94, 1965.

RAPOPORT, R., and R. N., 'The dual-career family: a variant pattern and social change', *Human Relations*, pp. 3–30, 1969.

RAYNOR, J., *The Middle Class*, Longman, 1969.

RIESMAN, D., *The Lonely Crowd*, The Free Press of Glencoe, Illinois, 1956 and 1961.

RIESMAN, D., *Abundance for What?* Chatto and Windus, 1964.

ROCHEBLAVE-SPENLÉ, Anne Marie, *Les Rôles masculins et féminins*, Presses Universitaires de France, Paris, 1964.

ROSE, A. M. (Editor), *Human Behaviour and Social Processes*, Routledge & Kegan Paul, 1962.

ROSE, H., *et al.*, *Management Education in the 1970s: Growth and Issues*, National Economic Development Office, H.M.S.O., 1970.

ROSEN, B. C. (Editor), *et al.*, *Achievement in American Society*, Schenkman Publishing Co., Boston, 1969.

ROSENBERG, M., *Occupations and Values*, The Free Press of Glencoe, Illinois, 1957.

ROTH, J. A., *Timetables*, Bobbs-Merrill, Indianapolis, 1963.

ROY, D. F., '"Banana time": job satisfaction and informal interaction', *Human Organization*, pp. 158–68, 1960.

RUNCIMAN, W. G., *Relative Deprivation and Social Justice*, Routledge & Kegan Paul, 1966.

SCHEIN, E. H., 'How to break in the college graduate', *Harvard Business Review*, pp. 68–76, 1964.

SEELEY, J. R., SIM, R. A., and LOOSLEY, E. W., *Crestwood Heights*, John Wiley, Chichester, 1963.

SHIBUTANI, T., 'Reference groups and social control', in Rose (1962).

SMIGEL, E. O. (Editor), *Work and Leisure*, College and University Press, New Haven, Connecticut, 1963.

SOFER, C., 'Conflict between colleagues', Paper read to the VIth World Congress of Sociology, Evian, 1966.

SOFER, C., *Men in Mid-Career: A Study of British Managers and Technical Specialists*, Cambridge University Press, 1970.

STACEY, M., *Tradition and Change: A Study of Banbury*, Oxford University Press, 1960.

STOETZEL, J., 'Une étude du budget-temps de la femme dans les agglomérations urbaines', *Population*, pp. 47–62 Paris, 1948.

STONE, G. P., 'City shoppers and urban identification: observations on the social psychology of city life', *American Journal of Sociology*, pp. 36–45, 1954.

List of references

STRAUSS, A. L., *Mirrors and Masks: The Search for Identity*, The Free Press of Glencoe, Illinois, 1959.

STRAUSS, M. H., 'Deferred gratification, social class and achievement syndrome', *American Sociological Review*, pp. 326–35, 1962.

TAUSKY, C., and DUBIN, R., 'Career anchorage: managerial mobility motivations', *American Sociological Review*, pp. 725–35, 1965.

TURNER, R. H., *The Social Context of Ambition*, Chandler Publishing Co., San Francisco, 1964.

TURNER, C., 'Conjugal roles and social networks: a re-examination of an hypothesis', *Human Relations*, pp. 121–30, 1967.

UDRY, J. R., and HALL, M., 'Marital role segregation and social networks in middle-class, middle-aged couples', *Journal of Marriage and the Family*, pp. 392–5, 1965.

UDRY, J. R., *The Social Context of Marriage*, J. B. Lippincott, Philadelphia and New York, 1966.

WATSON, W., 'The managerial spiralist', *Twentieth Century*, May 1960.

WATSON, W., 'Social mobility and social class in industrial communities', in Gluckman and Devons (1964).

WAUGH, M., 'The changing distribution of professional and managerial manpower in England and Wales between 1961 and 1966', *Regional Studies*, pp. 157–69, 1969.

WHYTE, W. H., *Is Anybody Listening?*, Doubleday, New York, 1948.

WHYTE, W. H., 'The wives of management', *Fortune*, October and November 1951.

WHYTE, W. H., *The Organisation Man*, Jonathan Cape, 1956 and Penguin Books, 1960.

WILENSKY, H. L., 'Work, careers and social integration', *International Social Science Journal*, pp. 543–60, 1960.

WILENSKY, H. L., 'The uneven distribution of leisure: the impact of economic growth on "free time"', *Social Problems*, pp. 32–68, 1961.

WILENSKY, H. L., 'Orderly careers and social participation: the impact of work history on social integration in the middle mass', *American Sociological Review*, pp. 521–39, 1961.

WILLMOTT, P., and YOUNG, M., *Family and Class in a London Suburb*, Routledge & Kegan Paul, 1960.

WILSON, A. T. M., 'Some sociological aspects of systematic management development', *Journal of Management Studies*, pp. 1–18, 1966.

List of references

WYLLIE, I. G., *The Self Made Man in America*, Signet Books, New York, 1964.

YOUNG, M., and WILLMOTT, P., *Family and Kinship in East London*, Routledge & Kegan Paul, 1957, and Penguin Books, 1963.

YUDKIN, S., and HOLME, A., *Working Mothers and Their Children*, Michael Joseph, 1963.

Index

Acton Society Trust, 78; *see also Management Succession*

'The adjustments of married mates' (Bernard), 203

A.E.I., 6

ambition, and anticipatory socialization, 20–22; effect of marriage on, 23, 60, 63; thwarted, 36, 37; related to efficiency, 38; related to family life, 97, 198, 251; lack of, 97–9; of managers' wives, 122, 176; of American managers, 179, 237–8; as central middle-class value, 237–42; attitude of managers to, 252–8, 261; mentioned, 1, 25, 100

America, career patterns in, 17; definitions of 'success' in, 34, 237–8, 241, 242; definitions of 'failure' in, 34; management education in, 37–8; salary structures in, 85, 86; home life of managers in, 120; working mothers in, 127, 134; middle-class community life in, 141, 160, 162, 165; duties of managers' wives in, 165, 177–83, 189, 193–4, 226; marriage patterns in, 198–9, 202; mentioned, 35, 39, 40, 43, 111

Association for the Advancement of State Education, 165

Axelrod, M., 141, 161, 165

Bailyn, L., 222

Barnes, J. A., 144

Bechhofer, F., 9

Bell, C. R., vii, 9, 14, 22, 154; *see also Middle Class Families*

Berger, P., 16, 44, 142, 205; *see also* 'Marriage and the construction of reality'

Berlew, D. E., 24

Bernard, J., 203; *see also* 'The adjustments of married mates'

Beyfus, Drusilla, 200; *see also The English Marriage*

Blackpool, 121

Blau, P. M., 44, 140

Blood, R. O., 120, 201–4, 223, 226; *see also Husbands and Wives: the Dynamics of Married Living*

Blue-Collar Marriage (Komarovsky), 111

boredom, 120, 121, 128, 129, 153

Bott, E., 111, 173, 200, 203–4, 218, 219, 226; *see also Family and Social Network*

Box, S., 22

Bracey, H. E., 141; *see also Neighbours*

Britain's Married Women Workers (Klein), 129

British Institute of Management, 35, 37, 38

Brownies, 163, 167

Burns, T., 25, 26, 144

business schools, 264

Index

Cambridge, University of, vii, 6, 8, 10–12, 52, 229, 261

Canterbury, viii

capitalism, 106, 263

The Captive Wife (Gavron), 128

careers, mobility in, 5–7, 10, 22–3, 27–30, 32, 46, 48–68, 70–77, 238–9; as source of social stability, 17; and career patterns, 17–20, 22–34, 78–107, 283, 292–3; and achievement of personal aims, 18, 33, 37, 81–9, 92–107; long-term commitment in, 18–19; and anticipatory socialization, 20–22; and marriage rates, 23; and early job challenge, 24; competition in, 24–5, 42; promotion in, 28–9, 292; and management selection organizations, 30; demotion in, 31–2; and company commitment, 39; and 'life styles', 40–43, 252–8, 279; decision-making process concerning, 59–61, 85, 104, 106, 283, 284, 294; 'luck' as factor in, 94, 97, 99–104; service experience as stimulant to, 99; of managers' wives, 109–19, 121–2, 126, 128–39, 175, 195, 203, 222, 271, 276, 281; as source of identity, 149, 151, 175; affected by wife's behaviour, 176–94, 196–7; and fringe benefits, 195–6; effect on marriage of, 200, 202–3, 206–35, 237, 242–51, 260–62, 285; wife's attitude to, 222–35, 242–51, 258–78, 290; as central focus for middle-class life, 237–42; definitions of

'success' in, 252–9, 283–4; motivating forces in, 258–68; and expansion of British management, 263–4; mentioned, 1, 3–4, 14, 142

The Changing Roles of Men and Women (Dahlstrom), 114

Cheshire, 56

children, managers', and career mobility, 23, 54–9, 62–5, 67, 76, 127, 233; education of, 54–9, 62–5, 76, 87, 97, 241, 285; friendships of, 67, 151, 219, 227, 282; and father-child relationship, 90, 158–9, 214, 230, 234–5, 251, 258–60; and mother–child relationship, 109–23, 128–39, 153, 157, 206, 211, 224–5, 228, 272; and participation in community life, 148, 163, 164, 168, 178–80; and participation in family life, 169–72, 213, 221, 231–2, 281, 285, 298; and participation in company's social functions, 184, 189; and company fringe benefits, 195; marital relationship centred on, 208, 213; managers' ambitions for, 209–10, 229, 252–7, 261–5, 280; mentioned, 25, 93, 95, 104–7, 198

China, 238

Christensen, H. T., 203

church attendance, 112, 141–2, 162, 164, 251, 274, 284

Cicourel, A. V., 13

Clark, D. G., 11, 78; *see also The Industrial Manager: His Background and Career Pattern*

Classification of Occupations, 1960, 69

Detroit, 161
Diogenes, 205
Downs, A., 34
Dubin, R., 34, 259; *see also* 'Industrial workers' worlds: a study of the central life interests of industrial workers'

Eastern region, 51–3, 74
Edinburgh, 287
education, and managers' courses, 10, 11, 264; and career patterns, 19–22, 47–50; school, 19, 21, 48, 71, 78–81, 84, 85, 90, 96, 99–101; university, 19–21, 23, 48, 71, 78, 81, 83, 90, 109; and anticipatory socialization, 20–22; technical, 23, 48, 71, 101; American management, 38; of managers' children, 54–9, 62–5, 68, 76, 87, 106, 209–10, 213, 254–7, 280, 284; at evening classes, 60, 80, 101, 168; received by managers' wives, 62, 66, 76, 91, 108–10, 114, 118, 127, 131–2, 154–6, 163–4, 182, 188, 191–2, 234–5, 266–8, 271; by correspondence course, 91; as means to material success, 240, 262–3; mentioned, 3, 35, 42–3, 160, 202
The English Marriage (Beyfus), 200
entertaining, 122–3, 176–82, 187–94, 224, 227–8, 285, 291, 294
Essex, 61, 209
European Economic Community, 241, 267
The Experienced Manager – A Major Resource, 35–8

'failure', definitions of, 34, 38, 118
Families and Their Relatives: Kinship in a Middle-Class Sector of London (Firth, Hubert and Forge), 147
family life, company benefits and, 1; sociological studies of, 3–4, 13–14, 111; career mobility and, 5–6, 46, 54–68, 76, 238; 'partnership marriage' and, 16; promotion and, 19; educational process and, 21; related to efficiency at work, 38; related to ambition, 39–41, 60, 93–4, 103, 249; and managers' childhood, 81, 168–9, 171, 207–10; and 'styles of life', 95, 104, 168–73, 190; as source of stability, 106; highly valued by managers' wives, 118, 129, 268; related to community life, 141–2; affected by fringe benefits, 195, 196; managers' attitude to, 198, 201, 203, 213, 215–17, 219, 222, 229–31, 237, 252, 293; mentioned, vii, 9, 30, 33, 37, 44, 289
Family and Social Network (Bott), 111, 200, 203
Firth, R., 147; *see also Families and Their Relatives: Kinship in a Middle-Class Sector of London*
Fogarty, M., vii, 4, 118, 123; *see also Sex, Career and Family*
Ford, J., 22
Forge, A., 147; *see also Families and Their Relatives: Kinship in a Middle-Class Sector of London*
Fremlin, C., 131; *see also* 'The wider life'

Index

Index

Manchester, 61, 78

Mant, A., 35–8, 40; *see also The Experienced Manager – A Major Resource*

marriage, and 'partnership marriage' ideal, 16, 168; and career mobility, 23, 51, 53–67, 70–71, 73–7, 150; and discussion of job prospects, 59–61, 84, 85, 92–3, 104, 106; as source of security, 86–8, 95, 121; effect of managers' careers on, 110–11, 136–8, 200, 202–3, 206–35, 243–51, 260–62, 265, 285; of American managers, 120, 177–83, 198–9, 202; and participation in community life, 163, 165, 167–73; importance of company's social functions to, 187, 197; attitude of managers to, 198, 200, 205–35, 260–62; attitude of managers' wives to, 198, 200, 205–35, 243–51, 254, 257, 261, 265–8, 272, 277–8, 280–81, 303; theoretical approaches to, 201–6; mentioned, 1, 25, 89, 133, 294

'Marriage and the construction of reality' (Berger and Kellner), 16, 205

Martin, N. H., 28

Matthews, D. G. J., 111

M.B.A., 264

The Middle Class (Raynor), 238

Middle Class Families (Bell), 9

'Middle Class Values' (Pahl), 238

Midlands, 51, 52, 74, 102, 166

Miliband, R., 46

Mitchell, J. Clyde, 145, 204;
see also Social Networks in Urban Situations

mobility, and 'spiralling' process, 5–6, 10, 22–3, 49, 67, 238–9; wives' attitude to, 7, 53–67, 110, 136, 232, 261, 276–7, 282; social, 9, 10, 20, 21, 207, 238, 240, 242, 259, 264; career, 27–30, 32–7, 46, 48–68, 70–77; effect on friendships of, 150–54, 174, 175; and participation in community life, 163, 167; of American managers, 177, 179; effect on marriage of, 206, 208, 211, 216–19, 221, 224, 227, 232–3, 265; mentioned, 1, 94, 186, 237

money *see* salaries

Moore, W. E., 33–4; *see also The Conduct of the Corporation*

Myrdal, A., 127, 128

national service, 96, 99–101

Neighbours (Bracey), 141

Newcastle, 101

newspapers, 14, 16, 21, 30, 87, 91, 101–2, 279

Norman, J., vii

North East region, 81, 84

North West region, 51–3, 74

Northamptonshire, 15

Northern Ireland, 51, 65

Northern region, 52, 53, 55, 57, 58, 62, 65, 74, 233

Observer, 14, 101

Organizational Careers: A Source Book for Theory (Glaser), 4

Orzack, L. H., 259; *see also* 'Work as a "central life interest" of professionals'

323